E
183.8
.I8
N48
New World journeys : contemporary
Italian writers and the experience
of America / edited and translated
by Angela M. Jeannet and Louise K.
Barnett. -- Westport, Conn. :
Greenwood Press, 1977.
    xxiii, 2   p. ; 22 cm. --
(Contributions in American studies ;
no. 33 ISSN 0084-9227)
    Includes index.
    Bibliography: p. [241]-24
    ISBN 0-8371-9758-9
    1. Public opinion--Italy--Addresses, essays,
lectures. 2. United States--Foreign opinion,
Italian--Addresses, essays, lectures. 3.
United States--Civilization--20th century--

(continued)

NEW WORLD
JOURNEYS

Recent Titles in
Contributions in American Studies
Series Editor: Robert H. Walker

New World Journeys

CONTEMPORARY ITALIAN WRITERS AND THE EXPERIENCE OF AMERICA

edited and translated by
Angela M. Jeannet and
Louise K. Barnett

Contributions in American Studies, Number 33

GREENWOOD PRESS WESTPORT, CONNECTICUT
LONDON, ENGLAND

Library of Congress Cataloging in Publication Data

Main entry under title:

New World journeys.

(Contributions in American studies ; no. 33, ISSN 0084-9227)
Bibliography: p.
Includes index.
1. United States—Foreign opinion, Italian—Addresses, essays, lectures.
2. Public opinion—Italy—Addresses, essays, lectures. 3. United States—
Civilization—20th century—Addresses, essays, lectures. I. Jeannet,
Angela M. II. Barnett, Louise K.
E183.8.I8N48   301.15'43'973   77-14144
ISBN 0-8371-9758-9

Library of Congress Card Number: 77-14144
ISBN: 0-8371-9758-9
ISSN: 0084-9227

First published in 1977

Greenwood Press, Inc.
51 Riverside Avenue, Westport, Connecticut 06880

Printed in the United States of America

Acknowledgments

The authors and the publisher wish to thank the following for permission to excerpt and translate copyrighted material:

Italo Calvino for the article "Hemingway e noi," *Il contemporaneo* 1 (November 13, 1954): 3.

Danilo Dolci for excerpts from "Alcuni appunti su esperienze educative sperimentali in USA." Unpublished notes, 1973.

Giulio Einaudi Editore, Turin, for excerpts from Cesare Pavese, *La letteratura americana e altri saggi*, Turin, 1959, and from Giaime Pintor *Il sangue d'Europa*, Turin, 1950.

Aldo Garzanti Editore, Milan, for excerpts from Guido Piovene, *De America*, Milan, 1953.

Ugo Guanda Editore, Milan, for excerpts from G.A. Borgese, *Atlante americano*, Modena, 1936.

Istituto Gramsci, Rome, for excerpts from Antonio Gramsci, *Note sul Machiavelli, sulla politica e sullo stato moderno,* Turin, 1955.

La Nuova Italia, Florence, for an excerpt from Giorgio Spini, *America 1962*, Florence, 1962.

Giuseppe Laterza e Figli S.p.A., Bari, for an excerpt from Gianfranco Corsini, *America allo specchio,* Bari, 1960.

Arnoldo Mondadori Editore, Milan, for excerpts from Margherita Sarfatti, *L'America, ricerca della felicità*, Milan, 1937, and from Elio Vittorini, *Diario in pubblico,* Milan, 1957.

Fernanda Pivano Sottsass for excerpts from *America rossa e nera,* Florence, 1964.

Giuseppe Prezzolini for excerpts from *Tutta l'America,* Florence, 1958.

G.C. Sansoni Editore Nuova S.p.A. for excerpts from Emilio Cecchi, *America amara,* Florence, 1940, and from Mario Praz, *Viaggi in occidente,* Florence, 1942.

Giorgio Soavi for excerpts from *America tutta d'un fiato,* Milan, 1959, and from *Fantabulous,* Milan, 1963.

Mario Soldati for excerpts from *America, primo amore,* Florence, 1930.

"Introduction (to Italian Criticism of American Literature)," by Agostino Lombardo was first published in the *Sewanee Review* 68 (Summer 1960). Copyright 1960 by the University of the South. Reprinted by permission of the editor.

"Do you like America?"

. . .

Its name endures. If it didn't exist, we would have to invent it.

Giorgio Soavi, *Fantabulous*

The reader of this anthology will undoubtedly be struck by the obvious, abiding fascination which the United States holds for Italians. Seldom does an encounter between cultures yield so detailed and abundant a documentation. The writings of Italian intellectuals on America turn out to be an expression of admiration, puzzlement, and—at times begrudging—love for a land of mythic potentialities and for an experience charged with significance.

It is in that same spirit that this collection has been made.

Angela M. Jeannet
Louise K. Barnett

Contents

Introduction

1

In any work concerned with Italian attitudes toward America, the first ambiguity lies in the very term *America*. The name variously, and most often concurrently, refers to a mythical presence *and* to a political entity: to America as the collective symbol of a promise, *and* to the power of the United States; to a legend one wants to believe in, has to believe in, *and* to a còmplex, specific, historically defined nation. But that very ambiguity is what makes the American experience rich, haunting, and multifaceted. One should not—and could not—separate the dual identities subsumed by the term, particularly when speaking of the reactions of Italians to anything "American." What is important, however, is to be conscious of that fact, to try to distinguish the components of the extremely complex reality of America as it is reflected in the Italian mind, and then to evaluate any statement made about America on the basis of these recognized ambivalences.

If, as many have already said, America is the necessary projection of the old European dream of a palingenesis of the human (read: Western) spirit, if America tantalizingly offered man a second chance in a new Eden, then the groups most likely to pursue the dream of a new beginning in a land of unlimited opportunity had to be those living in the continuous, inescapable horror of either physical want or political oppression. Quite appropriately, the history of American immigration confirms this supposition, while at the same time exposing contradictions and ambiguities of the most varied kinds.

The years between 1820 and 1920 witnessed a phenomenon whose magnitude has been noticed but only sketchily explored. During this period, millions of Italians migrated in a desperate search for relief from want. From 1861 (the year in which records began to be kept for the newly formed Italian nation) to 1940, approximately 9,842,000 people left Italy to go beyond the oceans, while many more millions spread into Europe and the Mediterranean countries. At the turn of the century, the peak of the movement, 600,000 people left every year, fleeing in all directions. From another perspective, the records of the U.S. Immigration and Naturalization Office reveal that approximately 5,096,200 Italians were admitted to the United States between 1820 and 1967.[1] These figures explain why very few people living in Italy today do not have at least distant family ties with citizens of the United States. Unfortunately, it is only today that serious, organized efforts are being made to document, evaluate, and preserve the many aspects of Italian immigration to the United States. This applies also, to a greater or smaller extent, to all other ethnic influxes of the late nineteenth and early twentieth centuries. Studies are appearing now. Yet, even those most often focus on the emergence of an ethnic-American culture, leaving in the background what is most intriguing but more difficult and perhaps impossible to recapture: the early immigrant experience, the immense pain out of which a new society was born.

What is important to remember here is that those masses of Italian immigrants, particularly the waves of the years between 1880 and 1920, had a very definite mythical image of a land called America, although they knew nothing of the literary myth of America and even less of the philosophical implications of the concept of the "noble savage." The immigrants came from subcultures that had minimal contacts with the intellectual life of their own country. They were victims of a class system and were often illiterate, but they had learned of America in other ways, above all from the oral sources of their own culture: the example of the first emigrants, their messages to those at home mailed from distant cities, the songs and tales about transatlantic voyages, and perhaps the legends from semireligious sources—telling of continents rich in gold—which are an essential part of European folklore. Most of all, America was born out of their despair and out of their need to believe that a place existed where all persons could recover their rightful dignity. This dignity was not something abstract. Rather, it had to do with adequate food, schooling, work, money, and justice. In contrast to a view of human destiny as manipulated by hierarchical forces and by fate, static and necessarily, naturally unjust, there survived in the immigrants the certainty that somewhere one could be master of one's own life.

With very few exceptions, highly educated Italians were not among the throngs entering the United States during the period of intense immigration. The few who did visit the States before 1930 were in some ways unusual, such as young Camillo Olivetti, whose letters from America (dating from 1893 to 1909) have recently been published. [2] What were the intellectuals doing that prevented them from paying more than passing attention to the phenomenal event that was taking place? All that is available on the subject of emigration in traditional sources (novels, plays, and the like) are a few sentimental allusions to the "unfortunate emigrants" and unrealistic vignettes of the land of their destination. [3]

The Italian middle class at this time was totally absorbed in the politics of new nationhood which it accurately viewed as its own achievement and as its exclusive reward for the long struggle to achieve national independence. Class divisions as drastic and as dramatic as racial divisions in the United States caused either outright hostility and contempt toward the disinherited, or a callous and self-serving unconcern with the desperate solution to flee the country on the part of the younger and more daring poor. Compassionate and far-sighted political observers did point out the unfairness and the dangers of the intolerable social inequities, and the damaging drain of the new country's human potential. But their warnings went unheeded.

World War I and its aftermath further polarized the country. The coming of age of the Left, and the birth of the Fascist party, marked the beginnings of a new era which came to a close only in 1946 and which clearly showed that the bourgeoisie was utterly hostile to social reforms and deathly afraid for its however petty privileges. Little thought was given to the peculiar relationship that necessarily develops between two countries and two cultures linked by a major migratory flow—if we except a politically and national-istically motivated effort by the Fascist regime to regain the Italo-Americans' allegiance.

Yet, that massive social phenomenon was going to have far-reaching repercussions on all Italians; that is the reason why we wish to point out its importance here. It was the Italian migratory movement, above all, that contributed, for example, to creating the differences in the experience of America between the French and the Italian intellectual elite.[4] It was difficult for the Italian intel-lectuals to approach America as their French counterparts did, relying extensively on the Edenic myth and on the image of the "noble savage." There was that, but there was also much more that they knew and did not want to know about America. As the 1930's came and Italians began to travel to the United States as observers, they were very much aware of the fact that thousands of people from the same peninsula, Italy, had preceded them on that route, under quite different circumstances. They knew, or guessed, what that experience of America must have been for the "other" Ital-ians. They were torn by conflicting emotions, often unacknow-ledged: a sense of vague uneasiness about the image of Italians abroad, which was also their own image now, a sense of guilt and disbelief, curiosity and bewilderment, in discovering the country that had absorbed so many. In some ways, America was a miracle, the mythical manifestation of a very un-European opportunity. But that also devalued America in their eyes. Because of the elitist edu-cation they had received inside a closed and well-established class, uncritical of its own time-honored perceptions of what constitutes culture, they were ill-equipped to admire a country that served as a receptacle for the poor, the ignorant, the less valued human re-sources of their own country, the place where illiterates could amass fortunes. The Italians' inability to look at America as a truly "other" country, unconnected to their own tormented and divided culture, is obvious, for example, in the pages of such a fine writer as Emilio Cecchi, or of such usually sophisticated observers as Giuseppe Prezzolini and Mario Praz. Only later, with Guido Pio-vene, was thoughtful expression given to the experience of America as a liberating force for the middle class as well and as an escape from the stifling atmosphere of the Italian culture which remained partly provincial, conventional, and stratified even after the fall of Fascism.

The emotional burden we have described is not a significant component of the attitude of younger Italian writers. Mass migration ended in the early 1920's, and important social and political changes have taken place in Italy and in the United States. Italo-Americans have emerged as a new group with individual characteristics, in some ways quite removed from the bitter roots of emigration. This may explain why, given also the more frequent conventional contacts between Italy and the United States, the Italian writers of today tend to approach America in a more "professional" manner, limited and specific. They view political life and customs with objective interest and see American culture as a laboratory where experiments foreshadowing the future of all the Western countries are being conducted. Or, like Michelangelo Antonioni in *Zabriskie Point*, they freely move on to a poetic contemplation of America as the mythical place for our culture's apocalypse and improbable new genesis.

It was not so much Fascist ideology that prompted some Italian visitors in the 1930's to view the United States negatively. Rather, it was the reverse: their inability to accept, or even appreciate, values and customs that were repugnant to them made the Fascist ideology and its nationalistic rhetoric more attractive. A pertinent example is the reaction of Italians from different backgrounds to American technology. The Italo-American is presented by the Italian observer as naively impressed by and often obnoxiously proud of American technological prowess. The very things and attitudes that had liberated and vindicated obscure Southern peasants appeared to the Italian visitor as unwelcome "equalizers," as props in a nightmare, evidence of a basically less valuable materialistic civilization.

It seems as though (and this is by no means a unique experience in recent Italian history) the dispossessed had to be the pioneers, in their own way. Under the pressure of physical necessity, they turned to alternatives that forced them to discover other realities. It did not matter that the historical reality of the United States—even more than the reality of Brazil, Argentina, or Canada—should utterly differ from the myth. They had found a way to break the isolation in which Italian society was wasting. In contrast, it took the bitter outcome of the rise of Fascism to start Italian intellectuals questioning and to push them on to their own discoveries.

As Fascism became the ruling party in Italy, several things happened which influenced the shape of intellectual life and the themes of literary works written during this period. First of all, the young intellectuals experienced in their own minds, and at times in their own flesh, repression and humiliation. The loss of human dignity, which had different connotations for the intellectual and for the peasant, was now a reality for both. Intimidation, beatings, censorship, emerging anti-Semitism, and a progressive closure of all avenues of exchange with other countries fostered anti-Fascism among the intellectuals. The outlawed Leftist parties found new recruits and allies outside the proletariat. It was also at this time that political persecution often entailed periods of *confino*, a favorite tool of Fascist repression, which caused Italian intellectuals to "discover" the South. What they found was a metaphor for a social and political reality, a land wasted by exploitation, the loneliness of fields and villages abandoned by the men who were by now "Americans," a world "other" from theirs, a world where injustice and powerlessness had always been givens. The accuracy or fairness of such perceptions was beside the point; it was the discovery that counted. As the whole region—geographic entity but, even more, personal experience and mythical presence—was explored by "outsiders," the names of the Italian South and the name of America started appearing together in the pages of the same books or in books by the same authors. What interests us here are the parallels and the contrasts between the two themes of the South as a "somewhere before," a somewhere before history, and America as a "somewhere else," as well as the now obsessive preoccupation with the American experience of the dispossessed. The South as the realm of Necessity and America as the realm of Freedom became a binomy as frequently evoked and as peremptory as any basic pair of opposites. Later, the Italian South and America were going to become two historical entities, more pragmatically and perhaps lucidly observed, but quite different conditions were required for such an evolution in attitudes.

The connection that developed in Italy between anti-Fascism, awareness of long-standing social injustices, and the myth of

America in its double perspective—that of the hungry peasant and that of the angry intellectual—is at the root of a phenomenon which the American reader may find puzzling: many of the sympathetic observers of the American scene from the 1930's to our day are Leftist intellectuals. This should be no surprise. The dynamic qualities Italians thought they detected in the American experience—the rejection of the crudest forms of hierarchy, the contributions to the anti-Fascist struggle, and the various other political factors mentioned earlier—all contributed to fostering interest and admiration toward America among the intellectuals of the Italian Left. Later political events have only added to the ambiguities and the contradictory quality of Italian feelings toward America.

2

Although scattered observations can be found earlier, most of the attention which Italian writers paid to America is quite strikingly concentrated in the 1930's and the early 1960's. Political reasons of a different sort seem compelling in both instances. The Italian situation generated interest in the United States in the 1930's, while in the 1960's the American political climate provoked a new period of concern.

For the earlier decade, as Dominique Fernandez has pointed out, the great value of America to Italians was as an *altrove*, something other than Fascism.[5] For the Fascists as well, America presented itself as the prominent example of otherness, but of a negative sort, a bad example that Italians must not emulate or even show interest in. Thus, it is especially in the light of the differences between the two countries—pointed up by the official position—that writers of the 1930's view the United States. Not all of the writers about America in this period—like Cesare Pavese, exiled to Calabria for championing American literature, or like Giaime Pintor, killed in the Resistance—were militantly hostile to Fascism. Nevertheless, given the narrowly nationalistic view of culture espoused by Mussolini's regime, and its implementation in the form of censorship, the publication of any book about America at this time must be regarded as a political act.

If knowledge of America was discouraged under Fascism, after World War II it became all too easily obtainable. American culture in its least attractive forms invaded and occupied Europe. The myriad products of American technology, the most immediately obvious and the most eagerly propagandized facet of America, reduced the meaning of America to a crude materialism that intellectuals abhorred. If formerly banned American classics could now be readily purchased, so could a host of ephemeral authors. In this postwar milieu, a number of the enthusiastic *americanisti* of the 1930's recanted, for their cherished myth of America had been displaced by a vulgar reality. At the same time that contact with American culture in their own country displeased Italian intellectuals, cold war politics almost completely alienated their former sympathies with American political ideals. Singlemindedness, inflexibility, provincialism, and lack of worldliness in American leaders appeared much less attractive to Europeans than the same characteristics had appeared to be earlier in American fiction. Throughout the 1950's, America was perceived as filling her world power role with little grace.

The election of John F. Kennedy and the subsequent domestic troubles of the United States reawakened and sustained a new wave of interest during the 1960's. To Italians, as to other Europeans, Kennedy was an enormously charismatic figure whose "New Frontier" programs suggested a return to the positive potentialities that America had traditionally embodied for Europe. On the other hand, the problems that had remained dormant during the 1950's surfaced explosively at this time. Great hopes and great difficulties conjoined during this decade to stimulate a revived Italian interest in the United States.

In addition, it might be useful to recall that the Italian "economic miracle" was underway, in contrast to the unhappy stringencies of the previous decade. With the spread of prosperity, travel to the United States became more feasible, and Italians could imagine the American standard of living within their reach, if not yet entirely in their grasp. For a wide-eyed and humanly envious contemplation of American wealth, in time Italians substituted a critical appraisal and frankly emulative attitudes.

More recently, America has emerged as an example and as a

warning to other countries. The negative aspects of American life—its violence, and the pollution and waste coexistent with it—are seen as the potential image of a world others do not want to see actualized elsewhere.

3

From the time of De Tocqueville, Americans have benefited from the insights of perceptive, and at times hostile, foreign observers whose outsider status has given them valuable perspectives on American culture. The writers brought togethei here both challenge and confirm the American self-image, record and analyze phenomena that we either take for granted or ignore, and make us aware of similarities and differences between their sensibilities and ours. The focus and scope of their studies differ, but all exhibit a genuine desire to explore and understand our culture. These Italian intellectuals write in the tradition of De Tocqueville: they give us a carefully observed portrait of ourselves and their own response to it.

As Donald Heiney has stated:

The American reader will hear a strange place mentioned that is called America; often it seems to have little to do with the prosaic place where he marries his wife, raises his children, and eats his corn flakes. Eavesdropping on the private dialogue between Italian writer and Italian reader, he may have the strange sensation of overhearing a conversation about himself between two other people. Eavesdropping is rather dishonest but it is also fascinating, especially for those who—like all who hope to know themselves better—have a profound curiosity about the lives of others.[6]

Lacking the immigrants' obsessive economic motivation, or the desire to remain in the United States permanently, the intellectuals—that is, the educated, generally professional writers—express wide-ranging and spontaneous reactions to American culture. Given the sophistication of their background, and discounting their sometimes biased perspectives, they desire to assess the United States' possible uniqueness, to compare it with the European experience and to determine its value for Italian culture. America as a political entity, a technological laboratory, a people, and a literature is the subject of the Italian writers' reports.

This anthology offers both a wide spectrum and a representative selection of the writings of Italian intellectuals on America. Its purpose is to introduce a number of distinguished Italian writers to the American reading public and to make available their descriptions of and reactions to America. The majority of the writers, whatever the extent of their reputations in Italy, are virtually unknown, even to an educated American public. Some names, however, will be familiar. Mario Praz, for example, is widely known in academic circles as a critic of English literature; while the novels of Cesare Pavese and Italo Calvino are finding a growing audience in this country.

In choosing material, we have been guided by considerations of originality, interest to an American audience, and enduring value. Inevitably, a work written about the United States by an Italian for Italians will contain explanatory data of little interest or novelty to Americans. Similarly, much of topical importance in the past, much of the material from which this compilation was culled, is now hopelessly dated. At the same time, a number of observations, even those thirty and forty years old, seem surprisingly insightful and at times prophetic.

In grouping the selections under four broad headings, we have intended to impose some organization on a welter of observations, reactions, and anecdotes. Instead of presenting all excerpts from a given work together, we have found it more valuable to indicate recurrent motifs and common areas of interest among the writers as a group. A biographical headnote is given for the first selection of each author.

NOTES

1. This figure includes repeated admittances of the same immigrant. The data given here derive from two articles: G.L. Monticelli, "Italian Emigration: Basic Character and Trends with Special Reference to the Postwar Years", and J. Velikonja, "Italian Immigrants in the United States in the Sixties." Both are included in Silvano M. Tomasi and Madeline H. Engel, eds., *The Italian Experience in the United States* (Staten Island, N.Y.: Center for Migration Studies, Inc., 1970), pp. 3-22 and 23-38.

2. Camillo Olivetti, member of a landowning Jewish family, was a

Socialist in his youth, in the best tradition of a Piedmontese intellectual elite which much later was to become a hotbed of anti-Fascism. He initiated the Olivetti commitment to an enlightened industrial paternalism which his descendants have remained faithful to. His letters reveal a curious, warm, and thoughtful personality.

3. On this topic, see Constantino Ianni, *Il sangue degli emigranti* (Milan: Edizioni di Comunità, 1965), pp. 335-343.

4. Dominique Fernandez briefly alludes to this at the beginning of his book *Il mito dell'America negli intellettuali italiani dal 1930 al 1950*, A. Zaccaria, trans. (Caltanissetta: Sciascia, 1969), pp. 7, 14-15.

5. Ibid., p. 7.

6. Donald Heiney, *America in Modern Italian Literature* (New Brunswick, N.J.: Rutgers University Press, 1964), pp. 6-7.

CITYSCAPES

I

Not surprisingly, it is the sheer size of the United States and the variety of terrain it encompasses that have impressed Italian visitors most forcibly. Those who attempt to be comprehensive have dutifully visited points north, south, east, and west and have seen—not always with admiration—the Grand Canyon and Niagara Falls. The West holds a particular fascination for these visitors as the most distinctively American section in terms of the land itself. For the Western European, accustomed to a highly cultivated countryside, it offers the least familiar kind of topography—an immense stretch of sparsely populated space, which provides a pleasurable confirmation of the awesome mythical dimension Italians have attributed to America. For Guido Piovene, whose *De America* is a monumental study of the United States, this western landscape has a rich suggestiveness:

It is sublime because it is inhuman: It is abstract, impervious to man. It is never wise, but exalted and absorbed in itself. It is never ancient, not even with an antiquity of millennia. It is astral, geologic, anterior to life. It has no age, like monsters. Nature is admirable in other places because of its affinity with man; here, because of its aloofness. . . . When speaking of America, one must remember that the most modern nation in the world includes spaces such as these, deserts that remain barren or are colonized by necessity. America includes the cruelty of an essentially lonely nature where no one dreams of resting in the open air, a nature dominated by a mythology devoid of characters, of true personifications and even of divinities, ruled over by Powers and Forces. It would not be credible if Americans were not carrying it inside them, if their character were not in part shaped by it, either through resemblance or contrast.

American cities also inspire awe because of their size, but unlike the great spaces of the West, it is vertical area which impresses here. All visitors find it obligatory to consider the skyscrapers of New York before turning to other sights. A number of writers see these imposing *grattacieli* as an embodiment of the American passion for what is colossal and prodigious. Few feel entirely comfortable with the Manhattan skyline. Its "architectural pyrotechnics" reminds Emilio Cecchi of the Tower of Babel. Cecchi believes that like that prideful edifice, the skyscrapers will fall, and men will recover their sanity about buildings.

After skyscrapers, Wall Street, Harlem, and the Bowery often elicit comment. The fascination of the unfamiliar operates in all these subjects, and again, a certain impression of size contributes to their interest for these visitors. Wall Street overwhelms because of the tremendous business interests centered there, the Bowery openly displays a large number of unfortunates, and Harlem's concentration of blacks strikes the Italian writer. In addition to these well-known areas, the writer's own experiences, usually involving some description of the city life-style, are treated. These naturally vary far more than the places visited. Nevertheless, some degree of uneasiness tends to be a common denominator, aptly summed up by the title of a section in Giorgio Soavi's book *Fantabulous*: "What to do to keep from going crazy."

Skyscrapers

EMILIO CECCHI

America amara, 1940, pp. 12-17

Emilio Cecchi (1884-1966): A member of the conservative Florentine intellectual elite, Cecchi was a prolific and influential critic and essayist. An authoritative scholar of English literature, he contributed two classic volumes to the field of English studies: *History of English Literature in the Nineteenth Century,* (1915) and *English and American Writers* (1935). He also wrote art criticism, concentrating on Tuscan artists of the fourteenth and fifteenth centuries, and translated several of Bernard Berenson's works into Italian. In the 1940's, he became a member of the prestigious Academy of the *Lincei.*

Cecchi's refined, in some ways limited, sensibility expressed itself most effectively in short texts in prose, particularly in travel notes. As he came in contact with cultures far removed from the closed, sophisticated, beloved Florentine environment, he reacted in two contradictory ways. On the one hand, he was an unusually perceptive observer, a visitor at once aloof and full of romantic empathy. On the other hand, he often reacted to the unfamiliar with diffidence and skepticism. *Bitter America,* an account of two visits to the United States in 1930-1931 and in 1937-1938, became a classic of its genre. The Italian title evokes other well-known titles—Mario

Soldati's *America primo amore*, for example, and a famous Tuscan folk song, *Maremma amara*, which also speaks of the sorrows of emigration. *America amara* underlines the disillusionment with the American myth felt by an intellectual who, unable to appreciate some of its positive elements, was instead sensitive to its negative aspects: the lack of cultural sophistication, the brash defiance of tradition, racial oppression, and the dull uniformity of a life-style that had been held up as a fabulous promise.

Providing strikingly different perspectives, Cecchi's and Soldati's books were the lenses through which many Italian readers saw America, a fascinating and bitter presence, for a long time.

It was Bernard Berenson who, upon arriving in New York by sea and seeing the first skyscrapers, compared them to the towers of San Gemignano. This is an appropriate enough comparison even today and one that has almost become a motto or a proverb, so that, just as in the case of a proverb, no one remembers the author of it or imagines that it had an author. Another American pilgrim, Henry James, who held a personal grudge against America, could not repress sarcasm at the sight of the first skyscrapers. He said that to him the profile of New York brought to mind only "a comb that has lost many teeth."

I once queried Berenson as to his views on the architecture of skyscrapers. I had the impression that he could not make up his mind to admire it, or even to recognize in it a style in the making. Skyscrapers interested him, but not as architecture; they interested him as scenery. The distinction isn't sophistic. In the frescoes of Antonio Veneziano and of Gozzoli in the Camposanto of Pisa, or in the Tower of Babel of Breughel, the backgrounds are architectural messes. But they perform a suggestive and romantic function as scenery with complete success.

Years ago, I used to enjoy discussing the skyscrapers of New York with Meyer Shapiro, of the Department of Fine Arts at Columbia University. On one such occasion, it was hot enough for sunstroke, and in the washed-out dawn one could see on terraces the forms of sleepers stretching and rising from improvised pallets. Shapiro's opinion was even more severe than Berenson's: for Shapiro, the masses of skyscrapers represented only the extreme swelling of contemporary daring and Babylonian monumentality. They were, he said, the bastions of a Valhalla over which twilight hangs and on which, sooner or later, the end of a world will be celebrated.

I listened to these ideas along Riverside Drive, near the neoclassical tomb of General Grant. One fact appeared incontestable: in American building a new organic principle, a new rhythmic pattern, is not visible, whereas architectural styles have always originated in a characteristic and decisive element, a formal cause which is lacking here. There is nothing here which might correspond—in a new order—to the column and architrave of the Greeks, to the Roman or to the Renaissance pillar and arch, or to the ogive curve. Nothing is here from which, as from the themes of a fugue or a symphony, developments and combinations of an exact and infinite variety might be generated.

The skyscraper is not a symphony of lines and masses, of voids and solids, of forces and stresses; it is, rather, an operation of arithmetic, a multiplication. Carried entirely by a vertical thrust, which has certain gothic affinities, it provides only the material for a mechanical problem: how to push this thrust to the highest possible point and keep it there. The skyscraper is not a living thing, like a classical building which is poised under its weight with human naturalness. It is a ghost, an apparition, an explosion congealed in the middle of the sky. On the brief cliff of Manhattan, if we overlook the old towers surpassed and in part torn down, in the space of a few years rose the Chanin (54 floors), the Chrysler (77 floors and 1,020 feet), and the Empire State Building (102 floors and 1,332 feet). Until the crash came and put an end to these architectural pyrotechnics.

Intellectuals, aesthetes, and professors of fine arts do not seem to be overly persuaded that the skyscraper represents an effective spiritual conquest and not a paradox of the construction industry. But here the moralists have their say. In *Rediscovery of America* by Waldo Frank, the polemic against the skyscraper is an essential part of the criticism of the entire American civilization, with a number of very perceptive pages. The skyscraper is not the innocent and solid expression of civic power, but the expression of a proud and isolated economic supremacy. It is the bell tower without a bell of a materialistic religion without God. Baronial fortresses of the plutocracy, skyscrapers resemble in all respects the medieval towers of the nobles, armed one against the other within the same circle of walls, and only united against the community, the *res publica*.

Peaceful people can pretend not to hear, or they can shake their heads at such arguments. In any case, the solemn spectacle of the skyscrapers (as architecture or scenery) was created to astonish and amaze, for when all is said and done, the skyscrapers were made with ingenuity and audacity, with millions of dollars, and with steel. They were not castles of ideas and words. Then new men began to speak. No longer the critics subtly nourished with the quintessence of ancient art and no longer the reformers and the preachers who, in order to find support for their own ideas, would gladly deny the evidence, but men who were knowledgeable—those who had invented the skyscrapers and had constructed them, perfected them, and made them famous—began to speak.

Frank Lloyd Wright is one of the greatest architects of America. A pupil and follower of Louis H. Sullivan, he designed the Wainwright Building, which may be considered the grandfather of skyscrapers in the same way that the cupola of the Brunelleschi is the grandmother of cupolas. Wright published a book, *Modern Architecture*, decrying the "tyranny of skyscrapers," even while the last chains were being tightened and the last coats of paint were being given to the Empire State Building. His are responsible opinions because they are spoken by an American builder who wages war against skyscrapers, the pride of his country, thus risking his popularity and his earnings. His fondness for such opinions cost him thousands of dollars.

Wright is not a prisoner of tradition. He views Greek and other related architectures, when transplanted to America, as pagan poison. He judges the architecture of the Renaissance to be nothing more than a replica of Roman and Greek forms. He considers the apse of Saint Peter's to be nothing more than a grandiose sculpture. Not even Le Corbusier is so curt. On the other hand, Wright does not hold illusions about cardboard box buildings and playing card towers, while recognizing the fact that skyscrapers in certain places may well serve a certain need and become examples of organic and truly modern architecture. For the time being, in America, the skyscraper has torn up the city. Its rigorous and obsessive patterns have mechanized its dwellers. And if living in buildings of one hundred floors forces one to lead a distorted and crippled life, there is no doubt that those buildings are a mistake.

In 1930, in New York, vertical traffic was greater than horizontal traffic; that is, elevators carried more people than automobiles, buses, streetcars, and subways combined. It's a madness for verticality. Meanwhile, the automobile and telephone, with their continuous development, tend to reestablish the horizontal line, or as Wright calls it, "The line of domesticity, the meridian of human life." The skyscraper has neither aesthetic nor moral beauty; and it does not have a great future. It is a financial speculation, an expedient. It realizes no higher ideal than to imprison thousands and thousands of people where several hundred could stand, in order to exploit land and property values.

Wright foresees a time when people will come into the city at ten and go away at four, three times a week. That is utopian. But what is realistic in this utopia—the desire to transfer family life to tranquil, airy, verdant environments—Italian urban life has anticipated by a decade.

The Tower of Babel, the stone giants of Nineveh and Babylon, fell; and the skyscrapers will fall. Already, disheartened, they have given up daring each other to go higher and higher. As happened in Nineveh and Babylonia, one day men will be content with the fact that skyscrapers are a morbid excrescence, a sin of pride worthy of Nebuchadnezzar, a madness. As for me, I am glad I lived in a time in which these sins, these madnesses, were committed because it might be only an illusory beauty, a fata Morgana, or, in Wright's words, a demonic beauty. But how can it be denied that skyscrapers are beautiful?

Falling on the street like the transparent shadows of glaciers, their vague and gigantic shadows, together with a gelid air, spread over the noise of the city that hushed silence which floats around cathedrals. Cells made of precious woods and crystal are lined up in their crypts, guarded by impassive black slaves. There is something subterranean about them, a feeling of a gate to the depths. Instead, we are carried off into the sky. The red numbers flashing in the elevator to mark the different floors seem to be the numbers on a thermometer registering the progress of a sudden fever, unreal and extremely lucid.

And that unexpected overflowing of nature at the top of the skyscraper! The land is like an immense map; the shores are scalloped with grey foam; there are wings of seagulls, and patient boats on banks of clouds. On stormy days the entire structure vibrates and hums like a violin string. But the poetic charm of skyscrapers is nocturnal, which would seem to confirm their dark and magical essence.

In New York, they illuminate skyscrapers with sober taste, with lights less diffused and varied. Lighting is more suggestive when it only touches the tops which are magically enveloped, against the black sky, in a Rembrandt-like flicker of pale flakes, now and then vibrating with more vivid scintillations. Traveling West, in Chicago, the colors multiply: reflectors completely envelop the mass of the buildings in blue, greenish, and orange rays; or the light grazes the surfaces, etching the vertical skeleton and its dark flutings which resemble snowy gorges or lunar basalt formation.

Perhaps because the rock is not steady as in Manhattan, where it rings like steel under the pickaxe, or perhaps because of the tenacious memory of lethal earthquakes, in San Francisco the skyscrapers do not rise as high. The oriental spirit of California liberally dispenses special effects and colors. San Francisco, seen by night in the distance along the waters of the bay, looks like a tray of sweets and candies, with pink slices of watermelon sprinkled with a sweet white frosting.

Among some recollections by Sam Brannan, who in 1849 was foremost among the California pioneers, there is one of the most airy imaginings of modern epic. In the flux of goldseekers, the deserted hills of the bay were populated with "houses" made of cloth: "At night the effect of those transparent houses was extraordinarily fantastic; suspended like huge Chinese lanterns on the dark slopes, they gave the impression of an amphitheatre, lit from within." This today is San Francisco.

The encampments of the pioneers, the tents of Biblical armies have disappeared. The skyscrapers will disappear. We are happy to have been in time to see them.

Skyscrapers at a Standstill

G. A. BORGESE
Atlante americano, 1936, pp. 27-34

Giuseppe Antonio Borgese (1882-1952): Until 1914, Borgese was a literary critic and a journalist. After World War I, his novel *Rubè* (1921) enjoyed great success and was published in translation by Harcourt, Brace. Other novels followed. Then, there was a long sojourn in the United States (1931-1948) prompted by Borgese's anti-Fascism. During that period, he taught Theory of Literature and Italian Literature at the University of California, Smith College, and the University of Chicago.

American Atlas, a selection of travel notes written between 1931 and 1934, shows Borgese to be a witty, humorous, and independent-minded observer of the American scene, at a time when few Italian writers knew it intimately. It is a quaint America that he describes, the America of the Depression, before worldwide expansion, a country exciting and remote.

The "Empire State Building" is the name of the newest and loftiest among the buildings soaring over the city's skyline. On the oversized chessboard which opens up as if on a platter before the approaching seafarer, and where a chess game is being played by giants, that building stands out among the other chess pieces as the Queen.

Overwhelming in size, it doesn't have to show off with frills; just as it is, square, serious, sober in color, and without ornamentation, it still dominates New York's skyline. The topmost tip, or pylon, more varied and brilliant, soars up from the last floor; it is properly called a pylon, because it seems that dirigibles could be anchored there. Others, however, say that the wind would tear airships apart up there in that savage sky.

The inlay of white metal, going up longitudinally from bottom to top, melodiously expresses this infinite ascent. Inside, the vestibule with its shining, smooth walls is a pattern of fine marbles, of reflecting surfaces and arabesques. The work is thoroughly modern and occidental, and yet it evokes the labyrinthine veinings, the geological hieroglyphics which the Byzantine architects wove on the walls of their cathedrals, selecting one by one the slabs of stone and marble. Silently and smoothly, local and express elevators zoom up and down, from floor to floor and from zone to zone. In two minutes you are at the top. Up there, leaning on the parapet, what do you see?

Especially in the evening, when it is difficult to distinguish what we see, this view is unforgettable. The stars barely shine here and there through the dark mist of the sky, but the land below us is an immense light show, thicker and lighter in spots. Here is Manhattan and the dazzling glitter of Broadway and Times Square; there is Brooklyn, the immense dormitory of the metropolis, where those who work on the island, after crossing the infinite bridges at sundown, gather around the table, around the radio, or turn off the lights, one by one, then by masses. Yellow constellations, galaxies of reflections, mile-long processions of headlights penetrating the darkness, grow dimmer and dimmer, stretch out, and disappear towards Queens, beyond Flushing. The horizon is black. In sudden spurts, you see a pool of darkness expand, in an eclipse of lights; a large one lies still in the heart of Manhattan—Central Park undoubtedly. They, the pools of darkness, even more than the million lights, invade our vision little by little. A dread rises from them, as if from whirlpools; a vague breath of vertigo tells us that straight down under our eyes is an abyss.

Greater than all. *World's greatest*. The building higher than any ever built on the face of the earth. Higher than the highest bell tower, higher than the Eiffel Tower. Higher than the royal site of the pyramids.

Every time the European feels these superlatives flutter like flags, extolling the material and technological preeminence of America today, he averts his eyes and ears. Out of superiority, out of envy. Certainly the Greek did the same in front of the colossi of Roman engineering, the walls and the arches.

Yet, since the world began, the great have loved huge things: to construct the most majestic cathedral or the grandest mausoleum, or, when they did not know what else to do, to amass the greatest pile of stones. Energy of spirit has always aimed to actualize itself in mass, in the enormity of matter; God did not create toys, but the universe. Only later, feeling must liberate itself from mass. This laboring of huge masses straining toward their own meaning, this stuggle of matter towards the expression which saturates it, can be grasped at first glance: it is the first spirituality of America.

One hundred and two floors is the height of the Empire State Building. The common passerby, throwing his head back, asks: how long will this record last? when will there be a building, a factory, of one hundred and ten or twenty floors? And he thinks to himself that it will be soon, tomorrow.

But perhaps, this may instead be a point of arrival; perhaps here also, as in other things today, there is a pause, a break. The Empire State Building will probably keep its number one position for many years. For now, such as it is, the skyline of New York is destined to remain: no longer is it an impetuous becoming, but an accomplished fact, a linear diagram added to the physiognomy of the world. I would suppose that the returning American reentering his city from the ocean would be able to recognize the almost unchangeable crest for a long time, the alternation of the peaks and precipices of unequal masses. Just as the Second Empire fixed the appearance of Paris, thus—I imagine—the decade after World War I has substantially fixed the shape of New York.

To finish, to attain perfection: this has always been the aim of man and of every one of his arts. Translated into visible terms, into architectural equivalents—the most socially expressive of all the visual media—the problem is: at what height, at what level of the atmosphere, will we touch the *ubi consistam*? at the hundred and twentieth floor? the two hundredth? We will have to stop at some point; or so the very nature of the human mind causes us to believe, for it doesn't know how to conceive of the infinite all at once.

There is a point, impossible to estimate beforehand, at which matter grown beyond measure demands measurement, in which hyperbole wants to bend into a parabola, and, in short, the house puts on the roof. The impossibility of extending the progress toward nothingness indefinitely has already been established, and, in architectonic terms, since the time of Babel.

At first, well-known objective and natural conditions—the urgency of business and traffic on a limited surface, the fabulous cost of land—encouraged the vertical thrust. Alone, in the middle of the giants of Wall Street, stands the building of the Morgan bank, only a single storey in Renaissance style; it has the solitary pride of the superpower that doesn't even need to exploit its area.

To these conditions of fact were added, perhaps, the memories of gothic architecture, of the spired churches that the puritan settlers carried in their hearts. And certainly, compounded in time, geographical suggestions were added: these immigrants, these groundbreakers of the wilderness, these builders of bridges, had on one side a boundless ocean and on the other a boundless continent. Between the two equal immensities there surged in them the impulse to compete in an aerial direction, which made it possible to look at nature from up high.

Then came the emphasis on the sublime and the habit of emphasis: the thousand arms of Briareus raised in the air just to be seen—until the summit of stone and metal was built just to hold up high, higher than anything else, a belvedere.

In the trends of taste also and with other results, three moments can be distinguished. There was a time when these buildings pretended to be what they were not, copying the base and the cornice from a Venetian or Florentine palace, and stretching between one and the other thirty or forty smooth floors, like the extension of a dining room table. Secular, commercial, and bureaucratic structures imitated medieval castles and churches; most intrusive of all is the mass of the popular five and dime store which, if it were a cathedral as it almost seems to be, would be the greatest cathedral in the universe.

All of a sudden came awareness, independence. What was new was no longer ashamed of being such; it did not beg for masks. Suddenly there was a search for a daring new style, for capricious embellishments, for a jingling, unheard-of-gaiety. The last master-piece of that genre is the skyscraper of a great automobile company, truly the jewel of New York, a minaret, a lighthouse, from whose summit, which is a cone of scales, the pinnacle darts like an arrow: a lunatic arabesque, a fantasy of surprising grace, which forces that serious sky to smile.

But the truest and most characteristic of New York, its best, is in the third direction taken by taste: in that style which is essential, in that hidden or suddenly revealed grace that is given to buildings by the balance of masses, by the equilibrium of quantities. Some of these gigantic palaces, made of nothing more than walls and windows, can enchant with the suggestion of alternate series of filled and empty spaces, with the enveloping ubiquity of their hundreds of thousands of windows. Or the white walls, flattened by certain lights, have an overwhelming appearance of glaciers. The necessity of space, technical contingencies, or above all, the obligation to pull back the top floors in order not to steal light from the sky-scraper opposite, give incredible positions to these conglomerations of cubes, blocks, and protuberances. A geometric fantasy—primitive and new—takes the place of the old decorative rhythms. These progressions of triangular, receding terraces, these stairways in the sky with cyclopean corners, would have set a Wagner on fire. These earthy masses, at first sight brutal, have souls, hold surprises of perspective, have shoulders and glances, like Sphinxes.

Above all others, the geometric impression prevails, and more than that, arithmetical, algebraic. The series of windows are rows of ciphers; the corners are symbols and signs. One walks as if in the middle of the clarity and mystery of a book of mathematics, leafing through logarithmic tables. The entire city seems at times to be translated into a hyperbolic numerical operation, of which we will want to know the result.

Numbers—numbers are everywhere; the abacus, the Pythagorean tables, more than the alphabet, seem to be the key to this civilization. The number of the street, the number of the avenue that crosses it, the number of the building, the number of the floor and of the apartment, the telephone number, the license plate number: in this circle of numbers is inscribed the profile of each one of these however many millions of beings.

The shining river of nightly advertisements on Broadway is a numerical aggregate: light upon light upon light, red upon green upon red, without end. And a numerical aggregate, light upon light, wheel upon wheel, is the terribly monotonous fun of Coney Island, the largest Luna Park in the world, and the most desperate.

Extension, expansion, elevation: every quantitative value demands a pause, a soul searching. At the apex of a collective pride which reaches to the sky, the human being feels the need to find himself again, even if he must do it by humbling himself.

The Quintessential City

G. A. BORGESE
Atlante americano, 1936, pp. 19-26

One may call "city" a series of houses and gardens, pleasing houses and fresh gardens, which stretch for miles like a long poem in alternate rhyme. Certainly, the duet has its charm, varied as it is a thousand times between leaves and shutters in the cities of cottages. Paris seems to everyone to be the model and paradigm of modern cities. Yet, its central thoroughfare, the great boulevard from the Louvre to the Etoile, with its fountains, arches, and flowering trees, imitates delightfully the form of a park. But the city supremely, quintessentially city is this one—New York.

In the same way that desert and virgin forest are nothing if not nature, New York is nothing if not city—a conglomeration of people.

Forget the sea; forget the green land. The ocean, physically not far off, is foreign to our sensibility, to our sense of smell. I say sense of smell! as if here, on this pavement which is in its own right a sea of coagulated tar, one could smell the odor of the rocks of Posillipo—it doesn't enter through any pore into our life. The two powerful branches of the river, Hudson and East, which surround the island on which the center of New York rises, must certainly have charms of their own for familiar eyes, but at first sight, under the flabby and irritated August sky, it doesn't seem to matter whether they carry water or oil. Just across from there, when you get to a pier on the river or to a tenth floor with the right visual angle, you can see the hills of New Jersey rise, a paradise within reach of weekend vacationers. But their straight lines and monochromatic green, almost of an unfinished landscape, don't say much to us. They seem rather points of reference and natural geometric forms than living nature. In any case, the whole of the city doesn't see or remember them except on Saturdays.

Middle-aged men still remember the time when there were luxuriant trees in Central Park—leafy, shady—vast conifers and other rare species. The smoke has asphyxiated them, and now nothing grows except trees of meager height, of a skin-deep green which looks ready to peel, in ringwormed meadows whose only adventures in color are the black children who play there, perhaps still untouched by the curse of knowing that they are rejected. You might wonder why geraniums and morning glories are never seen blooming on windows and balconies, why it is so rare to see a flower smile through a window (even florists stock more cactuses and thorny plants than roses and cornflowers, and sell only flowers in oblong boxes which look like coffins for tiny corpses). Or you might feel like criticizing the facades of the houses because they are decorated only with awnings striped off-white and brown or off-white and green, frowning and dazzling, like long rows of eyebrows, window after window, and with outside metal fire escapes like contraptions for gymnasts. Then the ladies here will remain thoughtful a moment and will answer you that it is very difficult to keep a vase of flowers in New York, where storms arrive suddenly with cyclone violence, devastating everything. That is true, but something else must also be true: that the moral climate of urbanism, no less than the physical climate, has reached such an extreme here that it discourages whatever aspect of souls and things does not fit in with it.

No, you no longer think of idyllic retreats, of pauses. Between humanity and nature here a curtain is drawn, invisible and ineluctable. We let the clouds and the smoke of the skyscrapers up there mingle with each other. We wait, without looking up, for one of those tropical storms to arrive, as if from another world. Galloping towards evening on tempestuous winds, they hover over the city, burst down drowning it in an almost hot wave, and then fade away over the ocean or toward the prairie. Here one doesn't look up. New York is a city only in the way that Dis is a city.

This is the paradox: that on the threshold of an immense continent such a city should have risen, a city with narrow spaces, where tenements stand on tiptoe, or even on stilts, in order to all fit there, where it seems that the outlines became elongated and thinned because of the impossibility to spread out and therefore caused the whole to achieve the effect of gothic hyperbole.

The natural origins of this unnaturalness are well known. They are the unique configuration of this natural port at the mouth of the Hudson, where any ship, however titanic or gigantic, loses majesty, where ten fleets could gather without crowding; as a consequence, the convenience, thus the necessity, of packing offices, houses, markets, and stores on the little island of Manhattan which commands the entrances of the port; and, finally, the almost metallic solidity of the rocky subsoil, miserly as to vegetation but clutching unshakably the foundations of the most audacious buildings.

Out of these natural conditions rises the vertical thrust of New York architecture. But, once it has risen, it is no longer nature, but spirit; no longer necessity but expression: it is eloquence and poetry. New York is proud of itself, acknowledges its own countenance, exults. From this springs the rhetoric or sublime expressionism of vertical architecture.

Grattacieli: skyscrapers is the exact word, with its intonation between boldness and light irony. Buildings is the generic term. Building! how can it be translated? Edifice, construction, structure? They are all flat synonyms; none of them gives the release, the pride, which overlays this common objective word here. "Building" by now means to build for the sake of building, Babel-like. The word, perhaps untranslatable with this connotation, will persist in all languages, as the words pagoda or pyramid have been preserved.

Here is the second paradox: the everyday, and yet always surprising, meeting of extremes. New York, the metropolis of the West, can evoke oriental recollections in the mind. This obsession with quantity, this gigantism of superimposed cubes obscuring the sky, is oriental. A Hebrew prophet of twenty-five centuries ago landing here would rub his eyes and recognize in these forms the same forms familiar to his visions of Babylon, haunted and full of execrations.

Third, fourth, nth paradox: they are syntheses of opposites, more or less analogous to what has been said about the meeting of

East and West, results of a human will so ruthless that through too much force it contradicts itself, does an about-face. For example, of the great modern cities this is the most modern. Yet, where will we find something similar to this city, that is nothing else but city, all stone and windows, with nothing green, all men, all will, all defense, all attack, and no rest? Not certainly in Paris and London, such as we see them today. If anywhere, we will find a parallel in the old walled-in cities, in the military cities of antiquity and the Middle Ages. Unarmed at first glance, not crossed by troops in uniform, it has another dimension which shows it to be fortress-like, fearsome and armed, although its castles and towers turn out to be only the buildings of corporations, banks, and real estate speculators.

Another example is the aspect, which can be religious or not, of the cityscape. We Europeans know cities dominated by a royal palace and other cities crowned with a castle, and others still, innumerable in our land, ordered around a cathedral: courtly cities, warrior cities, Christian cities. Here there is nothing, naturally, which attracts attention in the first or second sense; but the religious monuments also are in the background, crushed as pygmies, or almost, among the giants. Therefore, arriving in New York and seeing this crowd of sharp-topped giants move toward us almost staggering from their own hugeness, we believe they are the fronts of temples and bell towers full of bells and prayers. Instead, we find they have nothing inside but elevators and typewriters. We then feel a pang in the realization of being a foreigner, almost like the Christian traveler does in front of the cupolas and minarets of Istanbul.

This transposition of values is in no place felt more strongly than in the enigmatic, narcotic oasis of Trinity Church. Trinity Church! Church of the Trinity. By its spires navigators recognized the little city, puritan and faithful, the modest colony which the modest name of New York suited well—just as San Marco and *la Salute* showed Venice to navigators.

Now it is hidden, encapsulated within the phantasmagoric system of the skyscrapers of Wall Street, of that center of finance and banking. The soil on which it rises and the small open plot that remains next to it and that allows it to breathe have a value useless to speculate on in figures. Certainly, no one thinks or will ever think of touching it; it remains intact and protected, like a sacred spring. Near it remains intact the little garden with two acacias which almost throw some shade and the ancient little cemetery with some monuments and ornate eighteenth-century tombstones. Within it sounds the organ, undisturbed by the clamor, almost as if it were concealed in a catacomb.

From here, looking up as you go out, we can measure how far we have come, how far New York has come; New York, whose humble colonial name seems to be now so inappropriate, and which should rather be called Manhattan, by the great nasal, pioneer, barbaric-sounding name of its central island; or Atlantic City, a name usurped by a beach nearby. We can also measure how far Protestantism has come, from its religious pessimism to this burst of secular energy. All these towers of capitalism surrounding us look down on Trinity Church and do not even see it.

Manhattan's towers. I don't remember who compared New York's skyline to San Gemignano's: the greatest to the smallest, the rock to the gem. In a general way, any view of an ancient city filled with towers resembles New York. And that also is strange because inside the circumference of the Commune each powerful family raised its tower against its neighbor and rival. Here, in the bosom of the open community, in the supposed republican equality, each magnate raises his tower with capricious arrogance, higher than his competitors, and he carves on it his name as if on a monument.

Parallels

G. A. BORGESE

Atlante americano, 1936, pp. 222-223

In other times, in the years of the "open door" policy, when a steamboat discharged from its flanks every day a mass of human beings abandoned to chance, this city was a crossroads, a web of meetings. Different peoples marched down its streets with a pluck which Pelizza da Volpedo could have rendered pictorially. The city was then all movement and generous openness: a gate to the future. Now its merchant towers at times take on the air of military defenses, from which invisible arrows rain down on the shipwrecked fleeing other continents who are trying to come ashore; if the fugitives can set foot on land, they are received with a courteous ticket of sojourn which fixes the date of departure six months thence. Exclusion by race has spread a veil of staticity over certain zones of the city; sections which were bustling twenty years ago now look exhausted, with large areas of silence. You could imagine grass growing in the cracks of abandoned stone pavements. You can feel a shivering air of decadence in these marginal pools of immobility. Rushing ahead with foreboding, you can already imagine a time when it will be possible to say: old New York.

It is then, when you are in such a mood, that the parallel structure of this singular city becomes strangely obvious. As a general rule, this city has no squares, no curves, no domes. It stretches out in a system of straight lines, right angles, and perpendiculars—a last simplification of a Roman city. Its center, if center it is, is the so-called Times Square, only a ganglion, a more congested crossing upon which, stuck like a pin, is the building of the newspaper that gives it its name. The avenues, even thirty miles long, are cut by transversal streets, which are much shorter, much as you see in some fish skeletons. The transit system, ultrafast above and below the ground in the longitudinal direction, is slow and antiquated along the transversal lines, as if this imbalance also were to point out the difficulty of making up a new society out of this warehouse of human crowds. Is perhaps the famous melting pot of peoples rather a cylindrical tube where the various social and ethnic substances remain one lying on top of the other without hope of fusion? The races touch but do not mingle; whites and blacks, blondes and brunettes, coexist in an atmosphere of lukewarm tolerance without knowing or loving each other. On the interminable sidewalks, too, each person is just a transient, and meetings are only chance ones. This lonely walking, these lives running on parallel lines, are so much a part of the soul of this city—where more trusting generations once dreamed of building a perfect community.

A World Within a City

MARGHERITA SARFATTI

L'America, ricerca della felicità, 1937, pp. 8-11

Margherita Sarfatti (1887-1961): Writer, journalist, and ardent Fascist, Sarfatti was the author of a well-known biography of Mussolini, translated into English in 1925. Nevertheless, she was forced into exile by the laws against Jews. Her visit to the United States, recorded in *America, the Pursuit of Happiness*, took place in 1937.

In spite of a style heavy with literary allusions which fatigues the reader, she showed originality of thought, genuine curiosity and enthusiasm about the "new world," and a great empathy for the individuals she met. She spoke of "future shock" before the term ever appeared, and she toyed with a view of technological inventions as man's extensions of himself, a notion which today's readers associate with Marshall McLuhan.

The spectacle of this rigid geometry, which can depress a romantic spirit, fascinates me as a creative act of the will, cast in cement, etched in stone, rigidified in steel, and polished in granite and marble. Every channel of the parallel streets is intersected by the cut of the other channels, at 90° angles and at fixed distances: the famous "blocks" . . . equal at the base, unequal in the height of the buildings which shoot up like plants or frozen water sprays. From the height of these buildings, swarming below, is the magnificent sight of the incessant but changing wave of millions of mechanical toys. One block—two—three blocks—look! Every car stops obediently, as if controlled by the same lever. Through the interminable streets, the north-south blood flow stops; into the emptiness swarm the corpuscles of the east-west arteries. One block —two blocks—three blocks—the sistole and diastole of the enormous pulse suddenly stop, suddenly change. Some tiny car still slips away beyond the corner, with the insolent impunity of the small, under the pretext of being too far into the intersection to stop short. It is "the stealing of a block," intoxicating to the mischievous, although the serious cars maintain the impassive discipline of regular troops. In the evening, from the hundredth floor of the Empire State Building, all New York changes from red to green at every street corner, three minutes in each direction, over lanes that go on for miles and miles, from one river to the other, from the boundless plain to the enormous sea. And all the cube-shaped shadows of the mechanical toys, each with its yellow headlights, there, way below in the chasm, move or stop, stop or move, according to the rhythmical breathing of those millions of alternating lights, through thousands of streets.

These skyscrapers, these avenues, these lights, this mechanism of the city—interlocking, prearranged and coordinated—spring up almost from nothing, almost through an impromptu act of will. They seem to erase the image of the old, long-lived England with the affable imperialism of its cities formed through centuries of sedimentation. It may happen that a cool-headed second look will cancel the profound and warm flow of the intuitive first impression. A little information estranges you from instinct, but a great deal of knowledge leads back to it, and one returns with meditated conviction to the first divination.

"New York has no past." "America—a country without history." "Americans—a people devoid of traditions." The mental laziness of those who do not know America or its history, other than through two or three glib textbook formulas, gives credit to and at the same time overworks these insipid commonplace statements. Thus speak those who are not interested in the past, except to throw it in the teeth of the present and denigrate it; and those who, deprived of a living sense of tradition, consider it an embalmed mummy in bandages, without references, without changes, without active continuity with the present!

In my opinion, few histories are as interesting as that of America, if by "history" one understands not only a chronological measure of defunct millennia, but a succession of related events, rapid and insistent, which stretches from the past into the present day.

New York is a city overflowing with history. Americans are the most varied people and the richest in traditions. They have visible new traditions; and traditions, like the Manzonian "ordinances," are all the more obvious and intransigent when newest. Moreover, well rooted in their subconscious, Americans possess all the traditions of their continents of origin—Africa, Asia, and, above all, Europe—which they carried with them to germinate and grow anew.

U.S. Hotel

MARIO SOLDATI

America primo amore, 1935, pp. 165-171

Mario Soldati (1906-): Soldati came to the United States as a student on a scholarship in 1929. When the scholarship ended in 1930, he worked at menial jobs in Depression-era New York so that he could remain in the United States for another year. He called the book recording that experience *America, First Love.*

"America is not just an area of the world. America is a state of mind, a passion. And any European may, all of a sudden, start yearning for America, revolt against Europe, and become an American" (*America, First Love*, p. 212). Those were important words, which established a certain view of America quite removed from Cecchi's stance as an observer. They echoed the feelings of many a well-educated, restless, rebellious young Italian—the beginning of that sense of suffocation which Italian intellectuals learned to know so well under Fascism. Within the impoverished reality of a post-World War I Italy—financially, ideologically, and culturally impoverished—the image of America began to represent an escape from provincialism, from the restrictions of tradition, from the self-conscious sense of defeat and humiliation upon which the *Duce* was able to raise for awhile his fragile vision of imperialistic conquest.

In the late 1920's and in the 1930's, after being the dream of salvation for thousands of the poor, America was becoming the land of discovery and estrangement for the children of the Italian bourgeoisie—their "first love."

Soldati later became a journalist, novelist, and filmmaker. Today he is a familiar personality on television in Italy.

A hotel corridor in America always looks somewhat abandoned and sinister, whether because of the indifferent glances of travelers, the superficial cleanliness, or the long rows of identical doors. A prison corridor is scarcely different. But how many European hotels, especially if they are old or second class, have corridors varied with arches, recesses, steps, and other age-old architectural caprices? In this way they offer a completely human domicile. They are truly hotels—refuges, shelters. More welcoming, even if the bathtub doesn't work so well; more civil, even if less clean, than the perfect American hotel.

The elevator unloads us in the silence of a very long corridor—narrow, deep, plush. We walk along searching for our room number as if in a nightmare. No chance to meet up with a maid.

In Europe, the hotel corridors are the place of gossip, the meeting point of maids and porters. This, too, is humanity. But in the corridors of American hotels the maids irrupt from basement workrooms at a given hour. In uniforms with blue and white stripes, and with their muscular bodies and ruddy faces, they seem rather to be platoons of nurses. They throw open all the doors. They open all the windows. They change all the sheets. With buzzing machines they absorb all the dust. They have finished. They disappear. Until the same hour of the next day, the corridor is deserted.

We go forward. Our room is still far off. We advance defenseless against invisible and inimical presences. Today in the United States armed assault is the most common event in the news. Give the bandit a place as safe as this corridor. *Safe*: secure, clean, without danger of failure.

Nevertheless, the impression of dread made by the American

hotel corridor lies elsewhere: in its silence, its narrowness, its length, in the apparently infinite rows of convex metal doors, the geometric exactitude of the construction. Because we truly are in a rational construction, in an exclusively logical reality, between walls which no longer have anything unconscious. But they have the diabolical characteristics of abstract logic, of Absolute Consciousness.

Everything serves a purpose. Everything is justified. The thick carpets, in order not to disturb sleep. The indirect lighting, in order to rest the sight. The convex doors, double, bivalvular, in order to hang up your pants in the evening without going out into the corridor and find them pressed in the morning without the girl from the hotel presser's coming into your room and disturbing you.

Comfort. Service. . . . Magic words in America. It's a reasoned repression of the instincts, a perversion, we would say. Let the girl come in, wake you up, disturb you! What an adventure of human relations. What authentic comfort and service. Nothing is less practical than the extolled American practicality. It isolates, chills, frightens. It reduces human contacts to echoes, reflexes, shadows. Sometimes, as in this corridor, it removes them to the point of making you doubt their existence. To the point of saturating things with magic. To the point of endowing them with a spectral supremacy.

The dread of the American hotel corridor is actually a fear of the devil. With which we enter our room quickly and lock ourselves in.

The smell of American hotel rooms. A smell not unpleasant, but sad. Perhaps it is the overlapping, the mixture of scents of people who have stayed there. Shaving cream, skin cream, toothpaste, talcum powder, face powder, hair lotion, etc. All the complicated paraphernalia of the American toilet. All the cleanliness, all the chemical layers with which even the lowliest traveling salesman defends, isolates, rationalizes his own body. The aridity of those poor lives seems to hang on between the walls, suspended in the dense perfume of a cake of soap. You can almost hear the echo of gloomy jokes and empty laughter.

The floor is covered with a thick layer of green plush. The walls are bare, crisply covered with cream-colored plaster. And decorated with two or three prints. If the room costs twelve dollars, they are copies of eighteenth-century French prints. The usual little scenes. Alcoves, embraces, shadowy recesses, pastorals, ladies, maids, and gallants. *Les confidences. La lettre. La jolie bergère.* And certainly they will suggest to American guests a sense of luxury, of lasciviousness, of corruption, Very "continental," they would say, with an adjective that they love, between the ironic and the envious. Very continental, that is, very European.

But whoever can pay only seven dollars must be content with fox hunting scenes. Hounds, horses, red livery: copies of nineteenth-century English prints. Finally, whoever pays no more than three dollars must suffer the full American severity. Behold respectfully the classical subjects of New England: the White House, the Lincoln Memorial, Mount Vernon, the Washington Monument. Or, at the most, the Potomac and the Battery "as they once were."

The desk, the bed, and the bureau roll on rubber wheels and can be moved without difficulty by a child. The room is very small. But whoever wants the bed against the left wall rather than the right or vice versa can effect the change in half a minute. Usually the bathroom is also small, but always completely equipped. A waterproof silk curtain, pink or green or blue, closes the shower stall.

A whole pamphlet would be necessary to enumerate all the attractions—all the features, merits, and specialties—of an American hotel room. And the blue night light. And the radio in every room. And the newspaper of the city where the client lives slipped under the door every morning with the compliments of the hotel manager.

Yet, all this service, instead of soothing or mitigating the stay in a strange room, oppresses. It does away, it is true, with the impatience for hot water that doesn't come, the nervousness over the light switch that doesn't work, but also the reactions, tastes, and personal life of the traveler.

Americans aren't aware of this. Precisely because they aren't aware of it they suffer terribly. It's a sadness that they don't admit. A gloom that only a European can see in them: especially when they joke; when they believe that they're having a good time; when they insist on having had *a very good time*: happy hours.

And the hotel room?

The best they ever had in their life. . . .

And the bed? how did they sleep?

Fine! Very well!

But it's a "fine" too nasal (pronounced fain), too monotonous, too identical to the innumerable *fines* that all Americans say every day, for it not to sound rather like an enormous frustrated desire for happiness. Still, there *was* something new, a marvel.

What?

The iced water tap. *O boy, that was hot*! . . .

Hot. Caldo. It is also used for sexual, exciting. Perhaps, given the scarcity of real excitements, it comes to signify simply pleasing. And then, even refreshing. Sometimes in vocabulary there is all the history, all the psychology of a people. In this absurd adjective is all the boredom of a summer afternoon in a Chicago hotel room.

There is nothing to do. You don't know anyone. It's hot. You throw yourself down on the bed but without the desire to sleep. What is it that gleams, there in the corner? You go to see. *Iced water* is written on the enameled knob of a long nickel-plated spigot. Iced water. Are you thirsty? Not very. It doesn't matter; drink a little. Make the water run between your fingers. What a nice pastime! *Good time*! *Fine*! *Hot*! After a few minutes, even this discovery no longer has anything exciting about it. Across the open window the courtyard can be seen, or rather a section of the courtyard from the height of twenty or thirty floors. The bottom and the top of the skyscraper are visible only if you lean out from the windowsill.

Thousands of windows. Thousands of cells identical to ours. But what solitude! In each cell, on each desk, is a large black book—the sacred Bible. With that staging, no wonder it makes an impression. *There is a God who is watching you. And here is his Will*. How many times a trembling hand will have opened the magic Book! A desperate glance. It will have read condemnation or hope. The wanted criminal, who fears for his life, holed up, hidden in one of the 50,000 hotel rooms, how many times during the long hours of tedium and terror must have had recourse to it. Technological progress doesn't destroy the tragic religiosity of Americans, but feeds it. And how many times other men will have thrown down the terrible Book. And will have opened the desk drawer.

In every room, in the drawer of every desk, beside the ink, pen, and paper, is an envelope, nice and stamped with the name and address of the hotel manager. "In case of suicide." *American Efficiency*! Efficiency, always American Efficiency! This time it is well said. Let us join the enthusiastic universal recognition.

It is marvelous how the walls of celotex, the double doors divided in half, and the plush of the carpets deaden noise. Not even your next door neighbor would hear a gunshot.

And then, next to that envelope in the drawer of every desk is a card. A handsome yellow card. DO NOT DISTURB. . . . The guest, if he wants, hangs it outside his door.

Don't worry, sir. You will not be disturbed. Go ahead and shoot yourself.

Red-brick Baltimore

MARIO PRAZ

Viaggi in occidente, 1955, pp. 214-215

Mario Praz (1896-): A prominent Italian critic and scholar of English and American literature, Praz is identified with the introduction of American authors to the Italian reading public of the 1920's. He held the chair of English Language and Literature at the University of Rome until his retirement, and is a member of the Academy of the *Lincei*.

Praz's experience as a traveler in the United States during the 1950's is reported in *Travels in the West*, but he is better known to English readers for his translated critical works, *The Hero in Eclipse* and *The Romantic Agony*. Generally, Praz's approach to American literature has been negative; he finds the absence of a long literary tradition to be a serious difficulty for American writers. His travel narrative reveals him to be similarly uncomfortable with the United States as a place, one which he finds large and lonely, without compensating attractions.

"Red" would be a good adjective for Baltimore as it is for Bologna. There is even a lonely brick tower, tall and thin in the middle of an open space, which could make one think of the famous towers of Bologna. This tower, with its shape like a truncated cone, actually looks more like a chimney than a tower, and if it were not for the round battlements that crown it, it would easily reveal its utilitarian origins: for it was used in the melting and cooling of lead projectiles. As for the red color of the nineteenth-century houses in Baltimore, down the still numerous streets where they can be found, it is not so much a brick red as it is a paint red, which goes from a hot to a cool red, here with orange tones, there with blue tones, and at times veers toward a livid red, a muddy wino red. The houses are low, with flat fronts, like the ones around the British Museum in London; they are the plebeian colonial offshoot of that metropolitan aristocracy. The houses on St. Paul Street near Mount Vernon Place are an exception, for that is the better section of the city and the colors are spread with more taste. But as one moves farther from the center of town, the southern and western districts display exactly that humble appearance with a crowd of little houses painted in lively colors, next to each other, like little toy houses.

I must say that here in America the comparison between houses and toys comes spontaneously. This is not so for today's skyscrapers but for the little houses of the first settlers and for the white frame houses built at the beginning of the nineteenth century next to their little church, also made of wood, clustered around the village green, amid tall trees, in so many New England towns.

Loneliness in the City

MARIO PRAZ
Viaggi in occidente, 1955, pp. 212-214

How lonely and lost one can feel in America! A colleague of mine came here from Italy to teach in an American university and fled like a madman after three weeks. I cannot agree with what he did, but after having been here I can understand it. The only remedy could be the one de Maupassant resorted to in order to dispel the sense of loneliness he felt at nightfall. Actually, a scholar from Eastern Europe whom I happened to meet succeeded in getting used to the environment or at least surviving in it (although he still has a foreign accent after thirty years), thanks to the American women who felt attracted to him. The woman you hold in your arms can be a substitute for the land that's disappearing from under your feet. But not everyone can play the ladykiller and the Don Juan.

Here it is impossible to build ties with a city. In our old Europe a city, however few traditions it may have, soon becomes your companion, your mother, your lover. Not here. Here you are alone among machines. Can a skyscraper be close to you as an old palace would be? The very dimensions of the skyscraper are unreal and do not communicate any hint of the sublime. If you look at them with the eye of a Swift in the land of giants, the famous skyscrapers of Manhattan are a collection of bottles and decanters; or, if you prefer a more noble term of comparison (but the cheapest bottles have been ennobled by Morandi's brush), they are an agglomeration of crystals. A skyscraper makes you think on second thought, if not at first glance, of how certain death would be if one jumped from one of its windows.

What to Do to Keep from Going Crazy GIORGIO SOAVI

Fantabulous, 1963, pp. 12-16

Giorgio Soavi (1923-): Soavi, a journalist and poet, has been a frequent visitor to the United States. His first collection of journalistic pieces on the United States, *America All in One Breath*, and the later *Fantabulous*, are the product of his two encounters with this country in the late 1950's and early 1960's.

Soavi belongs to the generation after Soldati's— certainly a more open, flexible, and cosmopolitan one. The society which Soavi discovers is recognizable to the reader (or should be); it is yesterday's America, the one Americans found so dull.

Yet, Soavi, too, tells us that he had dreamed of America before actually discovering it. For him, as for Soldati, America was a "first love," and his journey was the consummation of that love. And again, what a shock it is for this cool Italian visitor to come face to face with American reality, a journey of self-discovery within a cultural context.

I simply went out on a rather cold and windy March evening, in spite of being dead tired, because I had tried to talk politics with some American friends to whom politics seems to be everything, absolutely—their totally absorbing hangup. Could I possibly go to bed right away now that I live in New York? Even though the city jumped in front of me and sometimes swayed violently like the ship

I was on when a hurricane made it bend to one side in the middle of the ocean, a hurricane of force eight or nine, as it was written in the captain's bulletins. I was carrying around that staggering force in the first few days, and now I lived on one of the highest floors of a skyscraper on the Hudson River, and the windy evening swayed dangerously like the ocean that I had already crossed. I needed other emotions. I left the hotel, joined my friend, crossing at various points that balance beam which is the city, first in a taxi, and then on foot for a long way. My friend's wife, a dancer, had already run off to her evening rehearsal, and we two went to the movies.

Then, a walk through the Bowery, but he was never at ease. He grabbed me by the jacket and prodded me on if I saw some drunk who wanted money to buy a beer. When I remained leaning against a ground floor window because I had heard the voice of a woman who was moaning, he reproached me. What was I to do? I was trying to understand something through this daughter or wife who was crying; it seemed different from the cries of my land. I looked at the stones of the house and the panes of the windows, too-horrible windows, with those fire escapes which wind like creepers along the façades of the houses and which I had dreamed about not only because of gangster films. The day before in a little room in a hotel near Sutton Place I had gone to find Gloria. Seated there on the bed, while she combed her hair and held two hairpins in her mouth, she made gestures like a mute or a cripple, craning her neck toward the window: "Look there, see? There are still bullet holes, and there, near your feet, on the floor, there is the mark of a third shot."

"That's all?" I asked. Gloria was laughing, but it was chilling, and then she explained that she had asked for months to have the glass changed, but the manager would not listen to her.

I leaned against that house, with my friend who was bending toward me and making signs of impatience. "Are you coming along or not?" he shouted. Then, unwillingly, I rejoined him and asked him to excuse my state; I was tired, couldn't wait to get home (let's go ahead and call it home, anyway). With those cries piercing my eardrums; well, let's skip the sentiment. Why go on about it? Well, finally, I told him that at least I didn't have any little bullet holes, and who can take aim at a window on the thirtieth floor from down there?

"But then if you're tired, we'd better go."

"Yes, we'd better," I answered, and in the meanwhile there's some little mutt who comes toward me shivering, who has no tail and only one ear. It must be the fault of this place.

"Well, see you tomorrow."

"O.K.; you understand? We are now going together to the square, on the bus, then you take a subway and ask. You have to get off at the Columbus Circle stop. From there you're just a step away, a few blocks."

"Right. I'll telephone tomorrow." So many things to do.

Instead of taking the bus, which never comes, I start walking; I'm crazy about walking, so off I go. What a strange square. Here where I am there is a great silence, not even a soul, and there, across the way, cars, buses, people—not people on foot, that's inadmissible. I cross the piazza, which is obstructed or marked in a number of places with many chains of traffic islands. I jump some and am making these jumps when from a corner, a dark corner, about twenty boys are almost waiting for me to fall into their arms. Now I see them well. They have the usual uniform—leather jackets, blue jeans, buckles on their caps, and cowboy boots. Ah, a gang. Just yesterday, another friend of mine who studies sociology told me he had seen them in action one summer evening right before his eyes. He had given a party and some friends had stayed late. From his house to the subway was a good way on foot, no money, so no taxi, and they had started off. But a few minutes after this, he hears running and then screams of pain. So he goes to the window just in time to witness a volley of blows, as only happens in the movies, and in two seconds, two boys are on the sidewalk under his window fainting and bloody. And then he told how one of those two had become blind because of the blows he had received. He wanted to be a writer and spent the first hours of his convalescence seated at a little table, next to his mother, who told him over and over, "Stop now; now you are beyond the margins of the sheet; go back; start a new line." Every day he improved and it almost seemed as if the problem was resolved. Instead, she became aware that her son was roaming through the house looking for a knife or a razor blade or a revolver to kill himself with. Then the sociologist explained: complexes, drunkenness, violence—what arms do they use? Elbows in the belly, elbows in the face, and above all kicks in the balls, this way a man can be incapacitated without fail. But why, why so barbaric? Well, he says, they don't know what to do, and if they find someone at hand who seems to be enjoying himself, they castrate him if they can. And usually they can. And the police? That's right, the police go around all the time, in fact, and stop those going on foot and ask them if they need help.

Alone in the square I looked around. They stood in front, not moving. There was a small chain to jump before finding an open space. In the other corner, far—200 meters—sped the colored cars, neon lights, the American colors, those images which so many times, bowed over a book of beautiful photographs or sunk in a seat in a movie theater in Milan, I had loved and desired to the point of identifying myself with them.

An about-turn and I ran out of breath up toward the cars and there felt safer. I dared to look back. The gang was there, like a cobra coiled or hidden behind a little pile of rags.

The cars grazed me. A taxi picked me up and I headed toward my refuge.

I took the elevator to my room. The elevator boy gave me a newspaper; I gave him a good tip and then I was home. There is New York—windows, river, the wild roar of tugboats, the lights that never go out, the guillotine clicks of the IBM electric locks, the noises of the Americans in the rooms nearby, the water glass wrapped in paper and sealed, the new little soaps. Something is wrong. My fear, the fear of experiences too strong, my effort not to waste the soap which these Americans leave daily . . . Bursts of wind reach up here, the wind is strong and the castle sways: after a night like this, do we want to imagine a great crumbling? A newspaper headline: American skyscraper breaks and crumbles. Eight hundred dead. Four hundred missing. All the participants in the Convention of Tailors of America perished in the disaster. What will become of me, what must I do in order to keep from going crazy between these walls? Simple: get dressed again and go out into the city; walk, walk; ask for help or go down to the bottom, down to the bottom, down to the bottom.

AMERICAN LIFE

II

General

Italian writers have reacted to all aspects of American life from institutions, customs, and language to individuals. Their impressions range from general views of large areas and types—such as the American "deity" of prosperity and the American woman—to anecdotes of specific experiences. Here, as elsewhere in their writings, the familiar frame of reference serves as an overt or implicit standard for explaining New World phenomena. Thus, Giuseppe A. Borgese, describing how an American refers to his wife, comments: "His wife is not for him 'my wife' or *la mia signora* as Italians say with their possessive pretension, but 'Mrs. Smith.'" Similarly, Margherita Sarfatti's characterization of America as "larger than life" is based upon an Italian norm that is never explicitly mentioned.

While some of the opinions come as no surprise—America's size and prosperity have invariably been remarked upon by most visitors from smaller and less wealthy countries—these selections are notable for their original insights and suppositions. Well before our own awareness was sharpened by the premonitions of energy shortages and a greater concern with natural living, Danilo Dolci listed the reliance on an artificial environment as a negative aspect of a school he visited: "Even though the children live near the light, the beach, and the ocean, they spend the greater part of their days with electric lights on." And who but an outsider like Borgese would regard the use of candles at dinner—a symbol of formality and sophistication to Americans—as a remnant of our pioneer heritage?

Italian writers are intrigued by a multitude of American types: puritans, gangsters, blacks, Mormons, business tycoons, Italo-Americans, and suburbanites—to name only a few. Individuals appear in these pages, but as might be expected, they are often regarded as representative figures. Thus, the observations found in this section are the more likely to surprise or put off the American reader—so much is arbitrary or incomplete.

One of the most frequently recurring characters is, quite predictably, "the American woman." But here the reader will find that, contrary to the often unflattering stereotypes prevalent in Europe, the Italian visitors are almost always genuinely admiring and at times quite perceptive. The male writers occasionally view women as potential conquests. More than one exemplar of Italian *machismo* has unhappily discovered that the freedom he remarked in American girls did not extend to sexual encounters; older women, divorced or with preoccupied husbands, were approached more successfully. Probably Mario Soldati's "Love in Brooklyn" is the classic example of an Italian-American romance. Emilio Cecchi's general statement on American womanhood is a classic of another sort:

Worshipping the Madonna at the altar, we feel freer and more at ease when facing women of flesh and blood. For the puritans it is different. Too proud to worship the divinity of the Madonna, they continuously run the risk of worshipping (or just about) the women in their own households. It's a bad trend.

The few women who have written about the United States view American women quite differently, both from the male writers and from each other. Margherita Sarfatti, a perceptive if wordy traveler of the 1930's, expresses admiration for her American counterparts, whom she views as courageous, industrious, clear-headed, and attractively independent. She describes them as the descendants of the pioneer women, determined to pursue happiness but at the same time hardworking and exquisitely compassionate. Fernanda Pivano, on the other hand, sees the independence of American women as rather disturbing. In the California of the early 1960's, the girls she met—beautiful, educated, "serious"—take the pill *and* guard their reputations in order to ultimately secure a husband.

None of the women she describes leads a totally successful life; Pivano senses a certain aimlessness and lack of purpose among them. Both the affluent unmarried girl and married woman seem vaguely dissatisfied: the girl waits for an undefinable "something"; the woman feels compelled to fill her days with activities that give little pleasure or sense of accomplishment. Through the eyes of an articulate foreign woman, we get a glimpse of the feminine society Betty Friedan chose as her subject at about the same time: women trapped by the most dangerous ambition, the traditional wifely desire for the husband's success, and the unreal expectations of complete fulfillment from perfect marriages.

Although the writers of this volume wrote about America in Italian, most did have a good to excellent knowledge of English. Moreover, since World War II, American English has heavily infiltrated a number of areas of Italian vocabulary—especially sports, music, and recent technology. No wonder, then, that several of these writers discuss the American language, most commonly with admiration for its vitality and richness. Borgese asserts that "American English is not a corrupted British English, but an English raised to the nth power," while Soavi lists words that have a distinctively American flavor and then coins one of his own to describe his entire American experience—"fantabulous."

Customs, Rituals, and Traditions G. A. BORGESE

Atlante americano, 1936, pp. 286-291

Someone who indulges in abandoning himself to the impulses of a fiery temperament would be rejected and lost in a very short time in America. That is probably the case because anger is considered here to be an anti-economical, negative, unproductive threat to the autonomy of other individuals.

Another forbidden feeling . . . is melancholy. There are poets, novelists and playwrights who deal with it on everybody's behalf; that is their province. The private citizen has no right to give vent to his sadness and to becloud the air everybody breathes. Tears and wails are crimes; confessions are barbarous. From the tenderest age, from kindergarten up, children are trained to smile more than the Japanese. "Keep smiling"—that American smile which would deserve a special chapter. The halls and the rooms of hospitals offer an incredible spectacle of stoicism, an artificial and uniform impassivity.

When we turn from the world of feelings to the minute pragmatic details, we find an etiquette unequaled anywhere in the world for its continually vigilant strictness. The newly arrived European who hears the traditional "How do you do?" immediately answers in proper English "Very well, and you?" but soon realizes that the question does not require an answer at all. To the first "how do you do" you respond with another "how do you do," since it is understood that elementary politeness requires you to be in good health and to refrain from indiscreetly inquiring about other people's health.

Respect for privacy is the reason why you don't say, as is done elsewhere, that you know someone because you met him at So-and-so's house. You will say only that you have met him. "To know someone" is reserved for more important situations; if it were used for a brief encounter, it would be the equivalent of a violation of personal privacy. On the other hand, the highest respect for the individual person is required in other ways: first of all, you must recognize people's faces and names. Absentmindedness and forgetfulness, so normal among us, are viewed here as offensive. The hostess certainly does not let her guests introduce themselves at random even if they want to; she meticulously introduces everyone. Each person, acknowledging the other's greeting, should repeat the other's name—if he can—to show that he'll remember it. However, as they do not want to encroach upon people's freedom and upon their own, they most certainly leave *à l'anglaise*, without even telling the lady of the house good-bye . . .

When speaking of themselves, they seldom use their titles, except perhaps professors. But they will always use their own names accompanied by the title of universal democratic dignity: "mister." When answering the phone, John Smith doesn't say "Smith here"; he answers by saying, "This is Mr. Smith." His wife is not for him "my wife" or *la mia signora*, as Italians say with their possessive pretension, but "Mrs. Smith."

This cult of the individual extends unconsciously, but very obviously, to other small daily occurrences. Consider, for example, the mail. Sending postcards with your private business in the open and available to the public eye is almost never done. But it's almost impossible to find lined envelopes in stationery shops; envelopes are usually transparent, the assumption being that no one will be curious about other people's affairs. I have already mentioned that there are no nameplates on doors of houses and apartments, but there is something else that needs mention: in this country, where everything seems to be made according to the criterion of the greatest possible comfort, it's generally very difficult to find house numbers, especially at night. They are hidden and unclearly marked, sheltered in a little corner where you have to go looking for them with a lantern. It is as if private homes were psychologically reinforcing the habit of keeping away from public view and from public curiosity. This is just a very small but clear example of the contradictions caused by the stubborn survival of historical trends in American life.

Here is another example, a more important one. Why, when they have so much space available, do Americans build houses with such small rooms and low ceilings? It would be inaccurate to attribute this phenomenon to economic reasons. Why, when they have so much electricity and gave the world the electric bulb, when they pour floods of light on streets and squares, why do Americans prefer to live in houses plunged in semi-obscurity, with thick, dark lamp shades which we Europeans find difficult to get used to, and which suggest a return to candlelit times? As a matter of fact, in the dining room we actually do go back to candlelight, for it is absolutely required from ocean to ocean that candles, dim and multi-colored, illuminate the table. And, finally, why—when they are so rich, at least those who *are* rich—do they prefer to move to camping grounds in the summer, places that are poor, uncomfortable, rough, and governed by a discipline and culinary simplicity that could easily be called Spartan?

Those are all colonial rituals. In their closed homes and in their open-air vacations, Americans want to find—consciously or unconsciously—the atmosphere, mystery, daring, and harshness of their first days in the New World. They reenact an almost sacred representation of their origins, a deeply instructive memento of that inspired individualism, limited and sharpened by every other person's individualism.

Under an appearance of anarchy, many essential elements of American life and customs—from emotions to manners, from cooking to language—have a Spartan sternness, a ritual-like rigidity. Now try to imagine this regularity and conformity of daily actions and expressions extended to every spiritual movement and need for expression. You will understand immediately why it is that Americans, in spite of their political freedom and legal anarchy, feel far from free. There is no country where the familiar complaint of repressed and oppressed souls is heard more frequently, although each may speak in general terms, most often hiding one's own personal grievances. In no country has Freud's research in the field of repressions become—as it has here—daily bread for even the most mediocre minds.

In theory, a stronger law would perhaps bring about, by counterbalance, a lightening of the weight of custom. Americans could regain in their emotional and expressive life some of the freedom of action they have surrendered to the State in other areas. Yet, we must not forget that such an hypothesis is in the area of pure and static theory. Actually, law and custom are tightly bound together; the weakness of the law is one of the many reasons for the dictatorial rule of American custom.

An American Deity

G. A. BORGESE
Atlante americano, 1936, pp. 296-301

. . . What does this American divinity resemble? Which one of our names would be appropriate for it? *Prosperità* would seem to be the Italian term equivalent to Prosperity, but this world's variety is made up of just such minute and profound differences.

One of our devotees of neoclassicism would carve her in the guise of allegorical Plenty: a maternal-like beauty, well-nourished and nurturing, cornucopia in hand. And perhaps the sculptor would not even fully understand the meaning of those two attendant divinities which he would add at the front end of the base: one called Opportunity, the other Chance. These words also seem to be easy and clear at first glance, and yet they are so different from their former selves! Opportunity or *Occasione* should have very little to do with the lady you "catch by her hair" or who "makes a thief out of you"; and Chance is very seldom mentioned when alluding to games of luck or to blind fate, with whom it is usually found associated in other languages. "Give him a chance" is an expression you often hear. It is said in a tone of encouragement by a superior or of straightforward sympathy by an equal, but it never points to a casual endeavor. It can only be translated with a periphrasis, such as "Give that man a way to pull himself up, to show what he can do." It doesn't mean "Give him the dice to gamble" but "give him a weapon so that he can fight."

Whoever has heard the speeches of political candidates and of their supporters knows with what seriousness and self-righteousness this trinity of deities is usually invoked: Chance, Opportunity, and Prosperity. According to local patriotism, America, much more concretely than what the Germans viewed as "the land of unlimited opportunities," is the place and time on the face of this earth where the greatest number of chances and opportunities is afforded the greatest number of human beings. To attain what? Prosperity, without doubt. And, without any doubt, there is no prosperity without wealth and abundance.

But plenty in America is not meant for enjoyment. It does not pour a horn full of delightful presents ("You understood me right," said Faust, the most American of all heroes, to the Devil; "I did not ask you to give me pleasure"). Rather, it is meant for enjoyment without pleasure, enjoyment for its own sake. Returning home from our tormented continent in the fall, American tourists speak of Europe as if it were a paradise of delights which they are leaving to reenter the disciplined laboratory that is their country. They are very careful not to imitate at home the pleasures they tasted during their vacation. America, if it is wealthy and as wealthy as it may be, looks more like a strange millionaire Sparta than like Sybaris. It has parsimonious meals . . . sprinkled with iced water. It has myriads of little wood houses whose unending uniformity is barely disguised by the sublime heights of New York, illusory triumphal gateway, where the skyscrapers more than palaces are actually a proliferation, vertically and cubically, of these very same little structures. Streets naively exhibit a stubborn melancholy and persistent humility as they open on both sides on an uncultivated, semideserted landscape dotted with simple little cabins. Luxury is found accumulated in public works and buildings, not in private dwellings which are almost never spacious and are seldom adorned with flowers in the windows or with laces and precious knick-knacks inside. One is surprised to find there, if at all, even a cage with singing birds or a cat purring by the fire. Americans have self-service; and cars, from New York to California, all dark, all well enclosed, with no . . . little good luck charm dancing in the rear window; and sports, which are more exercise than amusement; and dancing, which is the last resort for sedentary and ungifted people to practice some movement; and cleanliness, which is a hygienic practice and a social grace more than a pleasure; and the rule which forbids bad odors but bars strong perfumes; and beautiful women dressed more or less in uniform. Even free love, if and when it is practiced, is an obligatory acknowledgment of the severe and health-minded libertinism preached by a physiopsychological Jeremiah, Sigmund Freud.

Americans know that they do not know how to enjoy their own wealth and that their money is an end in itself. What does it serve then? Certainly not to be counted with avaricious claws, as it was counted by Harpagon; acquisitiveness may be American, but not avarice. It serves, generously, to be spent more and more magnificently for philanthropic or cultural causes; it serves, from the individual point of view, to know that it can be spent to live beyond the reach of humiliation and fear. Perhaps no trait sets the American apart in a more expressive way than his not using a coin-purse; it would seem to him a proof of an excessive petty concern with small change, which must be allowed to fall, nonchalantly, in some pocket. Poor or rich, all Americans agree on this. There is no real social difference between them because wealth here can give you an immense, overwhelming sense of power but not even the pleasure of feeling superior in caste.

Wealth is understood, above all, to be a means to autonomy and to courage. It is to be desired and pursued in order to avoid a spiritual ill or pettiness rather than because of the material, enjoyable goods it can buy. On a small scale, the clerk who hopes to buy more than the strict necessities of life by climbing one step, ten dollars more a week, is the spiritual brother of the great, old Rockefeller, who crushed his rivals and succeeded in amassing millions, spurred on only by the biblically inspired and Calvinistic impulse of a basically generous pursuit of "God's gold."

It may well be that in the last few decades, American wealth has lost, to a large extent, its awareness of moral and even religious roots; this is one of the reasons for its present decadence. But those roots have not died. It is a good thing for us to know it, if we want to grasp something of whatever actions the United States will take in the next few months and years, within the world's new arrangement. Whoever sees only materialism and business on this side of the Atlantic sees little and not very far. Whoever interprets thus the cry of "Prosperity," still echoing from the presidential campaign, must be ready for surprises.

Deep down, this term, which is one hallmark of Americanism, has a self-righteous ring. Their Prosperity is not a tranquil and monumental Goddess of Plenty but a dynamic, lean, and swift Goddess of Action. It is a quality, more than a possession; a movement forward more than a state of being. It would be appropriate to translate it with two classically Latin words: *Fortuna Virilis.*

A Meeting in Chicago

G. A. BORGESE

Atlante americano, 1936, pp. 35-41

You have heard, even you people far away, boasts of the magnificent and singular New York stations, one called Grand Central, the other Pennsylvania; with their vestibules, colonnades, corridors, galleries, shops, and displays—everything but trains. Actually, this impression of a trick, of dissimulation, which seems due to a sumptuous, traditional sense of beauty wishing to deny the harsh grey shapes of the trains, lasts only an instant. On second glance, along the walls of the large halls you discover the entrances, each with the number of the track to which it leads.

These entrances are relatively low and half-lit. There is no sight of arcades or a perspective of trains as far as the eye can see under the splendor of arc-lamps. You see only your own train (I was about to say your own coach); and even your coach is not especially notable since the sunken track lowers the steps to the level of the platform. There are few people: those who are leaving and a few more. There are no admission tickets to the tracks, and every time the permission of the station master or of one of his officials is needed. Newspapers, magazines, provisions, beverages—whatever you need you can get in the entrance hall, in the colonnades open to all. Down here, nothing of all that; here, a single operation is performed: departure. It happens at the predetermined moment, without turmoil, without emotional drama, almost without noise: a simple pulling away.

Yet, in its own way this simplicity is solemn, perhaps more suggestive than the travail and roar exhibited in European stations. It seems that not only practical and technical reasons have suggested to Americans this isolation of the train's departure and arrival from every other aspect of life, but a feeling peculiar to them of the grandeur and the majestic meaning of machines moving and of the conquering of space. Thus, paradoxically, the scientific agitation which smacks of the nineteenth century, that reverence in front of the "beautiful and horrible monster" of Carducci, which among us has cooled down, is again encountered here, where the mechanical structure of life must by now be a cold habit. A Whitmanian enthusiasm for the wheel and the engineer can recapture its primitive freshness. Whoever descends into this quasi-crypt, where the dark train prepares in silence to subdue thousands of miles, can have the impression of witnessing a serious and irretrievable moment of existence. Shades of old feelings rise again to your mind, unaccustomed words return to your lips; you almost feel like calling the train a "convoy."

Not that a lugubrious, sorrowful note is connected to it. For Americans, to depart is not to die but to live; it is their peculiar way of living. Out of ten observations and minute discoveries which could be made about the life and customs of Americans, at least five should be ascribed to this primordial and permanent mode of being peculiar to them—movement which is journeying. From the first beginning, from the first exiles and landings in this country, they have kept, willy nilly, the temperament of migrants and of colonists, an alienation from stability and repose, a goading curiosity about what lies beyond, the *plus ultra*. If it would be capricious and false to say that they are leaping back to a nomadic period out of the domesticity, the hedges, and the fortified walls of European man, it is nevertheless true that they are creating a new human type, that is neither sedentary nor nomadic, the forerunner of the race, the pioneer, the man ready to move. If every European recognizes his typical ancestor in the peasant warrior, every authentic American is ideally the descendant of pioneers.

This road I have chosen is the same that the pioneers in their covered wagons took—with rather greater difficulty. The railroad tracks, on which my train will take its smooth course of four nights and three days, were placed on that wagon road. It is a straight latitudinal line from Chicago to the Pacific, a belt of iron down the center of the country. It is called the Overland Trail.

But first, we must reach Chicago. There are no through trains from the Atlantic to the other coast. This lack, which seems strange in a country where everything has to be comfortable and quick, corresponds well to the configuration which the country was spontaneously given, making a pivot of Chicago, the capital of the Middle West, from which so many roads fan out.

The space between the Atlantic and the Midwest is covered in approximately a night and a day of travel. Hills high and low, robust swellings of the soil, leafy with a tart green, without the softness of vistas, follow us in incessant procession as the train forges on. Wide rivers, without the delight of banks, flow under our eyes with deep, compact waves; showers of rain beat down on them and do not even ruffle the surface. At dusk we are in Chicago.

Chicago! A flat, barbaric name, that English pronunciation has not blunted and smoothed at all—Chicago. In it, finally, in its exotic and vast sound, solitude and distance are heard. Here are no picturesque seductions of the Orient, as perhaps I will notice in San Francisco, with the Golden Gate open toward Asia, nor the fragrances of Europe which create an illusion riding on the breakers of the Atlantic, nor the names of cities and hills reminiscent of old England. The seas, the ways of the old world, are remote. In this umbilicus of the continent unforeseen innovations are fashioned. Although it is presumptuous and vain to predict the future, perhaps one will not risk too much who supposes that in the twenty-first century the name of Chicago will be greater and more noted than today. As in other times, Susa, Persepolis, and Peking were spoken of. As later people said Moscow, so one day people will say Chicago. A focus of earthly civilization, a first cause, a matrix of mysterious creation. Lawrence would say: a city of destiny.

I shall come back to Chicago through days and weeks to divine, if I can, its energetic thrust and the atrocious brewing of its crimes. Now I would like, at dusk, to have an instantaneous vision of it, to arrive at the shore of its Lake Michigan, boundless and turquoise like an ocean, to lose my way for an hour in its narrow streets, heavy with darkness and hellish energy. Here the victim falls, his cry drowned out by the noise, and the killer disappears into the eddying traffic.

So thought the superior part of my mind, while the other part, more biting and bothersome, was already agitated, thinking about the dallying between train connections, and more than that, the trek from station to station. But a traveling companion offered me some advice.

"I, too, am a foreigner," he said to me, although he spoke in correct English, even too much so, and softly, "but I'll be glad to be of help, if I can."

We walked together on the platform.

"Where are you from?" he asked, after a pause.

"From Italy," I answered.

"I, too, am a foreigner," he insisted, strangely, "from England. What do you think of this country?"

I parried with the usual stories: America is a great thing, and I can say I have been here only a few days and don't feel ready to judge it. (Perhaps I will never feel ready; phenomena of this size can be observed and verified. To give them a retail value is frivolous, even a little foolish, like someone who says he likes or dislikes tides, geological layers, phases of the moon).

But he, I believe, did not listen to me, and concluded mildly: "I prefer mine. I prefer my country."

Oh yes, England with its rolling meadows, dogs with curly hair, villas overlooking peaceful rivers, flexible and refined language! I thought of the ghosts of Sterne and Foscolo, who perhaps would not have known how to imagine a "sentimental journey" in America, a meeting here with a British citizen so sensitive and splenetic. And I thought to myself, Emerson the American philosopher, what would he say? No more than eighty years have passed since he wrote: "America is nothing more than the continuation of England." And they seemed to be lapidary words, carved forever.

It befell me to come to Chicago to discover Europe not as an idea, but as a reality of feeling. The melancholy Englishman felt closer to me, an Italian, than to his brothers here, who speak the same language. Certainly America is the continuation of England, its first-born child, but the mother now, looking at her excessive daughter, has reason to be dismayed.

Larger Than Life

MARGHERITA SARFATTI
L'America, ricerca della felicità, 1937, pp. 51-52

In the delirium of fever, in certain moments of excitation between lucidity and confusion at night, when insomnia borders on a
nightmare, it sometimes happens that we feel head, arms, and
hands suddenly become enormous and at the same time strangely
light. It happens also that we meet people who seem designed by a
pantograph, perfectly proportioned it's true, but in different dimensions from those of ordinary humanity. Take for example, the
6'5'' of the boxer Carnera. Even in Rome a beautiful woman para-
lyzes me every so often in midconversation. While I am extremely
intent on the interesting things she is saying, suddenly I catch myself, distracted and absorbed—perhaps for a minute but it seems an
hour to me—looking with extraordinary fixity at her high marble
forehead or at the space between her well-shaped ears and straight
nose. And then I rub my eyes; I must be seeing double, as in
dreams. It is impossible that this great thing I see is really true.

I have never been able to understand if the admiration for such
statuesque proportions is completely pleasing. It attracts me at the
same time that it defeats me, and it attracts me again because of
that very bewilderment.

America is like that woman—beautiful but larger than life.
Physically and morally, this different scale forms part of its originality. The phrase "the biggest in the world" seemed vulgar to me
before I came to America, like the *Kolossal* of the Germans, the
boast of quantity against quality, of matter against spirit, without
originality.

But it is not so. Now I know that "the biggest in the world" is the proper slogan, as they say there, the legitimate refrain and pass-word of American life. So genuine—human pride doesn't account for it. It flows spontaneously from things which it stamps with its imprint, from the landscape and from the look of places. It is sug-gested to men by nature and by the elements, by the earth and the sky itself.

Because of this it is true originality. Things that are so oversized, materially and intellectually, *are no longer the same*. Say what you will: it's a question of dimensions. One must recognize this axiom which is not generally admitted: size is an essential measure of pro-portion.

A miniature is something other than a little picture, and a fresco is not an enlarged miniature. A cat is certainly a feline and may even seem to be a little tiger of the domestic jungle, but the cat is domestic, and not a tiger, "because" it is small.

The leaning tower, reproduced pocket-size on a meticulous scale, has very little in common with the tower that rises in Pisa between the Duomo and the Camposanto, a flight of timorous little doves enclosed in tepid marble. Beyond certain limits, enlargement, even on an exact scale, does alter the proportions of things and makes them different in essence.

Two Facets of American Personality

MARGHERITA SARFATTI

L'America, ricerca della felicità, 1937, pp. 121-125

Two days in a row I was invited as guest of honor to a luncheon in the skyscrapers of the two major newspapers (rivals, naturally) of a large American city.

To be the guest of honor at breakfast, lunch, dinner, or tea in America is an enchanting though tiring business because of its solemn rituals. A good stomach isn't required, but nerves of steel and lungs of iron are. The crowd, noise, conversation, and smoke take away your appetite completely; you don't think about eating. At the end of the meal, delightful speeches, courteous and polished, are addressed to you. Almost all Americans know how to speak in public. They possess a genuine social eloquence, a tone between humorous conversation and academic discourse, playful but formal; then it is imperative to reply and with a courtesy equal to their politeness. Before and after the little speeches, there is a throng of introductions and handshakes, a shower of questions, and requests for autographs. The cordial enthusiasm that makes Americans dear renders this obligation delightful and instructive. You learn to know them, if by nothing else, by the tenor of their questions. Their frankness and the expansive fervor of those get-togethers abolish every residue of hypocrisy or studied social reticence. At the table and at the chess board you get to know man.

Of the two newspapers, the first was older and more important, with the prestige of a larger circulation, large earnings, and great respectability. As I entered the office of the publisher, who is also the owner of the largest block of stock (all kept in the family among the descendants of the founder of the enterprise), he greeted me with a welcome made solicitous by his affection for Italy, both ancient and modern. He did not know Italian but adored our poets; he spoke of his old school teacher, a good Dante scholar and translator of Petrarch. On his desk he kept the *Canzoniere*, in that professor's English translation, next to the portrait of his granddaughters, baptized with beautiful Italian-sounding names taken from Shakespeare. Then he showed me autographs of illustrious Italians and spoke to me about Rome, Florence, and Venice with a voice filled with emotion, as if he were confiding a love secret.

He was tall and robust, athletic but not stout, with thin grey hair and the ruddy complexion of blondes who remain outdoors without becoming tanned. With his watery blue eyes, thin lips, and roundish cheeks, a little fallen, belying his energy, he made one think of Scotland and the governor of Gibraltar, painted by Reynolds in the eighteenth century with the keys of the fortress in his hand. Not even in Great Britain had I ever seen an ancestor's portrait step down from the frame so vividly; the only change was from the red tailcoat to the grey suit jacket of today.

The office was exemplary in its order and tidy calm; not a pencil was out of place on the desks of the editorial staff. I knew of some of the editors sitting with us at lunch by their reputations as intellectuals or wits, but they belonged to that category of avaricious intellectuals who decant their wit only in printer's ink and don't waste a drop of it in gratuitous conversation. The entire dialogue was well bred and sedate, contained within the boundaries of convention without ever overflowing into issues that truly concerned any of us: a delicate interlude among the delicate mouthfuls of chicken salad, the prescribed food of traditional luncheons.

I asked myself—not without wonder—how such a considerate gentleman, with so much distinction, could handle that crude, indelicate reality that a newspaperman prepares for the public with a rapid pen, between the ticking of the typewrtiers and—in America— of the telegraph with its continuous printout, which incessantly distributes in every public or private office of any importance the news of the entire world; between the hellish ring of the telephone and the rumble of the linotypes, in the feverish hour when the galley proofs, the bundles of sheets, and piles of telegrams converge from every side on the unlucky editor.

All the clubs, and especially the women's clubs, of which I had been the guest across the States—literary, artistic, philanthropic, university, political, or simply elegant and social—had accustomed me to stormy dinner parties: a tumult, very obsequious to the laws of the toastmaster, the master or mistress of toasts who with a little hammer strikes the signal for silence and introduces the speakers in a fine hierarchical order, each of whom in turn addresses him first with a greeting and a word. Here, where men, and notably newspapermen, were in the majority, how come there was such unusual quiet?

I had formed my first ideas about American journalism as a child through the great Mark Twain. Not that I had ever misjudged *Journalism in Tennessee* as a piece of rigorous history, but that tale of bombs and pistol shots was too delicious not to embroider a little illusion on it. And here I was, in a thoroughly idyllic situation.

Bombs and pistol shots exploded around me, beyond every rosy Twainian expectation, during the luncheon of the next day. Or rather, I seemed to have been thrust into a needle case with all the needles turned up. This was a young and enterprising newspaper, which in the pride of its youth was on all sides threatening the respectable position acquired by its elder.

It was not a sedate family business, and young women—arrogant and bold—had a large share in it. The guests here were many and the greetings few, and no one lingered on childhood nostalgia and dear progeny. I had a fine job trying to find the proper fork for oysters among the silverware, thickly arranged around my plate, and the proper answers to the questions, fired thickly at me point blank. Where could the Giorgione of casa Giovannelli now be found, and what did I think of the NRA; what was the corporative state, and what impression did the great department stores of Chicago make on me; how was Balbo and how was the architecture of Italy?

Dear people, alive and vital, animated with genuine interest for everything, open to every idea, lavish with their own talents, and cordially human!

This contrast exemplifies the two principal types of the American mentality. The one type is almost southern, exuberant and rather aggressive, and represents the America of recent strata, geological sediments imported from all parts of the world. Above all, these characteristics are seen in women, emptyheaded in appearance only but in reality intrepid workers, full of energy and rich in initiative. They are spoiled only in one thing: they ask of life and wish to obtain with every effort nothing less than perfection and happiness— better still, perfection in happiness.

The other type of mentality, purely Protestant, dominates the classes of older wealth that form the directorial cadres of the country. Their example is not always followed, but even those who rebel and who perhaps mock it as an imposture and old rubbish, know that those values were the moral nourishment of the nation. They are the values one "falls back on," as they say over there, the values that give one support in moments of crisis. It is a mentality quietly conservative of fine manners and differentiated specialties. It shuns self-expression and reveals an "aristocratic" timidity toward the banality and ostentatiousness of words. But deep down, in this, too, similar to the English, it knows very well what it wants and where it is going; perhaps with greater concentration because its energy doesn't dissipate itself in breath.

The conflict of the two intellectual types exploded once, tragically, in the Civil War. Abraham Lincoln did not make war against the southern states because he wanted the abolition of slavery and they did not. But on the issue of slavery they were threatening to annul the great federal compact of the nation. There is no doubt that in constitutional and moral theory they had a full right to secede. Just as they had separated from England, so they could proclaim themselves independent from their brother states. In practice, they would have broken up the formidable bloc of a *pax romana*, not colonial but metropolitan. The secessionists would have reduced it to nuclear fragments, hardly independent from the influence of powerful European countries such as England, so near because of Canada, without a central axis, without the possibility of evolving its own civilization. North America would have splintered in a cloud of large and small republics like Central America. But Lincoln understood the tragic moment.

A Negro University

EMILIO CECCHI
America amara, 1940, pp. 205-211

In order to visit Howard University, to get an idea of the spirit of its teaching, I got references, some from promoters of the NAACP who, working against political and police hypocrisy, do their utmost to obtain less incoherent and less inhumane legislation for American Negroes.

At the beginning of 1938, there was for the nth time before Congress a proposed law against lynching, and it appeared that the time for passage was ripe. Roosevelt had solemnly committed himself to introduce a recommendation for this same proposal in the usual New Year's message, a speech that in some way is supposed to serve as a starting point and guideline for the work of the House and the Senate. As far as I know, Roosevelt's promise was acknowledged publicly by no one—least of all in America. If it were not for a scruple about indiscretion, I would name the participants in the colloquy and the actual words of the presidential pledge. The fact is that in the New Year's message he made not the slightest reference to the proposal against lynching or to related issues.

Thus, silently betrayed by Roosevelt, the proposal was postponed and then swept away in an audacious and stubborn maneuver of obstructionism conducted by senators from the southern states. It ended by disappearing from the agenda. While, at the closing of the first college semester of 1938 and the concurrent session of the 75th legislature, people feigned to rejoice that, after all, six whole months had passed without a lynching, lo and behold, in three consecutive days, at Rolling Fork, Mississippi, and at Arabi, Georgia, there were two very thorough lynchings—so thorough that the victim of the first was set on fire twice with gasoline in two places eighteen miles apart, for fear that once only would not be enough, and he would not be sufficiently dead. The first case did not even involve the oft-raised and much abused imputation of carnal assault, but a work dispute. The second was occasioned by a sixty-year-old drunk's resistance to the police.

From my conversations with the above-mentioned directors of the NAACP, I anticipated that the atmosphere I would find at Howard would be rather different from what I did find. The truth is that I had conversed mostly with elements of the old guard: men of the generation born around 1870 like J. E. Spingarn, president of the NAACP, or like the Negro poet and intellectual J. Weldon Johnson (who died in an automobile accident in Wiscasset, Maine, on June 26, 1938). These people had a profound and full realization of the problems of those ten or twelve million Negroes who, as it pleases God, live in the United States. None of them espoused the idea, as Garvey did, of pushing away with their rags and tatters in a special fleet in order to unload the Negro population in a new Negrolandia, thus creating another and more catastrophic Palestine. They live, these ten or twelve million, in the United States. Once they were heartily and solidly attached to the earth in the vast and solitary provinces of the South. The agricultural crisis, the bait of industrial salaries, and the pressure to escape which increases with every lynching orient these masses towards the North. The last fifty-three lynchings (twenty-six in 1935, thirteen in 1936, eight in 1937, six in 1938) occurred here and there in the southern States, with the largest number in Alabama (seven), Georgia (nine), and Mississippi (twelve).

Following the flood of Negroes into the manufacturing cities, these aspects of the problem have obviously been modified, but they have not lost their harshness. For a Spingarn or a Johnson, it can be understood how, within the tragic insurmountability of ethnic differences, everything feasible would come back to terms of social justice, of economic equalization, and, principally, of plain humanity. That meant to defend the Negro—farmer or urbanite— to educate him, to point out his qualities and his gifts, all the while keeping clearly in mind that he is a Negro and that, ultimately, he would also have to suffer a loss if he were to claim absurdly he was not one. . . .

At Howard University, as I have said, I arrived in a spirit that re-echoed such notes. But it was easy to see that people here took another tone. I talked with two professors, E. Franklin Frazier in sociology and Abram L. Harris in economics, both of them fairly young, very black, curly haired, and extremely vivacious. Their bouncy and playful aggressiveness in bearing and in argument had a sportive and animal-like quality. They were far from dumb, let us be clear. As a matter of fact, leafing through the excellent *Anthology of American Negro Literature*, edited by V. F. Calverton, I found that each contributed an essay to the sociology section. Through them the new generation, the one born around 1895, made its voice heard. I must confess immediately, however, that, although less apodictic, unconstrained, and optimistic, the arguments of the other generation which I had heard before seemed to me more authoritative and persuasive. By this other generation I mean the Negroes and Negrophiles, who cannot speak of the racial problem without a deep, Biblical melancholy.

In spite of the migratory currents mentioned above, the immense Negro majority gravitates to the South. For this reason, Howard University was founded and consolidated in Washington itself, under the direct protection of the abolitionist government and on the natural road from the southern States. Today, however, the students of Howard no longer come from the great southern agricultural regions. They come almost entirely from the industrial districts of the North and from the lake zone where the recent emigrants settled. In fact it is the uprooted and urbanized Negro, more than any other, who becomes a college student.

As may perhaps be surprising, the department at Howard which has made the greatest accomplishments is the department of chemistry. This, too, says something to us. Chemistry is a magnificent science with a boundless future, but with no moral liabilities and a strictly technical tradition. The spirit of a race is reflected and handed down more directly and intimately in other disciplines, arts, and doctrines. In Howard's curriculum, however, anything having to do with the Negro arts of music and poetry has a quite imperceptible part.

Harris, the younger of the two professors, declared with great finality that it was not at all their intention to cultivate and maintain these specifically Negro artistic traditions. It was understood, he maintained, that Negro writings were useless literature, the amusements of dilettantes or infantile stuff. The entire cultural and social effort of black people would have to consist, he said, of making themselves "American," melting and being absorbed in the famous racial melting pot of the United States.

In the turn that the conversation had taken earlier, their lack of loyalty and natural fidelity had already surprised me. But now we had reached something which could only be called fatuous cynicism and impudence. I wanted to ask the young professor, since he so resolutely rejected any racial connection, to explain how it was then that he found himself with a face so black. After that, we would have all tangled grotesquely in a fist fight.

What I mean is that there is something worse than the congregations of "Father Divine," with those tappings of nocturnal serums, yelpings, and canine abasements. At least the blacks of "Father Divine" are black. Completely black. They are proud of it, and from their point of view they are darn right. If it had been my lot to be black, I would have even wished to intensify my color with shoe polish. Those puss in boots who think to slip in through a false academic broadmindedness denounce the bonds of blood, of slavery, of color, and of poetry. Better, then, to invoke Canaan, the Jordan, and Uncle Tom's cabin. Better the wild shout of Claude McKay to his black brothers: "If we must die, let it not be like hogs . . . [but like men] pressed to the wall, dying but fighting back!" After all, after all, I thought, there is perhaps some college graduate, *summa cum laude*, who's sadder and more inglorious than a lynch victim.

American Life

GUIDO PIOVENE
De America, 1954, pp. 43-46

Guido Piovene (1907-1974): In his book *On America*,
the most extensive and probably the most significant account of the United States by a contemporary
Italian traveler, Piovene records his impressions
from a visit made in 1951-1952. A novelist (*Lettere di
una novizia*, 1942), essayist, and journalist—first for
the *Corriere della Sera* and then for *La Stampa* of
Turin—he brought to his travel experience a
thoughtful and thoroughly informed curiosity.
   Piovene dutifully covers most of the American
States. Out of this overwhelming encounter he
draws some important conclusions that show both
insight and the desire to come to terms with the
complexity of the dual presence America/United
States. His pages on the American landscape,
American institutions, American everyday life, and
the Italians' need to see America as the embodiment
of freedom from the crushing weight of the traditions and conventions of their own country are
among the most perceptive written by any Italian observer.

Even natural phenomena here assume proportions unknown to
us. The violence of nature and of its upheavals can be felt everywhere in America and can be noticed even in people and in their
politics. I was in New York one day when there was a big storm.

From my hotel I could hear the wind whistle as it blew, trapped among skyscrapers as if among Alpine valleys. Looking down at the street from my window, I could see four umbrellas, bent, torn, and abandoned. The trains had stopped, the routes were closed. The following day an American friend told me: "I spent a beautiful afternoon yesterday. Nothing was working, not even the electricity. It felt as if we were back in the eighteen hundreds."

It's a civilization which is frantic at times but deep down aspires to peace. It fights to achieve calm.

American life is not uniform; its variety is enormous. What we call uniformity is its reliance on a set of rules, similar to the rules of a club, which binds together the most diverse individuals. They are strict rules exactly because they must hold together people who are fundamentally different.

American life is not simple. Americans are naive and often childish, but not simple. Because of conflicting impulses, they are often confused, full of contradictions and shackled, therefore unhappy; they do not realize their complexity, and even less can they analyze it. This complexity is "simplified" at times, but in a totally superficial way, by impulsive bursts similar to the flames shooting up from a smoldering pile. This pattern is reflected in the life of the nation as well as in its politics, which often are incoherent and wavering until a powerful impulse simplifies them. What's strange is that Europeans accuse Americans of acting in a confused manner, while Americans in their turn accuse Europeans of having confused goals, particularly in politics. They are both right. The American "confusion" stems from the excessive strength of their impulses in relation to the reasonableness that should guide them; and by reasonableness I mean balance, sense of measure, clear will. The European "confusion" comes from an excess of reason in relation to an atrophied impulsiveness, which means that many reasoned alternatives are never simplified by sudden impulses; it is also the result of skepticism, cynicism, and, at times, insufficient honesty. Americans are confused as hesitating young people can be; Europeans, as old people are. As a result, American life is not yet cheerful. Even New York, while a lively city, is not a cheerful one. Life hovers between two extremes, excitement and lethargy, which are two aspects of the same heaviness. Life's complexity is often opaque, sleepy, unless it finds a physical outlet.

Finally, and this is important, American life is not moving toward a mass civilization or a working-class society. When we visit two or three of their industrial complexes with our readers . . . we will be surprised by the small number of workers compared to the massiveness of the installations. Machines are viewed as the liberators of the largest possible number of people, who can then be directed toward all kinds of other activities. That's why American society does not suggest a "working-class society," even in the large industrial centers. Rather than toward a "working-class" civilization, it is moving toward a civilization fragmented into multiple activities that are heterogeneous, often eccentric, and all equally acceptable.

I could go on and on. Somebody wrote, and rightly so, that the deep meaning of American life is not in the pursuit of happiness (that happiness for which Americans are not yet ready) but in the effort to protect oneself against pain. The determination not to suffer is stubborn; or, if there is a reason for suffering, the determination is to suffer no more. Their love of machines also goes back to that. They are loved as a means of softening the pain of living, as tools of tranquility. This accounts for the American love of home, the place of physical and emotional comfort. Americans have always gone to war with the dream that, once the job is done, they could go back home and never move again. Notice also what nostalgia Americans feel for the good old times. The dream of all Americans is to go back in time; they dream, it seems, of the maternal womb. Americans, after all, are the greatest consumers of candies and chocolate bars, which are not pleasures, but soothing, innocuous drugs to soften the impact of life. The mania of medical care has the same origin, as well as the mania of not growing fat, of not growing old, and the preoccupation about what to eat or drink or how to sleep. Everybody yearns for these means of protection, bottles and pills. Doctors find their most cooperative patients in America. There is often a hint of a *malade imaginaire* in Americans.

The day after the famous storm, some snow fell on New York. When I went out in the evening, I found the streets almost deserted and the restaurants nearly empty. Just a little snow had been enough to persuade the majority to stay home. But then American heroism and ruggedness also issue from their denial of suffering. It is this refusal that inspired America to build immense industrial empires and to thrust her toward daring initiatives. Everything in America aims at opposing suffering and at abolishing it. The will not to suffer is more efficacious and, above all, more deeply felt than the pursuit of happiness. It is the essence of a civilization which refuses to believe that suffering is good or that—as some say—it ennobles man, and which is convinced instead that suffering breaks man. This civilization is untouched by the cult of suffering and will not accept it. And now we can visit the Wall Street cemetery.

Anyone with even a superficial acquaintance with New York, even just from photos, knows that in the heart of Wall Street, among the skyscrapers as at the bottom of a well (in New York you often feel you are walking at the bottom of a well anyhow, especially at night, when the lights punch holes in the darkness without dissipating it) there is an old church, Trinity Church. It looks small when compared to the skyscrapers, and yet it is really the heart of the banking district. Next to the church lies an old cemetery, where people sit to rest or to have a snack. As I walked into it, my eyes fell on the tomb of a man who lived almost three centuries ago. The epitaph told the name and surname of the deceased, his age (ninety-two), and added: "Passerby, from this you may see how brief is life." At first the idea made me smile. Then, mulling over it, I found it thoughtful and beautiful. I remembered the exclamation of a Neapolitan lady who was his same age and who, knowing she was dying, commented in disgust: "What is this life, then? Just a look out a window."

The affronting brevity of life, that epitaph was saying, is not obvious in premature deaths (such a comment on someone who died young would merely be trite) but in the deaths of those who have lived long. Only then can we see how short that maximum span is; then death truly appears as an affront. More than anything else, that epitaph—old as it is—seems to touch the core of this civilization which is always pitted in a struggle against death, not against premature death or normal death, but against death in the absolute. This is why, facing American civilization even in its less appealing aspects, I feel drawn to it. For its refusal of suffering and of the mystique of suffering, which it expresses in good, bad, and contradictory ways—by nostalgia and futurism, by love of home and of adventure, of comfort and of an ascetic ruggedness. Daring heroism alternates with sudden, dangerous abandon in a confused pattern which never fully reveals what is predominant. Yet, its explanation is consistent: the determination not to accept suffering. It is the struggle against death which creates banks, skyscrapers, and industries; the cult of the doctor as well; and the desire to ignore death altogether. No matter how great, or how gaudy, petty, or unheroic its aspects, a battle is always waged against our sole, ultimate enemy.

Notes on Experimental Education in the United States (January 16-February 2, 1973)

DANILO DOLCI

unpublished notes

Danilo Dolci (1924-): Educated as an architect, Dolci was a member of the Christian community of Nomadelfia, an alternative experiment of communal living and child raising founded after World War II to shelter war orphans. Later, when Dolci became a writer, he was still concerned with education and social reform; he founded a thinktank—the *Centro studi e iniziative* outside Palermo—where he works today. He has the support of an international group of sponsors and sympathizers: several *Friends of Dolci* chapters are active in the United States. Dolci won the Lenin Peace Prize in 1959.

He is the author of numerous books, several of which have been translated into English: *Report from Palermo* (1959), *Waste* (1964), *A New World in the Making* (1965, rpt. 1976), and *The Man Who Plays Alone* (1969). In these books, Dolci discusses his own Sicilian experience against the background of a struggle for self-determination initiated by the Sicilian poor in the Palermo area. Dolci has helped develop and apply in the Sicilian context the techniques which the disinherited of the world have been painfully creating: "speaking bitterness" as the Chinese peasants once did, and engaging in collective action and civil resistance.

As revealed in these quick notes, Dolci's perspective on America is both specialized and very insightful. It suggests the Italian writers' ongoing interest in the challenge and potential which is America.

East Harlem Block Schools
1724 Madison Avenue
New York City   January 17

Positive impressions
—For each of the three classes (with respectively twenty-two, twenty-one, and nineteen children) there are three teachers: one is a professional, and two are parents who get paid and concurrently attend classes in education. In addition, there are some volunteers. The children usually have an affectionate relationship with the adults; they play freely.
—The effort is to absorb the parents into the educational system. Once a month (or every six weeks) there is a parents' meeting. *Up to 50 percent* of the parents participate. They prepare the weekly menu, for example.
—Most successful items: the cooking utensils, an aquarium with fish and shells, small animals, the children's drawings on the walls (when they paint they wear plastic smocks), a wardrobe with clothes for playing theatre, various materials for building (wood or plastic), a balance, a cardboard clock.

Negative impressions
—They have no garden, no open space to play in.
—In the afternoon, at 3:30, they have their windows closed and keep all their uncomfortable lights on.
—Plastic fruit on the tables.

Synanon
1910 Ocean Front Boulevard
Santa Monica (Los Angeles)
California   January 23

The work of the children is part of the work of the community of Synanon. The children, although they live in a separate wing of the building, are immersed in a kind of community which has chosen to be a society without violence, without smoking, and without drugs.

Positive impressions
—Stating clearly, from the beginning, that this is going to be a society without violence, tends in itself to eliminate violence.
—The residual potential for violence is defused by the discussions, which are a sort of "truth game": psychosocial training, a physio-psychological exercise in frankness, a tool to resolve problems relating to work, a sport in a disinterested sense, an experience in self-government, and self-expression.

. . . .
—Vivaldi music in some rooms—in the kindergarten area, for example.
. . . .
—Every morning the children talk among themselves. What underlies their exchange is the question: "How could this day be made interesting?"
—Underlining the fact that what counts is not the amount of time parents spend with their children, but the quality of that time.

Negative impressions
. . . the author speaks of the techniques of the "game," "reach" and "stew."
—During the "game" people talk about everything, as it comes. Two or three kids might speak at the same time, three or four shout all at the same time, keyed up and interrupting each other. One of them might try to speak time and time again, but the session is over and he never succeeds. Some mock other people; the little ones even make faces and obscene gestures. At times they scream hysterically, and at the end they all get up from their chairs acting as if they had just played a lively match.
All this could be explained as:
    reaction to the drive toward self-destruction—as it happens among drug addicts—which here discharges aggression on the other, rather then the selves;
    reaction of the person who has been so desperately alone that he would rather be insulted than ignored as usual;
    reaction to a society imbued with empty formalism, which

creates alienation, isolation, and addiction;

reaction of people who doubt, deep down inside, that there can be a solution to their problems;

reaction (as far as the teachers are concerned) to the lack of meetings in the traditional American school (50 percent of the cases), and to the kind of school assembly in which only the principal speaks (the other 50 percent).

We can believe what is affirmed by people who can attest to it that these techniques have been useful in a milieu where drug addiction is widespread. We must object when this approach is offered as valid for a new society. The frustration produced by too much talk is evident, both in the talkers and in the listeners. The therapy most often ends up by being an end in itself rather than implicit in a vital process. The atmosphere remains to a large extent the kind you find among ex-patients and patients looking for sport-like therapies. There is a hint of caricature in this spontaneity, which is mostly an outlet—in an atmosphere comprehensibly quite naive—fostering a situation like Noah's ark.

. . . .

—This experimentalism ("In a month everything might be totally different") rather than experimentation does not seem to have solid roots. It often appears to be closed in itself, a series of isolated empirical episodes.

—Each group of ten boys has a captain. Why a "captain"? They don't know. They think that the term was taken from the slang of the sports and the military.

—"The more serious things are discussed among the captains."

. . . .

—In the meetings of the eleven year olds, the teachers not only do not speak but they also do not participate.

. . . .

—Here again, even though they live near the light, the beach, and the ocean, the children spend a great part of their days with electric lights on.

People

Blue-collar Workers in
America   ANTONIO GRAMSCI

*Note sul Machiavelli, sulla politica e sullo
stato moderno,* 1955, pp. 329-340

Antonio Gramsci (1891-1937): Gramsci was one of
the founders of the Italian Communist party in 1921
and its leading theorist. Imprisoned by Mussolini in
1926, he died eleven years later.

Although he never visited the United States,
Gramsci frequently refers to this country in his writings because he viewed the United States as a laboratory where the options available to modern socie-
ties and the outcome of pursuing those options
could be studied in their actuality.

The major part of Gramsci's writing consists of
"notes" written during his long imprisonment. The
great knowledge and curiosity of this political
thinker, as well as his courage and endurance, are
made evident by his daily struggle to preserve the
keenness of a mind which the regime had vowed to
"stop from working." Polemic and reflective in turn,
all his work is an extremely personal dialogue with
an unseen audience. Recently, his *Prison Notebooks* and his *Letters from Prison* were published in
English translation for the American public, in 1971
and 1975 respectively. Giuseppe Fiori's biography of
Gramsci appeared in English in 1971. *The Modern
Prince and Other Writings* was published here in
1959.

Gramsci was not the only member of the Italian Left to express his interest in and admiration for America and to feel the fascination of American culture. Whereas intellectuals with Rightist leanings were more likely to be suspicious of the American myth because of its egalitarianism, the Left-leaning Italian intellectuals were most often attracted by America. This phenomenon may seem to be a contradiction only if we look at the surface, for both the American myth and the Leftist ideology held as a common assumption that there exist new alternatives to authoritarian regimes based on a static view of the human political condition. Against the spreading of Fascism in Europe, America reaffirmed ideals of freedom and self-determination. The United States also suggested a future characterized by industrial development and the power of the working classes. With Vittorini and Pavese, who lived longer than Gramsci and who did not write in the isolation of a jail cell, these and other dimensions of the American myth became enormously important but led in quite different directions.

Standardization of Work and Production

Trotsky's ideology was intimately connected with this complex of questions; I do not believe that this fact has been sufficiently emphasized. Its essential component, from the point of view selected here, was the excessive—and therefore not rationally valid—determination to assign a place of supremacy in the life of the nation to industry and industrial methods; to accelerate the establishment of discipline and order in industrial production; and to make the workers' way of life conform to the requirements of the work. Given the general approach taken in considering all the problems connected with his ideology, the latter was obviously bound to give rise to a form of tyranny, and therefore to the unquestionable need for its eradication. Trotsky's preoccupations were correct, but his solutions on the practical plane were radically wrong. A danger was inherent in that imbalance between theory and praxis, the same danger that had already become visible before, in 1921. The principle of coercion, both direct and indirect, in the planning of production and work was correct, but the form it had taken was wrong: the military pattern had become a damaging prejudice, and the workers' armies failed.

Trotsky's interest in Americanism can be seen in his articles, his inquiries into the American way of life and into American literature. Those activities were less unrelated to each other than it may have seemed, because the new work methods cannot be considered apart from a certain way of life, from a certain way of understanding and interpreting life. You cannot be successful in one area without obtaining tangible results in the other.

In America, industrialization and Prohibition are undoubtedly connected. The investigations made by industrialists into the workers' private lives, the inspection bureaus created by some industries to check on the workers' "morality," were all inspired by the needs of the new work methods. Whoever mocks such practices—even if they ended in failure—and interprets them solely as hypocritical manifestations of puritanism, makes it impossible for himself to understand the importance, the meaning, and the *objective significance* of the American phenomenon. The American phenomenon is the only major collective effort made, up to this date, to create a new type of man and of worker—and this at an unbelievable speed and with an awareness of the ends previously unknown in history.

The expression "awareness of the ends" may sound like a joke to whoever remembers Frederick W. Taylor's reference to "trained gorillas." For Taylor expressed with brutal cynicism the goal of American society: to maximize in the worker mechanical and automatic responses, to break the old psychophysical nexus inherent in skilled professional work—which demanded a certain active participation of the worker's intelligence, imagination, and creativity—and to reduce the productivity effort solely to its physical and mechanical components. Actually, these are not original novelties. They are only the most recent phase of a long process which began with the birth of industrialism, a phase which is only more intense than the previous ones and takes more brutal forms, but which will also be superseded by the creation of a new psychophysical nexus different in kind from the previous ones, and undoubtedly of a *superior* quality. A forcible selection will necessarily take place, a part of the old working class will be pitilessly eliminated from the work force and perhaps even from the world itself.

In this perspective, we need to study the "puritanical" initiatives of American industrialists of the Ford type. One thing is certain: they are not concerned with the "humanity" and the "spiritual potential" of the workers. Those elements are immediately done away with. The worker's "humanity and spiritual potential" can only be actualized in the world of work and production, in the sphere of productive creativity. They used to be highest in the artisan, in the "demiurge," when the personality of the worker was wholly reflected in the created object, when the link between art and work was still very solid. But it is exactly against that "humanism" that the new industrialism is fighting. The aim of the so-called puritanical initiatives is to maintain, outside the place and time of work, a psychophysical balance which will prevent the physiological breakdown of the worker, who is wrung dry by the new methods of production. This balance can only be purely exterior and mechanical, but it will become internalized whenever it is proposed by the workers themselves—and not imposed from the outside—by a new type of society, by appropriate and original methods. The American industrialist is concerned with maintaining the continued physical efficiency of the workers, their muscular and nervous efficiency. It is to his advantage to have a permanent force of technicians, a permanent and harmonious complex, because the human mechanism (the collectivity of the workers) is also a part of the industrial system which cannot be dismantled too often and which cannot have individual parts substituted too frequently without sustaining considerable losses.

The so-called high salary is related to this industrial need. It is the tool by which skilled workers trained for this system of work and production can be selected and kept permanently. But the high salary is a two-edged sword: the worker must spend the more abundant money "rationally" in order to maintain, renew, and possibly increase his muscular and nervous efficiency, rather than destroying or impairing it. So, the war on alcohol, the most dangerous agent of destruction among the work force, becomes a function of the State. It is possible that other "puritanical" crusades may be entrusted to the State, if private enterprise becomes inadequate to the task, or if an extremely deep and widespread crisis of the morality of the working masses explodes, as could happen in the event of a long and massive crisis of unemployment.

A question related to the one of alcohol is the sexual question: abuse and intemperance in sexual habits is the most dangerous enemy of nervous energy, after alcohol, and it is commonly observed that "obsessive" work practices cause alcoholic and sexual abuse. Ford's attempts to snoop into the lives of his workers by means of a corps of inspectors to control the ways they spent their salaries and how they lived is an indication of tendencies still "private" or latent. At a certain point these tendencies can become State ideology, grafted on the branch of traditional puritanism, purporting to be a rebirth of the pioneer morality, of true Americanism, etc. The fact most deserving of note in the American phenomenon in terms of these manifestations is the gap which has been developing, and will become wider and wider, between the morality and the way of life of the working class and those of the other strata of the population.

Prohibition has already given us an example of the gap mentioned here. Who could consume the alcohol which was bootlegged in the United States? Alcohol had become a luxury, and not even the highest salaries could permit its consumption by the masses of working people. The person who works for wages, with fixed hours, has no time to devote to a search for alcohol, to sports, or to evade the laws. The same observation can be made concerning sexuality. "Hunting" for a woman requires too much leisure. Among the new brand of workers we will have a repetition, in different ways, of what happened in the peasant villages. The relative steadiness of the peasant sexual union is strictly related to the agricultural work pattern. The farmer who goes home in the evening after a long day's labor wants what Horace called "easily obtainable sex." He is not prepared to lust after chance women; he loves his woman, who is reliable, always there, who does not play games and does not expect the comedy of seduction and violence in order to be possessed. One would think that the sexual function has thus become mechanical, whereas actually a new form of sexual union is born, one which is devoid of the bright colors of romantic claptrap made for the middle class and for the idle bohemian. It's clear that the new industrialism needs monogamy, needs a working man who does not fritter away his nervous energy in the frantic and exciting search for casual sexual satisfaction. The man who goes to work after a night of excesses is not a good worker. The excitement of passions cannot fit in with the chronometric precision required in assembly-line movements which must synchronize with the most accurate automatic mechanisms. This complex of pressures and direct and indirect coercion exerted on the working masses will undoubtedly obtain results, and a new form of sexual union will appear whose characteristic and fundamental traits will be monogamy and relative stability.

It would be interesting to know the statistical incidence of the phenomena deviating from the sexual mores officially endorsed in the United States, analyzed according to social class. In general, it will be noted that divorces are especially numerous in the higher strata. This morality gap between the working masses and more and more members of the leading class in the United States must be one of the most interesting and influential phenomena. Until not long ago, the American people were a people of workers; the "work ethic" was a trait ingrained not only in the working class, but peculiar also to the leaders. The millionaire who continued to be active until illness or old age forced him to retire, and whose activity took up a sizable number of hours out of his whole day, was a typically American phenomenon. He was the most unbelievable *americanata* of all for the average European. It has been pointed out that this difference between Americans and Europeans is caused by the lack of "tradition" in the United States, to the extent that "tradition" means, among other things, the passive residue of all the social structures obliterated by history. In the United States, however, the "tradition" of the pioneers is still recent, and the pioneer tradition means strong individuals whose "work ethic" has reached the greatest intensity and vigor, men who directly, and not through platoons of slaves and servants, entered into active confrontation with natural forces in order to subdue them and successfully exploit them. The passive remnants of history are the ones who resist Americanism in Europe ("they represent quality, etc.

. . .'') because they instinctively know that the new methods of work and production would irrevocably sweep them away.

But, if it is true that in Europe, under such circumstances, the unburied relics would finally be done away with, what has started happening in America itself? The morality gap mentioned earlier shows that wider and wider margins of social passivity are being created. It looks like women have a crucial function in this phenomenon. The industrialist keeps working even when he is a millionaire, but his wife and his daughters become more and more "luxury mammals." The beauty contests, the screen tests (remember the 30,000 Italian girls who in 1926 sent their pictures in bathing suits to Twentieth Century Fox), the theatre, by selecting among the world's female beauties and putting them on the auction block, foster a prostitute mentality; and the "white slave trade" is organized legally for the benefit of the higher classes. The women, who are idle, travel, cross the ocean back and forth, escape their country's Prohibition, and enter seasonal "marriages." We must remember that American sea captains were deprived of their authority to perform marriages on the seas because many couples married as they left Europe and divorced before reaching the American shore. Actual prostitution spreads, barely disguised by fragile legal formalities.

These phenomena, which are peculiar to the higher classes, will make it more difficult to coerce the working masses into conforming to the needs of the new industrial society. In any case, they create a psychological gap, and accelerate the crystallization and reification of social groups, making obvious their transformation into castes, as happened once in Europe. . . .

Taylorism and the Mechanization of the Worker

Thinking about the separation which Taylorism supposedly would effect between manual work and the "human dimension" of work, we can make useful reference to the past, exactly to the professions which are believed to be the most "intellectual"; that is, the professions connected with the reproduction of written texts for whatever form of diffusion or broadcasting: amanuenses before the invention of the press, then hand printers, linotypists, stenographers, and typists. Upon reflection, we'll notice that the process of adaptation to mechanization is more difficult there than in other

trades. Why? Because it is difficult to attain the maximum professional proficiency when one demands of the worker that he forget
or forego the intellectual content of the writing to be reproduced.
The worker must concentrate his attention solely on the calligraphy
of the individual letters if he is a scribe; or must break down the
sentences into abstract words, and these into characters, and rapidly select the lead pieces in their compartments; or must break down
not only the single words but groups of words in the speech context, grouping them mechanically into stenographic symbols; or
must attain the speed required of a typist, etc.

The interest of the worker in the intellectual content of the text
can be measured by his errors. In other words, it is a professional
defect. His qualification for the job is measured exactly in terms of
his intellectual noninvolvement, that is, on the basis of his "auto-
matism." The medieval copyist who was interested in the text
changed the orthography, morphology, and syntax of the text he
was copying and left out whole sentences he did not understand because of his limited education. The trend of thoughts evoked in him
by the interest he was taking in the text led him to insert glosses and
notes. If his dialect or his language was different from that of the
text, he introduced alloglottic nuances. He was a poor amanuensis
because he actually "rewrote" the text. The slowness of medieval
writing art explains many of these deficiencies: there was time to
reflect, and therefore mechanization was more difficult.

The typographer must be swift and must keep eyes and hands in
continuous movement; that makes his automatization easier. But,
if you really think about it, perhaps the greatest effort required by a
trade is exactly this, the effort that these workers must make to iso-
late from the intellectual content of the text—often very exciting,
and therefore causing one to work less and less well—its graphic
symbols; and to devote their attention to these only. However, such
an effort is made, and it does not destroy a man's spirit. When the
adaptation process is completed, what actually happens is that the
brain of the worker, instead of becoming mummified, reaches a
state of total freedom. Only the physical movements have become
automatic. The professional programming, involving simple movements repeated at a speeded-up rhythm, has been "stored" in the
nervous and muscular centers, leaving the brain unencumbered and
free for other activities. We walk without needing to think about all

the movements necessary for all the parts of our body to move in synchrony in the manner required by the activity of walking. The same thing has happened and will keep on happening in the industrial world for the basic gestures connected with manual work. We walk automatically and at the same time we think about whatever we want to think about.

American industrialists have understood very well this dialectic inherent in the new industrial methods. They have understood that the expression "trained gorilla" is just an expression. The worker "unfortunately" remains a man and even thinks more while he is working, or at least has much more opportunity for thinking once he has overcome the adaptation crisis, and if he has not been eliminated. Not only does he think, but the fact that he draws no immediate satisfaction from his work and that he understands that somebody wants to reduce him to a trained gorilla can channel his thoughts in not exactly conformist directions. A whole series of precautions and educational initiatives suggested in the books by Ford and in Philip's work offers clear evidence of such concern among industrialists.

High Wages

It's an obvious thought that so-called high salaries are a transitional form of retribution. The adaptation to new methods of work and production cannot be achieved solely through societal coercion. That one can do so is a "prejudice" prevalently found in Europe and even more in Japan; it is bound to have serious consequences for the physical and psychic welfare of the workers there. This prejudice, moreover, is based only on the endemic unemployment which is a phenomenon of the postwar period. If the situation were "normal," the coercive system needed to obtain the desired results would be even more expensive than the payment of high wages.

Coercion must therefore be skillfully blended with persuasion and consent. This aim can be achieved, within the patterns peculiar to a specific society, by a better redistribution allowing a certain standard of living which makes it possible to conserve and replenish the energies used up in the new type of labor. But as soon as the new methods of work and production have become common and widespread, as soon as a new type of worker has been created universally and the production apparatus has been further perfected, excessive turnover will be automatically limited by extensive unemployment, and high wages will disappear. Actually, the high-salaried American industry is still exploiting a monopoly based on their having the initiative in new industrial methods: monopoly wages correspond to monopoly profits. But their monopoly will of necessity be first undercut and then eliminated by the diffusion of those new methods both inside the United States and abroad (compare the Japanese phenomenon of low-priced products), and high wages will disappear at the same time as enormous profits do. Moreover, it is a known fact that high wages are tied to the existence of an aristocracy in the labor market and are not available to all American workers.

The whole Fordian ideology of high wages is a derivative phenomenon caused by an objective need in modern industry as it reaches a certain point of development. It is not a primary phenomenon. This fact, however, does not relieve us from the obligation of studying the importance and the repercussions of the ideology itself. To begin with, what does "high wages" mean? Are the wages paid by Ford high in relation only to average American wages, or are they high if viewed as payment for the energies which Ford's workers must expend in the productive effort and with Ford's work methods? No research of this sort has been made, to our knowledge, and yet it is only thus that conclusive answers can be given. The inquiry is difficult, but the very cause of such difficulty might be an indirect answer. The answer is difficult because Ford's skilled workers are very mobile, and this makes it impossible to establish an average rate of "normal" turnover among Ford's workforce to be compared with other industries' averages. But what causes this instability? How come a worker would prefer a salary "lower" than the salary paid by Ford? Doesn't this mean that the so-called high wages are less adept at reintegrating the work-energy expended by the worker than the wages paid by other firms? The instability of the skilled labor force shows that the normal competitive conditions in the labor market (wage differential) are effective only to a certain point as far as the Ford industry is concerned. The difference in average salary levels does not operate there, and neither does the pressure on the part of a reserve army of unemployed. That means that some new element affecting the Ford industry must be uncovered, a new element which is the true origin of "high wages" as well as of the other phenomena (instability, etc.). And it can only be that the Ford industry demands a selectivity, a specialization in its workers which other industries do not yet require, a new type of qualification, and at the same time an expenditure of work-energy and a level of energy exploitation within the usual time lapses, which are heavier and more exhausting than elsewhere; and which the wages paid cannot compensate for, cannot restore to everyone's satisfaction in that given society as presently constituted.

Once these reasons are given, the problem is whether the type of industry and the kind of work and production organization developed by Ford are "rational," and can and must be universally extended; or whether this is, on the contrary, an unhealthy phenomenon to be fought by union forces and through legislation. In other words, is it possible—with the material and moral pressure exerted by society and State—to impel all workers as a mass to undergo the psychophysical process of transformation which will make of the typical Ford worker the prototype of the modern worker? Or is such a thing impossible because it would lead to the physical deterioration and degeneration of the race, destroying the whole labor force? It seems that one can answer that the Ford method is "rational." That means that it should be used universally, but to do so entails a long process. A change in social conditions, as well as in mores and individual habits, is necessary, and that can happen not through simple coercion but only thanks to a blending of coercion (self-discipline) and persuasion. This strategy can also take the form of high wages, that is, of a promise of improvement in the standard of living, or perhaps, more accurately, of the opportunity to achieve a standard of living in keeping with the new production and work methods that demand a particular expenditure of muscular and nervous energies.

Phenomena similar to the ones caused on a large scale by Fordism also took place and are taking place in some branches of industry and in certain nonautomated factories, on a limited, and yet significant, scale. It has never been a simple matter to put together an organic and well-articulated core of factory personnel or a team of skilled workers. Now, once the top technicians or the team are assembled, their members, or some among them, not only end up by enjoying a monopolistic salary but are not laid off in case production stops temporarily. It would be wasteful to let go the components of an organic whole painfully assembled because it would be almost impossible to fit them back together again, and the reconstitution of the whole with new elements picked at random would cost considerable effort and expense. This factor sets a limit to the law of competition fostered by a reserve labor force and by unemployment; this limiting factor has always been at the basis of the creation of privileged aristocracies. Since there never was and still is not a law of perfect equivalence between the systems and methods of production and work for all the firms in a certain industrial branch, it logically follows that each firm is "unique" to a smaller or larger extent. Each one builds its own nucleus of skilled workers particularly qualified for that enterprise, knowing little secrets of fabrication or procedure, "gimmicks" that might seem minor in themselves but can have great economic impact if used time after time.

One can take as a special case in point the organization of work in ports, especially in those ports where there is an imbalance between loading and unloading of merchandise, and where there are seasonal peaks and lows. It is necessary to have an experienced crew always on hand, permanently settled, for the minimum seasonal work or for work of whatever kind. Therefore, you have closed employment rolls, with high wages and other privileges, as opposed to the mass of seasonal workers, etc. This also happens in agriculture, in the relationship between farm workers and daily laborers, as well as in other industries where low seasons exist either because of reasons peculiar to the industry itself, as in the clothing industry, or because of the bad organization in wholesale trading, when buying and selling are done according to cycles that are not synchronized with the cycles of production.

Al Capone's Barbershop

MARIO SOLDATI

America primo amore, 1935, pp. 153-158

I would have preferred to stroll around alone. But my friend and patron thought it would be courteous to give me as a guide Mic, the best of his men.

Mic was a Croat of around forty who had lived in Chicago for more than twenty years. Unlike what happens to almost everybody, even during brief stays, his expression had taken on nothing American. His face, thanks to its ugliness perhaps, had not been altered. It had remained typically Croatian: flat, wrinkled, yellowish. He had left Europe before the war and had never returned. He lived mostly with Italians and considered himself their great friend. He had also learned to speak Italian, he believed. But if I said *ragazzo*, he didn't understand; he only understood *guaglione*. He had learned a comical argot, a mixture of Neapolitan, Pugliese, Sicilian, and American slang.

He was employed by my patron in the capacity of supervisor, or better, as the man with the whip. Behind the counter of the employment office, every morning he handled alone hundreds of drunken and shouting bums. When he received a request for laborers, within a few minutes, ruthlessly and without mercy, he knew how to choose from those hundreds, forty or fifty workers. Then, across city streets and railway underpasses, he took them to the labor camps in perfect order. He cursed, insulted, struck them; he immediately discovered flasks of liquor, tore them out of their pockets, and hurled them away.

In every city, at the head of branch offices—in New York, Cleveland, Pittsburgh, Toledo, and Jacksonville, Florida—my friend relies on deputies of this sort. In New York he had in his office in the Bowery a Sicilian and two Irishmen. In Chicago, Mic was enough.

The introduction took place in the rear of the office, which was smoky, stinking, and sweaty like a police station. My patron, or—to call him what his employees called him—"the old man," had taken me there to Mic. He put me in his care. He told him to take me sightseeing through the city. Anyway, for that day there would be no more calls and they could close up the office.

The old man shook my hand, arranged to meet me that evening at my hotel, and went away. Determined, quick, elbowing the bums who blocked his way, he crossed the long dark room and went out. He stopped for a moment on the threshold, a large figure against the grey and foggy light of the city. He lit his cigar as usual, without cutting it. He drew two or three vigorous mouthfuls, then disappeared.

More than respect, Mic must have absolute devotion for the old man, because from first to last he was completely gentle, kind, and serviceable to me. With a dry and nasal voice he warned the bums that they could go on getting drunk and scratching themselves for today. To a dirty joke coming from the back of the room he replied with one worse. Then he turned to me, and with the clumsy kindness of the robber in the fairy tale when he speaks to the young princess, he excused himself for using such language in my presence, adding that unfortunately there was no other way to deal with that rabble. From the top of the counter, with two or three quick glances, he looked over the tattered crowd, and pointed out to me with a gesture, as if he was shaping an invisible substance above their heads: "They are tough people, you know."

Some exchange of insults between Mic and the "tough people"; some courteous explanation to me. And then—"After you, I am sure, after you"—he guided me from behind the counter to the door.

Mic's car, a four-door Chrysler, was outside the office. He invited me to get in, offered me a cigarette, and we drove off.

It was a little before noon. First of all, Mic declared that he would take me somewhere to eat—to an Italian restaurant in the old neighborhood of the Capones, right in front of the old barbershop of Frank Riccio, a friend and associate of Al's.

We crossed the Loop on to Michigan Avenue, and leaving behind the green fields of Northwestern University, we rapidly entered a section of the immense Chicago slums—dirty, dismal, with low houses and squalid avenues—which spread out behind the proud Chicago of the lakefront, the Chicago narrow but long, bristling with huge skyscrapers and facing the scintillating asphalt of Michigan Avenue. It's the same thing in Manhattan, where the rich avenues of the center, from Seventh to Lexington, are flanked by the miserable Eleventh, Tenth, Ninth, and Third, Second, First Streets; but between Fifth and Broadway, right in the middle of the prosperous zone, we have the formidable exceptions of Sixth and Bryant Park, and Babel-like cauldrons like Times Square, which make New York so much more human, or European, than Chicago.

Chicago is desperately divided. It can almost be said to be one street, one single very long splendid street, Michigan Avenue, behind which a disintegrating metropolis is crowded, sweaty and sad, where millions of men live in misery and degradation. In this respect perhaps, no other city represents America better.

Mic stopped right in front of Frank Riccio's barbershop. By this time, it had been closed for a year. The sign, white on a black background, could still be read: Riccio Brothers, Barber Shop. At the corner, the red and white striped pole, no longer moving, was dusty. The windows, too (in America the shops don't use shutters), were dusty—and empty. Stopping there we looked inside—vast, deserted, only the mirrors and a row of white chairs were left. The mirrors were very dirty. Looking closely, I noticed that one in one corner, down low, was cracked by the blow of a stone or a gun. A black gash, the tarred wall exposed, gave the impression of a wound; the pieces that had broken off were still scattered on the floor.

Fascinated, I continued to look around the inside of the shop, with my nose pressed against a window. Mic did not understand my reasons for looking or what pleasure I got from it, and the whole time he remained at my side in respectful silence. It seemed to me that, as the tip of my nose touched the filthy window, I was finally touching the famous criminality. No newspaper, book, or film about gangsters had been able to give me the feeling of that dust, that empty store, that broken mirror.

Through its poverty and vulgarity, the place conveyed something atrocious, epic. Thus, if you accost some well-known criminal, or some great businessman, what strike you first are his vulgarity, his pettiness, his spiritual squalor. Literature, newspapers, and gossip would have given you a theatrical idea of him; making you think of a Genius of Evil, a great Strategist and Swindler of Millions. But then (and almost always a few minutes of conversation and observation are enough), precisely out of that same humbleness and dullness you see emerge and loom large the man who kills, robs, and gives orders: from those very ashes arises the phoenix of a Dillinger or a Stavisky. Their epic tone lies precisely in their abjection. Their violence is only the result of their aridity, their powerlessness to be men.

The desperate grandeur of a crime is not revealed by the various tricks and pseudo-intelligent strategies that prepare it and try to wipe out its traces, but in the pitiful gash the bullet has made in the throat of the corpse, in the blood that has dripped along the collar, down the suit, to stain the floor—just ordinary blood, so easy and yet so difficult to shed. And the great coups of the celebrated businessman are not long, involved machinations, pawns moved with second and third intentions as in a chess game, but they are, for example, in a stockholders' meeting a fist struck on the table louder than all others; a telephone call broken off with an insult; an order given to the doorkeepers: "I cannot see Mr. X"—although Mr. X is a childhood friend, etc. For normal people (those who aren't born gangsters or financiers), these stupid little acts are the most difficult to perform. This is why America is so full of gangsters and big businessmen.

I continued to look inside the empty barber shop, almost expecting a revelation. Mic, immobile two steps away, ignorant of my thoughts, was not very different from that sort of people. And suddenly I felt myself to be fearfully far from my country, abandoned, defenseless, worse off than a pioneer of old among the Indians. They, at least, had killed to defend their land. They lived on the plains, surrounded by picturesque rites; they had arts and music. They were not barbarians with this spiritual barbarism, this invincible aridity.

Love in Brooklyn

MARIO SOLDATI
America primo amore, 1935, pp. 69-76

Suddenly she stiffened. As I continued to kiss her on lips thin and closed, she struggled, freed herself from my embrace, curled up in the back of the taxi, and held me back, pushing with her hand against my chest.

I asked her what was wrong, and in the flashing lights of cars that crossed our path I searched her face, ashamed in the disorder of blonde curls.

Rhythmic, swift, cyclopean, the girders of Brooklyn Bridge sped by the car window, opening wide in regular bursts to reveal the darkness and the great emptiness over which we drove suspended, and the far-off lights of the docks and the reflections on the river.

I looked at the immensity of the New York night and at my first American girl friend with the same eagerness. Brooklyn Bridge! Brooklyn Bridge! No longer abstract and glorious syllables as they are to the inexperienced, restless European, but alternately colossal girders that run toward me, and chasms of space that swallow me up. Only the eyes of the beloved when we are no longer thinking about them, but we look into them and kiss them; only the pleasure of the embrace of love equals the pleasure of losing oneself in a faraway country.

The girl in the taxi was only one element of this joy. Blonde, slender, strong, she was different from all the women that my adolescence had imagined. Completely ignorant about me, my nature and my past, she identified me at the most with Pugliese fruit vendors, Sicilian barbers whom, when she was small in her native

Dallas, she saw every day on the thresholds of their shops and called vaguely "Eye-talians." She had no idea of Italy. She had never heard the names of my native region—Piedmont, Turin.

I still spoke English very badly and understood worse, especially her definitely southern pronunciation (she had just arrived from Texas). But the amorous relationship between two people who don't understand each other's language is certainly purified of every intellectual structure, every sentimental complication. The affair either works or it doesn't. There are no possible tricks—unless that exotic love is in itself the most dangerous of tricks, the greatest of errors.

Mysteriously, she continued to push me away. She shook her head and eyed me dubiously. What had happened? I wanted to know. I insisted.

"Oh, this is not an innocent kiss," she answered.

At first I didn't consider the expression important. I thought it was the usual feminine resistance. Now that five years have passed and I begin to love America less and understand it more, I know that that answer had a quite different degree of seriousness. Anglo-Saxons, especially Americans from the southern States, see in the Negro guilt incarnate; they approach even the Mediterranean peoples—Spanish, French, Italian—with an obscure sense of sin. While in the kisses of their tall, blonde men they enjoy sparingly the perverse innocence of infantile and brotherly loves, in the kisses of dark immigrants they both fear and desire the masculine force of the adult and the stranger.

It was not an innocent kiss. With a look that was diffident and full of remorse, she asked me to leave her alone. I again tried to embrace her but now without conviction. Her repugnance, although I didn't understand it, had disturbed me. The love of a woman and of a foreign city suddenly appeared to me to be a nervous and intellectual impulse. For the rest of the way, we sat apart in silence.

And yet, that same night, in the miserable comfort of the flat where she lived with her mother, among the sad furniture of the living room, I recaptured, as if by enchantment, the desired illusion.

We lay on the sofa in each other's arms. In the next room her mother could be heard snoring, unaware of our presence. But even if she had awakened, she would have pretended not to hear us. At least the daughter guaranteed this to me. And it's true that every night for two or three months we used the living room with impunity.

Now what was it I had to be thankful for? Was it the Protestant's respect for the individual, the absolute acceptance of individual responsibility even between mother and daughter? Or rather, the mania for emancipation of the modern American woman? However, it was not the tolerance of the mother that more than anything else made me aware that I was in a faraway country.

The plaster on the ceiling that I looked at from the sofa repeated it to me with a happy and boundless feeling. The plaster, thin and very white. In the background, the window with its sash and draw drapes and lack of shutters. The built-in closet, polished, with one door. The shape of the light bulb and of the shade. The quality of silence, run through by the continuous static of cars and the distant rumble of the el. The invisible but tangible metallic quality of the place: iron girders, thermal tubes, electrical wires, a thick metallic cage barely disguised by the soft plaster of the walls. And that bitter smell of burnt rubber, that dry air as if in a power plant, which is the atmosphere of all American homes.

When I lowered my glance, I saw the spreadout mass of blonde hair that hid her face. I did not think of clasping a woman but *an American woman.*

Subconsciously, I indulged in a kind of singsong: who would have said so, eh? I am here, I am here, not in Turin, not in Rome, not even in Paris. New York New York Brooklyn Brooklyn. None of my friends is capable of imagining this room or this girl. No one in the world knows exactly where I am now. I could never return. I could die. The ordinary little living room, one of the infinite living rooms of Brooklyn; the ordinary little blonde, one of the infinite number of blondes in America: they have welcomed me from my oppressed and rebellious adolescence. And now they would shield me from going back. They would hide me from my own memories. The exotic blonde hair caressed me now, enveloped my face. It seemed to me that I existed only to feel myself different.

She was the last of twelve brothers and sisters. Once her brothers had started traveling through the country and her sisters had married, she found herself poor and alone with her mother in their native Dallas and had moved to New York, following an example and a hope then very common. She found a job right away in a bank on Fifth Avenue and earned enough to support herself and her mother in the modest flat in Brooklyn.

I went to pick her up at 5:00 in front of the bank. But she was often late, kept until nightfall doing extra work. She came out with eyes reddened by spending so many hours bent over figures. But she always smiled at me from a distance and came towards me with a bold step. Whether we ate alone and went to the movies, or joined a large and noisy group at some cocktail party, she remained invariably gay, vivacious, enthusiastic, seemingly full of confidence in the future and happy that New York had fulfilled all her provincial hopes.

With me every so often she was again bothered by puritanical doubts. In the middle of a kiss, she would pull back, as if at a real Negro who had surprised her asleep. But little by little (we saw each other every night), she began to lose her scruples. Finally she told me that it was too bad I wasn't a citizen; she would have asked me to marry her.

And perhaps, at some later time, it really might have ended in marriage, but one night we realized that we didn't love each other. We had taken the subway to get home. After a half-hour trip, we still had a five-minute walk. It was raining. It was spring. Along the broad dark streets, there were apartment buildings for blue-collar workers and clerks and shopkeepers. Vast empty spaces of building sites opened here and there, protected along the sidewalk by metal wires. The street we were walking down was called Bliss Street.

We walked by a large coffee shop all lit up. But one customer sat alone at the long shining white counter. Wrapped in a dark overcoat, perched on a stool, he was sipping through a straw from a glass full of pink stuff. We walked on, into the dark. I was thinking about the man in the coffee shop; I was looking at a fire escape dripping rain against the bright halo of a street light. I was savoring the unfamiliarity of the place, excited by my own estrangement.

Suddenly I felt a stronger pressure weighing on my arm. I could barely act in time to support her. Pale, with trembling cheeks, lips slightly parted, a vacuous stare, she let herself sink down to the ground like a dead weight. I picked her up in my arms to carry her into the coffee shop. Suddenly she came to herself, looked at me for a moment, and then, bursting into desperate tears, she rested her head on my shoulder.

I had had the idea that American women did not weep, or at least, never like ours did. I thought of their pride, their claim to equality with men. And now—

She cried for perhaps an hour without my being able to find out why. Finally, between sobs that became fewer, she stammered in her flat, very soft southern accent: "I always—wanted—to git— something in my life—and now—I know—I never will git it—and that's why—I'm crying."

Then she explained. From childhood her ambition had been *to go on the stage*—as ballerina, actress, singer, whatever might be done on a stage. But the last years in Dallas she had practiced tap dancing above all. Once in New York, she had been certain of getting started in a few months, but a year had already gone by and she had not seen the face of an impresario. Now she understood. It had been a dream. Finished, not to be thought of again. She would stay with her mother a few more years and then she would marry. She would have children and would live her life in some far-off city, in Ohio, Michigan, Illinois. Exactly like her sisters.

She walked at my side. She stared straight ahead, eyes full of tears, and every so often dried them with the soaked wad of her handkerchief.

I cheered her up with trite expressions. She smiled and thanked me, while continuing to stare straight ahead. She also looked at the street, where we walked, back and forth, for more than an hour. The wet asphalt. The reflections of occasional street lights. Down there, in the depths of darkness, the tranquil red and violet arabesques of a neon sign. The squalid grey facades, pierced by many windows and crossed by black zigzags, the galleries and ramps of fire escapes. Here and there, the great empty building sites. And an abandoned stand, green and yellow, glistening from the rain. Bliss Street.

It was no longer raining. A humid, light spring breeze had sprung up, and it reminded you that the Atlantic was a few miles away.

America! America! Perhaps she, too, who was born there, was—like me—fascinated and corrupted by America. I looked at her again. I saw her beside me—despairing, mad, alone. And then I understood. Human caresses would not have been able to console her. Nor could kisses dry her hysterical eyes, which had wept not for a thing, a person, or an emotion—but for a dream.

America! She loved the skyscraper of her bank on Fifth Avenue, the screen of the Paramount, the footlights of the Roxy, the top of the Empire State Building, and even the dark and macabre view of a street in Brooklyn more than she loved me or any other man. New York had disappointed her hope. It didn't matter. New York remained in New York in any case; Broadway, Broadway. And the disappointment had made its attraction grow even more. So it was with me.

I listened to the far-off noise of the el more than tò her sobs. I looked at the closed shop windows we passed by—yellow pyramids of grapefruits in mysterious shadow—more than at her suffering form. And I looked forward to the moment when she would have decided to go home and I would have gone back alone to the station of the el, walking lightly, quickly, through the deserted street; breathing the odor of the rain; and entrusting my face to the deception of the free American wind.

Masculine and Feminine Beauty

G. A. BORGESE

Atlante americano, 1936, pp. 191-194

Like it or not, the masculine type most frequently seen in the street—even in a mixed and multiracial city like New York—is the one that America has shaped and made popular everywhere in the world for the last decade, not only in Europe but also in Japan. It is the smooth-faced man, with a strong forehead and a square chin—the mask of the *Fortuna Virilis*, which is also borrowed from a classic ideal of the Renaissance, an ideal of Roman origin this time.

Feminine beauty is, on the contrary, an Hellenic-inspired ideal—not always attained, that goes without saying. As for beautiful children, it seems they have no other function than to resemble English children in Christmas story books, slender and tall like them, with puzzling hair which, rather than blonde, is transparent like a halo around their heads.

As is well known, the parameters of American beauty differ from the Greek on many points. The slope of the shoulders is different, as is the placement of the bust, and the blossoming of the body is more sudden at the branching out of the stem. The face is more striking if seen from the front than in profile, since the nose has a limited prominence. But what is identical is the tendency toward leanness and movement, the fact of experiencing beauty as a thrust which lends wings even to the wingless statues in museums of Greek sculpture. Strangely similar also is the concept of beauty as a collective type, a social model that disregards and does not like distinctive traits or individuality. Because of that, a beautiful woman here prefers to feel like a statue rather than like a portrait. She triumphs especially in mass gatherings, from school and sports events to chorus lines, where each woman rejoices in being like her companions. If one must make a comparison with flowers, she is similar to tulips, which taken one by one don't mean much, but clustered in a flower bed dazzle.

She remains young as long as she can. Then, as if by fiat, she moves into the category of middle-aged women, which is a totally different institution. Ages are separated by clear cuts, without nuances. As long as she is young, whether married or single, she is a "girl," which the Greeks would have called *korē*. The mature woman is rare; there is no rich, ripe fruit such as you find full of fragrance (and for so exquisitely long!) in European gardens, the beauty of forty and over, who a century ago used to be called *la femme à trente ans*. The American woman is twenty as long as she can. Her ideal is not the *femme fatale*, Carmen or Hedda Gabler, but the school girl, and almost the doll. That causes noticeable differences in wardrobe and makeup also. In a general way, Paris dictates fashion; except that this woman does not wear her dress, she moves in it. She prefers clothes that faithfully fit the pace of her movements rather than what looks elegant and sumptuously spreads when she sits down in an armchair. If at all possible, the bottles and the cases on her dresser are also European. Let the mouth become a carnation, let the cheek bloom like a geranium, but the eye shadow is lacking in the little arsenal. The dark rings, the passion blues, are not in.

Puritan modesty contributed, in a singular concurrence, to this rebirth of classicism. It taught to control emotions and first of all not to show them, favoring the proliferation of these smooth, fresh faces, in which innocence lasts and lasts, and eventually survives many trials. The eyes of the beautiful American woman are not to be looked at, but to look; they draw their luminosity from the sky, limpid, with no spark of expressiveness; eyes such as statues would want them.

Eve in America

MARGHERITA SARFATTI

L'America, ricerca della felicità, 1937,
pp. 192, 197-199, 202-204

The American woman has earned her own equality, and among
the rights she has earned is the right to the "pursuit of happiness."
To a man, this might seem a small thing. But a woman realizes immediately how this achievement is a heretical attack on the Latin
and European concept of femininity, and even subverts the unwrit-
ten, untouchable laws of tradition. Marriage, family, divorce—all
the things which in this area seem grotesque or admirable to us, all
the new and strange things we find in American culture, have the
power to surprise us because of the basic difference in concepts
they imply . . . .

Look at American women as they walk down the street—swift,
supple, and erect. Their movements, gestures, and words belong to
a being who is free by birthright, just like a beautiful wild creature
who was never tamed. The grace of European women, particularly
the Italian and the French, comes from the moving suggestion of
frailty, from the restrictions imposed by protective norms which
even the freest of women, even without wanting to, carries with her
as her own aura: the product of civilization, a melancholy awareness of limitations and denials. But the grace of American women
is spontaneous and rash, an untamed river, a natural force.

"The women of our countries," said a young French gentleman
who was duly divorced from one American woman and married to
another, have "a function in our civilization, which is to carry the
helmet and spear like a man's squire. There is no place for such a
woman in American society. Actually, I feel sorry for American
women. They live at the margins of this society, exploiting the male

or trying in vain to usurp his functions.'' The American woman is also generally accused of being hard, superficial, heartless, and fast, fast being an almost untranslatable expression, approximately meaning emancipated, brash, coquettish, frivolous, and a flirt, all of these terms in their weaker forms.

Appearances form three-fourths of reality and are almost always linked to the remaining fourth. Let's assume that the American woman is, as she seems, frivolous in her loves. This lovable *sauvage* turns out to be an extremely hard worker. She works in factories, on the farm, and in stores; she is typist, secretary, businesswoman, bank employee, artist, sportswoman, and homemaker with a disciplined, persevering, and enthusiastic strength. I believe that even her impertinence is dictated by necessity and is actually a virtue. She approaches her mate, teasing him and going a good part of the way, instead of waiting for him or even running from him coyly, Daphne-like. Can you imagine! Given the American respect for women she would have to wait till the end of time for him to pursue her.

It is the same thing when it comes to greetings. In Europe, a lady waits for the man to address her. In England and in North America, it's up to the woman to take the initiative with a brief nod of acknowledgment. Always and everywhere respect, timidity, and lack of time cause men to wait for the woman's initiative. She doesn't always get much satisfaction out of this task. The one who is approached has the choice to say no, to say yes, or to say no and let things happen. But if such is her situation when it comes to the perpetuation of the species, she should not be blamed for it.

Perhaps this explains the success of the Latin man in America. He is probably neither more amorous nor more exciting, and he is certainly less patient, than the American man, but he is more daring. He always considers taking the initiative with women to be part of the duties of proper masculine behavior. He can go from violence to gentleness, from a serious and discreet courtship to a nostalgic and playful one, expecting nothing, just expressing a vague nuance of regret. By so doing, he performs a reverse emancipative function. He gives back to the American woman the atavistic passive game, for which she feels grateful to him, at least for a little while. To her surprise she again finds the old defensive tactics. But when the arrogant Latin male ceases to be attentive, tender, and passionate enough to make his tyranny more pleasing than his submission, it may happen that she will believe she has given up something real for a shadow. The loss of her freedom and supremacy, and of the unconditional respect which she enjoyed among her compatriots, and especially the loss of that invaluable privilege—the right to take the initiative and to make a choice—seem to her renunciations that are not repaid by a presence at the same time more rare and less dear. Then the clamorous collapse of her marriage with a European often happens, for she is not bound by the fear of scandal, and she is not content with a discreet adulterous affair. No, she demands a divorce and happiness in legality.

* * *

The average female blue-collar worker . . . has an easier life here than in our country because the perfect collective organization saves individual pain and effort. It does away, it's true, with the happy individuality of our homes, even the modest ones, but that is another matter. To brown a cutlet with four little onions on your own stove might be more pleasant than warming up canned beef and gravy, but it still requires more work and more effort. The small working-class apartment in America is equipped with comforts, inventions, and appliances to save time and effort such as we do not even have in palaces. Middle-class women, however, are better off in Europe, where a little maid is not an extravagant luxury even for people with modest means, and where a university professor lives better than his American counterpart, even if he receives a smaller salary. Yet, American women of the intellectual middle class know how to be both Martha and Mary, homemakers and ladies of leisure. Even among average housewives, what a sincere desire to become educated! Their busy lives are actually so sad, devoid as they are of masculine presences. Marriage and family in America are an evening phenomenon. Husband and children lead their lives between office and club. The wife sometimes goes to her office and always to a separate club. In the morning she cleans house, in the evening she cooks and washes the dishes; in between times, she tries to keep up with fashion and culture and to keep herself pretty, with energy that would exhaust a European woman.

It was perhaps my personal good luck, and yet I do not think it is an extraordinary coincidence, nor can it be something that one can plan: I encountered in that country some of the most tender and strong examples of femininity that I have ever had the good fortune to admire. Women made of steel and velour, in the Martha Washington tradition . . . women who work better than men, in silence, ready to make sacrifices, and wholly devoted to a cause or to the man who embodies the cause. Tenderly altruistic, as European women also can be, they are even stronger in dissimulating their dedication and the toll exacted by their sacrifices, under a smile. I remember Mrs. M. of New York, a widow and mother of two sons killed in war, who was herself an amputee from an ambulance accident on the French front, where she neglected to care for herself in order to care for the other wounded. Petite, fresh, and slim, always extremely elegant, with two dark eyes lighting up her face like two misty stars under hair sprinkled with gray, that woman who suffered terribly was always cheerful and active. She directs a major periodical and heads many social and philanthropic organizations. She should not even have time to breathe, and yet she finds time to be hospitable and sociable, to be humorous in her indomitable courage, and to impart warmth and help. She never speaks of herself or of her work; nobody knows if she is in pain. When you see her, you think that all she has to do in life is plan surprises for her friends, who worship her.

In Washington, D.C., Mrs. K., a beautiful, intelligent, and very distinguished middle-aged lady, accompanied me on a tour which she had prepared with great care for me for three whole days. She was smiling and full of vitality, and yet I detected a secret anguish deep in her eyes; there was a shadow of exhaustion around her cheekbones and her nose which was unusually sharp. She told me that it was nothing, but I later learned that her husband, a politician and a prominent university professor, was stricken by progressive paralysis and that she, who adored him, treated him at home and cared for him personally. The night had been terrible, nobody in the family had closed an eye, the fatigue and the sorrow exhausted her. It seemed that that fragile woman ought to collapse at any moment. On the contrary, at the very moment I succeeded in eliciting from her a brief report made with the most reticent, rapid, and unemphatic words, she smiled to minimize modestly her secret torment. She tried to distract me, showing me the cherry trees in bloom, and the art works, in order to console me and to excuse herself for having revealed that pain . . . .

What About the Girls?

EMILIO CECCHI
America amara, 1940, pp. 257-260

Now I seem to hear somebody ask: "What about the girls?" A little patience, for heaven's sake! One thing at a time, and the girls will be along.

Here they are, in a rush, without hats. Many are in the cars of their fathers who go into the city to work; others with their own cars; or in pairs, in small groups, in large flocks. American student slang has a wide range of words to describe girls. But when they run around in groups this way, all alike, strutting, and when they crowd under the trees in front of the classroom buildings, there is no doubt: then they are called *heiferettes*, a word which suggests sun and hay.

They wear dresses with that typical neatness which in America more than elsewhere tends to level all women and to make it more and more difficult to distinguish social classes at a glance. The voluminous notebooks, books, atlases, rulers, and cases with which they are loaded down—even rather ostentatiously—indicate that they are students. But those who work as cocktail waitresses to pay for their studies dress as simply as the daughters of the wealthy. It looks as if blouses and skirts go directly from the trichromatism of the fashion magazines and from the shop windows to fit their bodies, all in the same manner, without a wrinkle and with anonymous, impersonal elegance. The bodies—slender, supple, all the right size, neither fat nor thin—also have an abstract and cold quality. Something about them makes you think of apples, all identical, all of the same color, and odorless as they are in the displays of California fruit sellers.

Whether for love of culture or for the simple desire to acquire social graces or to qualify for a teaching career, in many American universities girls constitute around two-thirds of the student body, with an even higher proportion in art history, languages, and literature. Women prefer the disciplines which among us once went under the rubric of "humanities." This does not mean that America is Helicon, but it does indicate that in this, as in other respects, America is a matriarchy. If in this case the phenomenon does not directly involve an exercise of power, but is instead a function of supply and demand, that amounts to saying that the incentive comes from women.

I do not wish to push this analysis too far, but in the cult of the Madonna, Catholicism exalted the instincts of man's veneration for woman, which, if left to themselves, could have degenerated. Catholicism has given us a sense of balance in that also. Worshiping the Madonna at the altar, we feel freer and more at ease when facing women of flesh and blood. For the puritans it is different. Too proud to worship the divinity of the Madonna, they continuously run the risk of worshiping (or just about) the women in their own households. It's a bad trend. It's not surprising that America has true and real sibyls and female popes, who head public cults with thousands of followers. . . .

Aside from these spectacular excesses, there is a background of chivalry in puritan asceticism. The tradition that gives such a large part to a woman in social functions, and men's gratitude for her strenuous collaboration during the hard times of pioneer life, have created for the American woman a situation which is, in some respects, a privileged one. All these things, and perhaps her keener moral sensitivity, have developed and refined certain qualities in her. She has remained more openminded and courageous; she has been freed, at least in part, from the obtuse conformity and the enslavement to opinion which Americans are subject to, partly from mental laziness and partly because they find it advantageous.

Today things are like yesterday. Eight or ten years of crises fill a country with disasters but do not change the ethical profile of a hundred million souls. It takes more than that to effect deep changes! And the American middle-class woman (all America is middle-class, high or low) always has her time for reading and her circles of "spiritualist science." Children and family don't count here as much as they do for us. Housework is careless, hasty. One of the many effects of this situation is the enormous influx of women into the universities, even though many, after they get their degrees, enter professions that are scarcely associated with university training. In these years, this is a frequent phenomenon for both men and women, and in Europe as well.

Movies and illustrated newspapers have revealed aspects of the college life of women: archery, gymnasiums, swimming pools. Perhaps because of all these bathing suits, Italians see little difference between a group of American students and a troupe of Hollywood starlets. But this is a conventional and mistaken idea, no less mistaken than the rumors about the fantastic, incredible things, that are supposed to have taken place in this or that university. Let us recall how the old anticlericals fed their imaginations with the mysterious deeds of the convents. What do you expect the college girls do? They dance; they have a glass too many at the major sports events; those who have one go out with a boy friend who is not, or at least not yet, a fiancé but a kind of anticipated *cavalier servente*, and who more than anything else helps her carry heavy loads of books and pays for movie tickets. They are concerned about the results of their studies, about ratings and grades, to the point of pique and of tears—big hot tears, almost incredible on those rosy cheeks. And they spend hours and hours, head bent, studying in the severe reading room of the university library, which is decorated with a series of copies of Velasquez.

Women and Men

GUIDO PIOVENE
De America, 1954, pp. 156-161

It's commonplace to say that relations between the sexes are not so smooth in America. Even Americans joke about it. A writer, Agnes Meyer, attributes this phenomenon to "immorality" and its consequences in the first half of this century, i.e., the estrangement from home, children, and permanent ties, the too-frequent divorces, and sexual freedom. But today that trend is disappearing in America. A new moralistic phase is beginning, in which there are strong pressures, especially from the Catholics, against divorce and birth control. Wanting children is again becoming one of the basic tenets of Americanism, just like sincerity, honor, and the cult of Lincoln. Youth seems to me to be basically home-oriented. Besides, the "immorality of the times" has always been the easiest explanation for all ills. It is necessary to understand why one gets the uneasy feeling in America that the two sexes too often have difficulty in understanding each other and that each is often unhappy with the other.

We already know about the importance of women in early America. The early years of America have been relived with every new emigration, like the one toward the West. There were few women in the West. In a society dominated by men who were violent and naive, and by fierce religious, racial, and economic struggles, women became the point of equilibrium, the adult influence, and the peacemakers in a community in turmoil. While the men acted, women directed them from their hearths. The law surrounded them with strict protective measures. American women have largely preserved their pioneer virtues. They are often more intelligent and more "intellectual" than men, and they are almost always more educated. They have a keen sense for economy and bookkeeping. They often work, for American life does not allow women to be only homemakers but imposes rigid social duties on every class. When they are good mothers, they are excellent mothers—sometimes too oppressive for their sons, so I am told, which must be a sign of their dissatisfaction. The American Mom is a national monument, the embarrassing object of a rhetorical cult. However, those womanly virtues have fostered, often through a degenerative process, an excessive and maniacal sense of women's own worth; a tendency to romanticize; mythomania; and narcissism, or more simply a self-infatuation—quite a lot easier to develop in a country where everyone is somewhat of a mythomaniac. All Americans actually live and are spurred on to overcome their problems by the "myth" of America.

The excessive sense of self-importance, the acute feeling throughout American society that one is in a perennial state of economic siege, and the danger of being discarded through divorce often creates—how can I say it euphemistically—an overdeveloped financial awareness. One of the striking peculiarities of night clubs is that the songs insist on the theme of the millionaire husband who gives furs and jewels. Or they insist on offering this advice: "Men are rude, ungrateful, and crude; at least get something out of them." Even the financial relationship between husband and wife—from what I am told—resembles the relationship between employer and employee, especially in the middle and lower classes. Generally, in American economic life, women serve the function of a spur and are often rather pitiless: men work, and women press them on. For this reason, a great part of American wealth falls into the hands of elderly, triumphant widows.

The American woman's sense of her rare worth can have other consequences. It can lead, for example, to a consistently calculating attitude toward the man she has selected. My readers may perhaps remember my report on a visit to a girls' school, Smith College. I said then that all girls who can, have a boy friend. In a society where you cannot be alone, the institution of the boy friend is accepted, even in the strictest milieus, and begins with infancy.

Everybody knows how strict American Catholic society is; yet, right in Washington, D.C., I saw an advertisement for a charity ball for little girls between twelve and fifteen, organized by nuns; the girls were invited to bring their boy friends. At Catholic as well as nondenominational universities, the girls have boy friends. In almost every family, the boy friend is allowed to come in the evening to pick up his girl to go out dancing. Speaking of my visit to Smith College, I said that girls often end up marrying their boy friends, and that is the point I want to bring up. As a teacher told me:

It's true that many girls marry their college sweethearts, but, generally, they take their time to do it. For example, once they are finished with their studies, they go to New York; they lead a very social life; they make every effort to have their photo appear in a magazine. Naturally, the ideal is a magazine like *Life*. That photo becomes the best card in the girl's hand. She goes back to the boy who's still back home; photo in hand, she makes him believe that millionaires want to marry her in New York; she makes him well aware of how much she'll be losing by marrying him. Then she agrees to marry him, but on certain conditions: so much income, and such-and-such standard of living; this or that house, and so many children. Remember, usually she makes an excellent wife.

Another effect of the American woman's sense of importance is her tendency to romanticize herself in order to make herself interesting. People who know tell me that many women have the habit of missing a rendezvous at the last minute; or they go to the rendezvous but just to say that they must run immediately and always for fantastic or mysterious reasons.

Finally, the American woman has a tendency to idolize her own body, which leads to frigidity, in other words, an extreme narcissism. Under this heading are the awe for science, a life minutely supervised by the doctor, the coffee and milk taken late at night "to cleanse" one's system, not laughing for fear of wrinkles, and reluctance about sexual activity. In a night club in New York, I noticed a radiant woman covered with jewels like an Indian idol. "See?" said my friend, and frankly I suspect that he was exaggerating, "in this city there are four or five women who are not afraid to ruin their bodies by making love. The men of the city have covered them with gold; they are wealthier than Croesus. That is one of those few, and now she has married a millionaire who's in Chang Kai-shek's retinue.''

The American woman also tends to believe that her body (and here again science has something to do with it) is like a foreign entity which can be manipulated at will. In the past, a girl frequently was in doubt whether she should reveal her premarital adventures to her fiancé. In Washington, I heard of a new version of such a dilemma. A girl had the protruding part of some of her toes amputated in order to wear smaller shoes. Now, the moral dilemma was: should she tell her fiancé, or should she let him discover it on his own? Apparently, the young man in question had once confessed in a conversation that he had a horror of women with cut toes.

Many men are not happy with women, and many women are not happy with men. The men are exhausted by their work. In addition, especially if they have a responsible—or at least a public—position, they are paralyzed by extreme caution. They are afraid of scandals and of blackmail, and they fear falling into one of the infernal traps of a life filled with menacing undercurrents. There is also an atavistic morality still alive in America, even amid the worst excesses, or, better, a morality which is the motivation for rebellions and excesses, so that in one way or another that morality has the last word. It fosters an exaggerated sense of the "responsibility" one assumes with any tie, of whatever nature; this feeling produces an instinctive fear of responsibility, of oneself and one's own scruples. For a number of reasons, external and internal, the life of men in this area is very difficult. Often there is a tendency to underrate the importance of sex, or conversely to exaggerate it, and to make a problem out of it; we know the vogue of porno books and films

. . . .

The European often detects a sense of coldness in American families, of which his presence is certainly not the cause, for there are no more hospitable people in the world. Perceptive Americans often have the same feeling, and they express it; literature about "dissatisfaction" abounds. We must remember that more than anywhere else, in America marriage is a social necessity. Life in this society is made for couples; the man who appears in public without a wife by his side, except in some less conservative milieus, has much less prestige. In spite of divorce, American life is basically more family-oriented than ours, with a tendency toward parenthood. Regardless of the "immorality" of the times, men start their families with an excessive sense of their obligations. The problems begin when a form of solidarity (often mistaken for love from the day of marriage to the day of death) takes the place of love. I have mentioned the habit, which is frequently observable in American families, of spouses praising one another. Innumerable husbands tell you, without being asked, "I owe everything to my wife," and the women jump to the defense of their husbands at the first suggestion of criticism, however mild. They really believe they love each other, without hypocrisy. Hypocrisy begins when the difference between our words and our thoughts is clear to us, and the American, trained to tell the truth, would hardly accept being a simulator. Cynical solutions, so common in Europe, are almost unknown here. Americans don't know cynicism; the very word horrifies them. Everything collapses when an accidental event reveals to two people who are sad, lonely, and bored in their togetherness, the point where simulation and cynicism could start. A novel written by an Italian in which there is a rather grim portrayal of a marriage created crises for some women who as a result discovered their own unhappiness in marriage. A trip to Europe has sometimes had the same effect. I know of an older gentleman who, after coming back from Europe, called his wife, telling her "I have discovered that we do not love each other," and then asked for a separation. Therefore, there is a sense of precariousness in American life, a diffuse anxiety, I would almost say a vulnerability vis-à-vis a book, a trip, or a meeting. It's understandable that women would try to protect themselves by their coldness, a strenuous defense of their own interests, clear agreements, and a secret bank account.

I have dealt with this subject with a certain extravagance. Doubtless, the facts I have mentioned are not the rule, and they do not happen only in America. It is true, however, that the quality of the relationship between men and women is one of the flaws in American life I referred to elsewhere, a question still awaiting solution, a question America is carrying along in its rush forward. A dose of spontaneity is needed, and I would almost say a dose of humility.

Come Back, Mary . . . All Is Forgiven

GIUSEPPE PREZZOLINI

Tutta l'America, 1958, pp. 98-103

Giuseppe Prezzolini (1882-): Prezzolini was at one time a writer and editor of *La Voce* (1908-1914), an avant-garde cultural and literary periodical. He left Italy during the Fascist period and taught Italian literature at Columbia University from 1930 to 1950. He is the author of numerous books on the United States which have been collected and reprinted in the omnibus volume *The Complete America* (1958).

The day before yesterday I opened up a newspaper to a three-page display, each with six columns of small print, that contained only names, one after the other, in alphabetic order. They were names of people sought by a savings bank, people who had left deposits of money years ago and had not reappeared since; neither they nor their representatives or heirs could be found. There were several thousand names. They ended in *ini, ani, off, chu, erz, son, or,* easily identifying them as Celtic, German, Anglo-Saxon, Latin, Jewish, Japanese, Chinese, or Slavic—from every part of the world. Several thousand men and women came here, about whom no one knows anything, nor can the police trace them, and an advertisement is placed to find them—not to do them harm but to restore money that belongs to them, with interest. An advertisement is placed as if they were not men and women, but dogs or wallets or glasses or bunches of keys or umbrellas, or I don't know what—one of those objects that easily gets lost.

If this was the most spectacular advertisement of this sort that I had ever seen, suggestive as it is of all the destinies represented by those names and initials, it isn't the only one that may be read in the newspapers of New York. Every day there is a curious column of inquiries for people, some of them legal and others sentimental. There are lawyers who are looking for heirs of people dead for many years, who give the last address and last news that they have had of them. There are relatives who look for some runaway from a family conflict, which can be guessed at between the lines of a necessarily cold announcement: "Mary, daddy and mama are looking for you; all is forgiven; come home." Or: "John, you are warned that mama is seriously ill; communicate with your cousin immediately." And there are the familiar dramas that emerge from a notice drawn up according to a legal formula, which makes us Europeans laugh: "My wife, so and so, having deserted my bed and board, I am not responsible for her debts," followed by the name of the husband and his address. Damn! a cuckold, yes, that is inevitable, but to be swindled in addition—that is, to have to pay the debts of the unfaithful party—that, no.

Seeing these notices prompts the question: Why is this the country of missing persons? Isn't it significant, perhaps, that so many people are lost in this part of the world where immigrants have come precisely to lose something, to leave something behind them, to create a new life for themselves, a different existence? This one left political oppression, that one religious persecution, another a crime, still another his creditors. But all, or almost all, with the premise of burning their bridges behind them, went where no one knew who they were, where they would have become something else, not because of or in spite of their past, but through the hope in a future or the certainty of a present. Once this separation was made, was not the desire to repeat it strong, perhaps, every time an obstacle presented itself and a test was failed? The past, this country seems to say, does not exist; it can be abolished. If your wife or husband bores you, get a divorce; if your father is opposed to your intentions, leave your family; if your creditor is insolent, change neighborhoods; if your name has some displeasing meaning or history, go to a judge and change it; if your conscience bothers you, sell your furniture and leave the city. There are so many other cities, just like the one where you live, near and far, with the same conveniences, and, as they say, with the same "opportunities." No one is looking for you, and so it is easy to make all traces disappear. There are so many people in the city that it closes again over the empty place left by the dead or by the living who pretend to be dead, just as water rushes to fill up a whirlpool, and air a vacuum. It is not a crime to give a name other than your own to a hotel, and, if you are not in trouble with the police, you can live your whole life with another identity. It has been calculated that 300,000 people are living here illegally, who slipped away from a ship's cubbyhole, deserted from a crew, entered under a load of coal, passed across a frontier without surveillance, came down from an airplane in an unwatched locality, or entered with a false passport. Of these a minimal part is seized by the police on the rare occasion of a street brawl, an automobile accident, a fire, or a denunciation—most of the time by a woman: "Look out, so-and-so does not want to marry me, but he is an illegal resident. Take him away, deport him!"

The country is so large. What a curious sensation one has when, after having traveled a whole day in a car or train, one looks at a map and becomes aware of having covered such a small part of it. Only an airplane seems to have the speed adequate to these distances.

In this enormous space, refugees from so many places create a curious sense of apprehension, unreality, and mystery. Immense forests, rivers like arms of the sea, plains as far as the eye can see like oceans, and cities that extend for miles and miles, all with their little houses. One doesn't know where the country ends and the city begins, with the buildings generally made of wood, still so near to the forest that it seems as if they might not need a vine in order to cover themselves with greenery, but that they could almost sprout branches, as if they had roots in the soil.

Who can know where you are and who you are? At times, lost among people so diverse, speaking a language that is not ours, with others who speak the same language but one we know is foreign to them also, a doubt arises as to whether we have changed, whether we are still ourselves. Then we try to say a verse in Italian or to joke in the mother tongue, almost to convince ourselves that everything that surrounds us is not a dream.

From slope to slope, the houses and woods and rivers follow each other along the great ribbons of the roads. How many places to run away to, to conceal whatever importunate guilt, whatever weighty crime. Who is it who stands near me on a train, who is it I meet on a path? Why did he come here, he or his parents; what fragments of existence are engraved on his nights, when he speaks only with himself? "Of every six people who are on your street car," I have read in a newspaper, "one has been in prison or will go there."

Who are those people in the automobile passing me now? A wife who has left bed and board, delinquents who have already been in prison or are going there, fugitives of countries far and near, or children of fugitives, people searched for by some savings bank and who have their own good reasons for not going to collect what is owed them?

But no, but no—my reasonable self keeps repeating—they are all fine people, regularly enrolled on the voting lists, who tomorrow will vote for La Guardia or for his rival. All fine people. However, of every six—

I don't know. However much I reason, I feel a certain over-looked mystery, which seems to me to spread from the automobile to the street, from the street to the woods, houses, and countryside. It is not a familiar countryside, and yet it is not new to me because every particular of the buildings reminds me of something I have already seen: a Greek temple, a Swiss chalet, a French castle, a German house, an English villa. All are impoverished, deformed, jumbled like a series of memories in a dream or like the elements of a surrealist painting where heads, trumpets, pieces of newspaper, factories, stars, and violins are found in a sacred and rigid conver-sation next to each other in space and yet, spiritually, astronomical distances apart.

And then I understand the secret of these places so strange and so unknown to my eyes, and the perplexity in which the faces and words of the inhabitants leave me as if they were, faces and words, translations of an interior face and of an original work that I cannot grasp, that perhaps existed, but in a distant, remote past, and now, reflected across many mirrors, had just cast the last glimmer of its spell on this country.

It is the country of surrealism, a country of fragments, residues, remnants, and shipwrecks, so abundant, so rich with seeds that have given life to a whole vegetation of houses and to an almost phantom-like population, and to poets of dreams like Edgar Allan Poe or of social mysticism like Walt Whitman.

The Dear Departed, or:
The Maid
GIUSEPPE
PREZZOLINI

Tutta l'America, 1958, pp. 706-711

Maria is a fine, attractive girl from Florence, who married an American soldier and disembarked at one of the New York piers a little while ago as a "war bride." Now she has a baby and an apartment. But she does not have a maid. This is a tragedy for an Italian woman.

Unless you are very rich, there is no maid. Nor is there any "service." Service, every personal service, is expensive—too expensive now for the great majority of American families, even the middle class.

A maid in New York earns as much as a university professor in Italy. When her working day is over, she rushes off without seeing her employers, just as the Italian professor who after he has finished his class hour rushes off without seeing his students.

Maria came by the other day to ask me for a book to prepare herself for her American citizenship examination. (Who was the first president of the Union? Who becomes president if the president dies? and other questions that for a recent immigrant float in the air like wisps of clouds). We also spoke about her domestic problems.

Many war brides are not doing well in America. They get along well if they come from the same class as their husbands, wealthy, and cultured. Otherwise, the differences are so great—difficulties of language, the foreignness of relatives, differences of customs— that love cannot patch over all the cracks.

Many war brides married when Italy was in an exceptional condition, when everything was destroyed and finding food and clothing was diffficult. The husband also was in exceptional circumstances. He had a splendid uniform, clothing that he had never had in his life. He drove a car, like the one he had dreamed of while looking at advertisements. He stayed in a good hotel. In short, in the midst of famished and poor Italians he was a kind of nabob, a magnate, a Lord God.

I don't say that all of the men took advantage of these circumstances. Many times the imagination of Italian women contributed to the reciprocal deception. They fell in love with that well-dressed soldier, that gentleman who took them to dine in the best hotels, that Lord God who made cigarettes and chocolate come out of his pocket like a magician. They got married. They traveled first-class on the honeymoon. They disembarked.

Here the disappointments began. The husband took off the brilliant uniform. He left the car which was as big as three little Fiats. He returned to what he had been before, such as the bride had never seen him—a simple clerk, a humble employee, a butcher, a traveling salesman, a diner-owner, an undertaker's assistant. The apartment was heated like nothing is heated in Italy, but it looked sad for whoever is used to the light of Naples or Rome. There was Italian food in the stores, but it was expensive. The in-laws were cold and perfect; you couldn't even argue with them. In church you had to pay to hear a sermon in Italo-American jargon. There was a car, but you had to wash and polish it every week by yourself.

And above all, there was no maid. Ah! how many times the war brides remembered Adele, Pierina, Mercedes, and Giovanna, who had followed each other in succession, each seemingly worse than the one before. This one stole, that one let the stew burn, the third talked back. . . . But what a joy to have them day and night when you have no one else. What a feat it would have been to be able to make them come here. Now my friend Maria is not at this point of desperation. She loves her husband, has learned to remain aloof from her in-laws, as much as possible, with beautiful manners, and she has a baby boy who makes up for many things. Besides, she is an intelligent modern girl and has known how to compensate for the absence of a maid with the means at hand. . . .

Every modern apartment naturally has what to Maria appeared

to be a novelty, that is, hot running water day and night, summer and winter, which is a great help. Her husband had also thought of some appliances which are the pride of an infinite number of families: the vacuum cleaner, with its array of tubes and brushes that make it work in every hidden part of the armchairs and in corners; the washing machine and the iron; and the dishwasher. The heaviest burdens of the housewife are reduced. Maria, however, has asked for and obtained more.

Maria has gotten an electric clock, central and silent, that she calls her brain or memory-protector because in the morning it not only wakes her with her favorite tune, but also turns on the electric lights, starts the radio, gets the coffeemaker going, and toasts the slices of bread in the automatic toaster. This servant dressed in a uniform of ivory and gold cost her only $12.50.

Maria need not get too tired preparing dinner because a simple mechanism that has more hands than an Indian divinity goes to work for her and beats eggs, grates cheese, crushes ice, transforms any vegetable into a puree, or a sauce, and can be washed very easily.

When she cooks, Maria has little time to lose, and so she uses a pressure cooker that cooks food in a third of the usual time. She roasts whatever she wants in a new electronic oven in which seven minutes are enough to make a potato soft and ten minutes to prepare a whole chicken. To have hard-boiled eggs you must be careful not to go beyond a minute and a half.

Her iron never scorches a fabric because it has settings for silk, wool, or rayon. All she has to do is to turn it on; it stops heating up when it reaches the right temperature.

She doesn't worry about public garbage collection because the garbage disposal not only swallows but pulverizes everything except diamonds (which generally aren't thrown down drains, even in America); bones and shells come out of that inexorable instrument minced up and are taken away. In short, Maria has learned how to organize her home very well.

I very much appreciate all those inventions that remove the little annoyances of life. Being of a stoic temper—some will say hard—I find that it's easier to bear misfortunes than the aggravations of life. A misfortune constrains us to remain firm against destiny, like demigods, while vexations make us feel that we are poor creatures. So I very much like what Maria has done. But the other day, when she came to visit me and to show me the progress of her baby (after having told me that she had bought a new tool for her husband, something that opens cans without letting air in and puts a kind of funnel there which makes it possible to use·them with ease), she spoke to me with a certain nostalgia: "Do you remember Adele? What a good girl she was, and so affectionate—"

Now, I remember Adele clearly. She was a large, flabby woman shaped like a barrel without a top, and every day Maria's mother had some new complaint about her and some new tale to tell me. "Do you know the latest about Adele?" I carefully avoided reminding Maria of these things. I just looked at her and sighed: "Ah yes, poor Adele—she was a really fine woman—a maid."

The American Family Is
Twin-engined GIORGIO SOAVI
America tutta d'un fiato, 1959, pp. 103-105

A European writer concerned with American life resists the suggestion of the word "matriarchy" with difficulty. With this word he explains everything—the vitality and initiative of American women, the unhappiness of the men, the crisis of love. In analyzing the relations between the sexes, the writer has recourse to expressions like "bitter battle" and "struggle without quarter." If he wants to be witty, he will say that in 70 percent of the cases, a Cadillac has a woman at the wheel; and in 65 percent it is the husband who washes the dishes. From what I gather, these little vignettes provoke a lot of laughter in Europe.

In reality, the prosperity of America is essentially based on the fact that women, as well as men, work. No family makes progress without the paycheck of two people. "Every American family," said an economist, "is twin-engined." The American woman adds her own salary to that of her husband, and this makes both ends meet. With her salary she pays for the small expenses of their vacations, books, and medicine for the children. If she wants to buy a fur coat, she does it with her own money, her own savings. Naturally, she no longer needs to play-act and stick counterfeit kisses on her husband's neck in order to buy herself two pairs of stockings or a new dress. The American woman now has absolute independence, complete freedom. She no longer grovels at the feet of her lord and master like a slave. Her life is chosen like that of her husband. Coercion and hypocrisy don't exist, and a perfect equality characterizes the rights of men and women. Do we want to call that "matriarchy?"

I don't know what else could be asked for in the American woman. She knows how to type, to speak in public, to dance the twist, to drive, to swim. She knows the name of President Kennedy's secretary; she knows who the Russian representative to the United Nations is. She goes to the threatre, reads a couple of newspapers every day, goes to Carnegie Hall, and, perhaps to occupy her vacation, studies languages. And this is not all. Since American men are generally withdrawn and a bit bad-tempered; since they are never aggressive or—least of all—full of desire, American women must also be responsible for eliciting romantic words and special caresses.

A Connecticut Weekend

GIORGIO SOAVI

Fantabulous, 1963, pp. 62-66

* * * *

The sea is grey after a day of sun. The light is still vivid, grey everywhere but blinding and brilliant, and the windows of distant houses reflect that harsh light. In the woods there are squirrels, and a woodpecker hammers on tree trunks like a machine gun; on the sea, there are wild ducks. These little animals live within reach. A weekend at Greenwich, Connecticut: on the shore there is a flimsy construction, Japanese-like, for the bathers who undress on the beach. Between the sand and the meadows in back there are little ovens with a grill for cooking steaks, the famous "barbecue." At the bend, there is a parked car, right on the edge of the sea, and on the seat a boy and his girl are embracing. Since in America women give the orders, she is the one who embraces, and he is the one with his head on her breast. The boy rests enraptured; the girl looks far away, straight ahead.

* * * *

New Canaan: Leo's house, an enormous old stable, now new and full of glass doors, empty spaces, armchairs and sofas, pictures, bottles, colors, photographs—the house of an artist. We go out into the garden while dinner is being prepared. Beyond the hedge there is a thickset man in blue jeans and a sailor's jersey who is sawing a trunk. Next to him is a pile of wood.

"He works on Sundays, too?" I ask Leo.

"Come on, I'll introduce you; he's a vice president of General Motors."

* * * *

After staying for five minutes with us for cocktails, at Amagansett, they happily left for their next cocktail party and then went home. At dinner with them, David remembered the Cowards. He took the old pale-yellow Delahaye and drove for ten miles. Then there were the usual cries of astonishment over the house, the interior decoration, the lawn looking like it had just been mowed. The cutting of the beautiful green grass caused Mr. Coward to speak of thousands of dollars, naturally. The company became livelier. They spoke of next summer, the thousands of dollars to be spent next year, next summer. They had had enough drinks. Dinners and parties were beginning. Jackie learned with pleasure that Sanders was going to the same party. They prevailed on him to leave his Delahaye.

* * * *

Sometimes, before my head became muddled, I would get out of the comfortable house and go to stroll through the garden or into the street. It was more beautiful and more genuine. Nature was there; one could even hear pastoral airs. America, with an Italian thirty yards away from the Americans.

* * * *

With Gloria at Amagansett, Long Island. We buy color postcards. Alongside these natural beauties there is American food—hamburgers, hot dogs. In every corner of America, bar or luncheonette, silent men, seated on stools, at whatever hour of the day, drink beer. In city or countryside every hour of the day, legions of women shop, making purchases furiously. I have never seen people buy the way Americans do. The elevators and escalators of Saks, Macy's, and Bloomingdale's spew out women, young and old, who swoop through the corridors and shop.

* * * *

I can't continue to refuse to drink. Now, at eleven in the morning, I'm going out to give a package to Gloria's friends. It's Sunday, and I find them in the living room. Between them there is a tray of ice cubes and a bottle of Canadian whiskey, half empty.

* * * *

Woods and rolling countryside, handsome thoroughfares and expressways, houses of the rich. Leo says that to build a boundary wall around the house of Philip J., the owner spent at least $10,000. They seem to be frightful figures; they have no effect on us, or too much of one. In the first case, since we are going back to Italy in a few months, it doesn't matter to us. In the second, if it were us, would we be capable of earning so much in order to spend so much?

Many of the villas are not very large. The architecture is traditional, the color white. There are also various modern houses, built in the latest style by Marcel Breuer, Philip Johnson, and others less famous.

* * * *

On Sunday morning in New Canaan people pass by dressed up and made up, in old cars, carrying signs for the fight against cancer; some applaud or laugh, smoking, on the curb. Everyone can fight against cancer while continuing to smoke. They smoke knowing, being aware.

* * * *

In these small provincial towns, funeral homes are very noticeable. In addition to the customary hearse, they provide motorcycles with sidecars. On the motorcycles are young men dressed in black who resemble policemen or Marlon Brando. . . .

* * * *

"Italian?"

"Yes."

"How long have you been in America?"

"Two months."

"Are you making out? Do you like American women?"

"Very much!"

"They're all the same—all well scrubbed, ambitious, boring, without nuances."

"Very beautiful, however."

"How are you getting along personally?"

"Badly."

"That's enough to drive you up the wall."

"Precisely."

"You are a good man."

"Thanks."

Women and Independence

FERNANDA PIVANO
America rossa e nera, 1964, pp. 251-262

Fernanda Pivano (1920-): A friend and protégée of Cesare Pavese, Pivano is a prominent Americanist, who has translated a number of American works into Italian and has written frequently about the United States. The title of her book, *America Red and Black*, reflects a desire to capture several facets of American life. Among her other books on American culture and literature are *La balena bianca e altri miti* (*The White Whale and Other Myths,* 1961), and *Beat Hippie Yippie* (1972). Her most recent work is *Mostri degli anni venti* (*Literary Lions of the Twenties,* 1977).

I am in a California hospital, visiting my husband, who is sick . . . . [There are] beautiful blonde nurses, made up like movie actresses and often with college degrees, almost all of whom own cars and are single (but certainly not spinsters). They are fine, efficient girls, serious, attentive almost to the point of pedantry, subject to a spontaneous professional discipline more than to regulations. They are bound by regulations on only two or three points: always to smile, to run all together to emergency bells, not to go away until the patient has swallowed the prescribed pills. They don't recognize other rules. They are "independent" here as in their private lives.

It is an independence which all girls here reach in a hurry: for once out of high school or college they are no longer provided for by their parents. This is not out of parental selfishness or lack of affection, but because the children themselves don't want to be protected. Their parents rationalize this by now general custom with the thought that the sooner their daughters learn to be free from them, the sooner they will manage for themselves in the eventual family misfortunes.

The daughters do not even try to rationalize their mania for freedom. Sometimes they say that they don't want to disturb their parents with their habits (the refrain is almost always that the parents can't stand the record player at full volume, or, on the other hand, that they ask them where they have been when they come in after midnight). Sometimes they say that it isn't fair to make the parents support them when they can earn their own living, and sometimes that they want to know new cities and new people.

They leave home definitively, and not for that type of "rehearsal" which is the college students' life away from their families. They go to live with a roommate in a little apartment—in order to share the expenses, they say, but in reality to protect each other when they are sick, and in general to find a substitute for the rejected protection of the family. When you ask them what difference there is between respecting the demands of their parents and respecting those of their roommate, they answer that in case of disagreement they can change roommates when they want to. But they almost never do. The stronger of the two in reality dominates the other, choosing for herself the best room and deciding what days the living room will be left free for the visit of a boy friend, etc.

Naturally, this matter of the boy friend is a great problem. An experienced woman in the huge Italian colony in California told me, horrified, of finding out one day that her daughter—a tractable adolescent, studious and domestic—had gone to a gynecologist to be instructed about a birth-control device. To maternal protests she had answered frankly: "But, Mother, all my friends do it. Would you rather see me in trouble?"

The girls never speak about these things, however. Sometimes, rarely, they confide in their mothers, more often in their roommates, but a stranger succeeds in entering their privacy with difficulty. A journalist, an editor of a magazine with a large circulation, told me: "The problem is that men want to marry girls who have not yet had sexual experience, but they don't marry them if they have not had this experience beforehand with them. Therefore we don't know what to do."

In reality, what they do, everyone knows, but it is incredible how the majority of them are preoccupied by what is still called reputation. When I protested, saying that there was a contradiction between their independence and that preoccupation, they answered: "Yes, but then we would no longer find husbands."

Thus, there does not seem to be a great difference between the aspirations of the pale, dreamy, submissive nineteenth-century girls and these tanned, bull-like creatures who carry their own luggage and wash their own cars, earn their own living, cook and sew, wash and iron, follow courses in film criticism on television, and take evening certificates in lifesaving. Beneath it all, the changing times have transformed the old saying "cherchez la femme" into the Americanized "cherchez l'homme."

To see if I was mistaken, I decided to question these girls a little more closely.

1

Norma, the head of a group of nurses, is a beautiful girl. She is blonde, has blue eyes and a smile that reflects the splendor and joy of the California sky. She seems to be a picture of happiness. When she puts down her starched cap and gets into her blue car, you can only think that she is driving off towards gaiety and thoughtlessness: towards freedom.

One day I went with her to the little house which she shares with another nurse. The house has three rooms, with a long corridor arranged with a built-in closet and a small courtyard that serves as a garden, large enough for a lounge chair and a barbecue pit. Scarcely inside the house, Norma became downcast. She took a shower in a hurry, leaving her uniform on the bed (where a sweater and other garments were already). She got dressed again, gulping down a reheated cup of coffee, and in the meantime answered the telephone. She left the cup near the telephone and a towel in the hall because passing through she saw the cat and went hurriedly into the kitchen to pour a little milk into a dish for it. Then she threw herself into the car, with a slightly bewildered look: "I must be careful not to arrive late at the doctor's."

The doctor prescribed some more pills in addition to those he had already prescribed for her, but he did not cheer her up. In the evening, in a fashionable restaurant, dressed in black and well made up, she found her smile again; but something remained quivering in her eyes. To put her at ease, I asked her if she had some program for the future. She answered that she didn't know. Perhaps next month she would be going to a hospital in a nearby city, or perhaps she would be registering for a course in advanced study, or perhaps she would be going to Europe to do typing. The house didn't matter to her; it was only rented and nothing there was hers. She had made the living room table by putting four legs on an old door, the closets were built in, she had not bought chairs because she liked to sit on the rug now that her parents could no longer forbid it. She could have all her belongings ready to go in a couple of hours. But she didn't know, she really didn't know, what she would be doing next month. Who knows, perhaps she would even be staying where she was. In the meantime, she had to take a week's vacation in her parents' country house; perhaps there "something" would happen and she would be able to decide.

Because Norma is the daughter of a wealthy engineer, she would have a pleasant and easy life if she remained at home, with parents she loves deeply and who adore her. She received her B.S. in natural science and at the same time took a three-year course in order to become a nurse. Then, at twenty-two years of age, she went back home to save the necessary money to go to Europe: perhaps to "forget" a broken romance, perhaps to satisfy her intellectual curiosity. The money for the trip—notwithstanding that her father had offered it to her—she earned working in an office of the Bureau of Health. There as an inspector of the living conditions of sick ex-prisoners she had experiences that would make you shudder. She found herself traveling alone in the bad neighborhoods of the city, going to charitable institutions and refuges for social outcasts. More through enthusiasm than through efficiency, she accomplished an excellent deed: for several months she dedicated her every effort to institutionalizing a pitiful adolescent idiot, the butt of pranks by neighborhood young men and the despair of a sister, also an adolescent. She did not rest until she had personally taken this girl to an institution for mental rehabilitation.

After working nine months to get together the necessary amount for the trip, she left and traveled in England, Wales, Scotland, Norway, Sweden, Austria, Switzerland, Spain, Italy, and Germany. In Germany, she ran out of money and took a job as a nurse in an American hospital. She stayed there a year and a half. She was very popular there, as I gathered when she fended off a joke of mine once, saying with a laugh: "No, no, I've had enough of boy friends. You have to have been a nurse in a military hospital for a year and half to understand that a little rest is also necessary."

But in Germany she did not know only popularity. She became a woman, and she learned to suffer. She fell sick through self-neglect, not protecting herself from the cold and relying only on her energy and enthusiasm. When she could take no more, she returned home. She came back slowly, on a ship, to get used to living without the things she had left behind. To take up time, she crossed America in a little Volkswagen that she had brought from Germany, and she arrived in California after three months of traveling.

Her parents were happy to see her again, but she stayed only two days. She got work in a hospital and went to live with a new friend, with whom she established the rhythm of "independent" girls in America. The rhythm of getting up at six in the morning, eggs gulped down while standing in the hall, clothes ironed in haste in the evening on the living room table, underwear washed on the day off, driving at night to get to a party. The rhythm of lack of sleep, meals rushed through to lose weight or to acquire time, of doing everything, everything, by herself.

I asked her if she was happy. She looked at me with amazement, pretending not to understand. I then asked if she lacked anything; she answered, "security." Security, she explained to me, would be hers with a husband; but love had brought her suffering, and she was fearful of suffering again. So she was waiting. "Something" would happen.

It was this expectation that trembled in her eyes, making her hesitant. But the next morning, when I saw her again in the hospital in an almost transparent uniform, her beautiful tanned face seemed to be one complete smile. And I understood that responsibility and professional efficiency are for her—and perhaps for other girls like her—a substitute for the security they lack in their private lives. Perhaps, I thought, this is the incentive that pushes so many girls to work when they might stay with their families. I then decided that I had to talk with some girls who had found conjugal security, to see if they were happier than the single girls.

2

Ruth is a young married woman, the wife of a doctor and the mother of three children. She lives in a development house, a kind of luxurious prefabricated house, with a garden, all possible accessories, and places for the children to play. The house is spacious, cheerful, and full of light, just as it ought to be for all the children in the world. In the backyard the youngest child can play in a sandbox, and the older ones with the rings and parallel bars of a gym. In their playroom they can spread out interminable rails for model trains, which are always broken or encumbered with the clothes of "sexual" dolls, as they call the realistic dolls dressed like adults instead of absurd children, such as was the custom during our childhood.

For herself, Ruth has a bedroom, a large living room, the yard for the barbecue, some built-in wardrobes for clothing, and an interminable cupboard for canned goods. It seems to be a house of abundance, joy, and serenity. Ruth is very attractive: tall, slender, with the short haircut of a sailor, efficient and quick as these American women know how to be. Her special charm, however, is the light black shadow around her large melancholy eyes.

One day she came to pick me up in her red station wagon to go shopping. She arrived at 2:05. "Hurry," she warned, "because the babysitter leaves at 2:00." In her youthful cotton dress she quickly jumped behind the wheel, and while she adjusted to the forced calm of local traffic, constantly slowed down by stop signs and the speed limit, she explained to me that her work ends at 2:00, and every day she is troubled by the worry that the children must remain alone waiting for her. Nor is it thinkable that the babysitter stay five minutes more; she has another job and can't be late. When she leaves the house, however, she takes the children to a friend of Ruth's nearby.

At a light, a little girl with a bookbag in her hand detached herself from a group of school children and with consummate care crossed the street and got into the car. It was Ruth's oldest child, coming home from school. Her mother had gone just a little out of her way to pick her up. After a brief stop at another house, to pick up the second child, left there by the babysitter, we went to get the little boy, who had spent the day with a friend. The mothers appeared at the door in their shorts or aprons, made up, smiling. The children rushed out in disorder, lively and self-sufficient.

By this time it was 3:30. With the car loaded with children, we arrived at Ruth's house, where she hurried into the kitchen to fix them a snack. "Now that I think of it," she said, "this morning I didn't have time to have breakfast." Perhaps she would have eaten something too, but she noticed that the babysitter had left the table half cleared off. So, she threw the scraps in the sink, ran the garbage disposal, put the plates in the dishwasher, and rinsed the milk glasses. "Hurry," she suggested again, "the stores close at 5:30." We arrived at the shopping center around 4:30; the children asked for an ice cream. When we went into the store where Ruth needed to buy a jersey for her husband, it was on the point of closing. "I'll take this one. If he doesn't like it, I can exchange it tomorrow," she said to the clerk who wanted to close.

When we got back into the car, I was gasping for breath, but Ruth was only a little on edge. "I must go back home immediately," she said, "the children have to eat, then I must prepare a dinner for some friends who are passing through." I tried to calm things down somewhat with a banal question as to where she had her hair cut. "I cut it myself," she answered. "I also cut the children's and my husband's." I asked her when she found time to do it. She told me that there is always time to do everything. She watches television while she irons, listens to the radio while she dusts, reads books while the dishwasher is on, sunbathes while she weeds the garden, writes letters while the children sleep, pursues her private studies in the evening between ten and midnight. In the morning she is up at 6:30.

I asked her when a little time was reserved to think. But I could not make myself clear. She answered that to the extent that appliances expedited family life, women felt the need to do other things with the time saved. In a vicious circle, without an end. "To do things" seems to be the goal of this lovely woman, the daughter of a famous Czechoslovakian surgeon, rich in childhood and well-to-do after marriage, who has no economic, social, or family worries and who has a responsible job in a medical laboratory. Is it possible that that slight black shadow around her eyes comes only from weariness? Yet, there is no doubt that Ruth has the security Norma dreams of: she has a charming husband who adores her and with whom she gets along well; she has three children—handsome, healthy, and good; she fits in perfectly in society.

"What don't you have, Ruth?" I asked her. She didn't answer. But later on, I understood what she does not seem to realize herself: her work of scientific research isn't enough for her; it's too anonymous.

I next talked to a girl who has chosen a more glamorous activity. I still had to find happiness somewhere in this America overflowing with money and well-being.

3

Alice introduces herself as a painter. She is not very young, has a fine figure, robust and subtly provocative, long straight hair, a face without makeup, fingernails without polish. She came to see me in the hospital because her husband, a writer of Welsh origin, had been told by his editor that I was here in trouble. Alice's husband is Norman . . . he smokes a pipe, speaks softly and little, has a great deal of tact, and a subtle and irresistible humor. When they came to see us for the first time, two rich Italo-Americans were with us: he with a shirt of red silk printed with Chinese horses, she a little plump and domestic, Italian-style. In contrast were Alice with her self-assurance and just the tiniest bit of insolence, wearing Japanese sandals and a gathered skirt under a low-necked blouse, and Norman with his torn and faded blue jeans. Their clothing seemed to be a recapitulation of the California anticonformist uniform of several years ago. Alice and Norman got out of an old red MG, with a dented mudguard and doors held in place by a strap; they brought a strange, enormous flower, from an exotic plant grown in their garden. They seemed to have stepped out of a documentary: they were perfect, without a false note, and the few things they were able to say in the uninterrupted shower of Italo-American words fit their appearance beautifully.

After that, they came almost every evening. Norman brought me the proofs of his book, and Alice some of her drawings. We became friends, and one day I went to their house. I expected to find the usual California house—the small villa with a few rooms, the living room separated from the kitchen by a divider, the backyard and garden with the barbecue pit, two or three lamps with shades (of the type that Americans come to have made in Italy to take advantage of the cheapness of handmade work). Instead, I entered a Spanish-style house with a square kitchen, without appliances. It had only wooden cupboards, a European stove, an oven without a clock, a sink without a garbage disposal, all of which were a little old and ramshackled but miraculously welcoming and warm—perhaps because the walls were of natural wood instead of being covered with white. The garden was also unusual: it had great flowering bushes and clotheslines and in the corners were two wooden cages, one where Norman works and the other where Alice paints. There was no wardrobe, for Alice owns only five dresses and Norman only two suits. Nor was there a supply of canned goods. Alice had learned to cook from a Russian grandmother, and she goes out to buy greens and fresh meat every day on a bicycle forgotten at her house by a friend.

This house, so far from the standard American conformity and so free of symbols of wealth, had a strange sense of freedom. It was clear that Alice and Norman did not lack anything, but it was also clear that they had consciously eliminated everything superfluous from their lives. The house is their property: to pay for it, Norman worked in the post office during Christmas holidays, day and night, and Alice did a season as a waitress in a luxury hotel. Now Norman works three days a week in a bookstore, and Alice two days a week in a library; the other days they live.

I asked Alice if she is happy. She answered: "I am learning to become so. I understood that to be happy here in America you have to free yourself from false obligations. If you aren't careful, you find yourself imprisoned by a thousand restrictions which in reality are imaginary." I believed her because I have never seen Alice tense or breathless, nor have I ever seen her uncertain or nervous. Very unself-consciously, she spends various afternoons in the houses of rich friends, but she does not envy them and she speaks of their swimming pools, Mexican furniture, and jewels as of things that don't concern her. When I asked her why she has never had a show of her paintings, she answered that she doesn't want to elbow her way; that if her work deserves it, perhaps in some way someone will recognize it.

Still, under this stainless steel armor, Alice, like Norma, Ruth, and so many others, also has a fear. This fear leaps in her eyes when she speaks of Norman's book. This courageous, intelligent woman has succeeded in freeing herself from all ambitions except the most dangerous one: her husband's success. Whether by this success she is thinking of her husband's happiness or simply a point of arrival is not clear; perhaps it represents both things, and certainly it is well-meaning. The point is that while she seems to be the picture of perfect equilibrium, she possesses a fear which, in reality, indicates that not even Alice is completely happy—and she, too, because of her relationship with a man.

Next, I talked to two women who have rejected this relationship.

4

Joan and Susan are both slender. They wear tennis shoes without socks and have the reputation of being very rude to overly aggressive boy friends. They are technicians in a chemical laboratory, with a small salary and no future. They react in horror to the idea of having sex with a man unless there is a great, a very great love, and they spend most of their evenings watching television or going to the movies with casual acquaintances. They were living in New York, but one day, with ten dollars in their pockets, they decided to come to California.

It was not easy to get them to reveal why they had fled. After many reticences and protests, however, they told me that they had left to get as far away as possible from their husbands, after having gotten divorced. The husbands were "destructive," as they say here: they didn't allow them to fulfill their aspirations; they were egotistical, and even irresponsible. I asked them if they had ever sensed these defects before getting married: a silly question, but they didn't complain. Susan told me that she had been married at eighteen, without knowing what marriage was and without knowing herself and her real aspirations. Joan told me that she had been disappointed by a fiancé and had deliberately married a boy who was his opposite. Both had tried to adjust to living with their husbands until they had children, but the children were scarcely born when they realized that family life was impossible. They had entrusted the babies to their mothers, had gotten divorces, and had escaped.

When I asked them if they were happy, they were offended, thinking that I was making fun of them. I then rephrased the question, asking them if they would not have preferred life with a husband to the loneliness and dreariness of their present existence. They vehemently answered no; but both hoped to find a marvelous new husband, one who was not egotistical, egocentric, or irresponsible. To find him they dated new men, at times believing they had met the new "great passion." They were always more fearful, always more concerned about their reputations—by now not so much for others as for themselves. At the same time they were spurred ever harder by the need to establish a bond of affection that in some way might fill their lives.

One evening, for Joan's birthday, friends in the vicinity organized a little party, bringing cakes and bottles of wine. At around 10:00 in the evening a general gathering arrived to give her presents. But by 10:30, Joan still had not appeared. As I learned later, in the afternoon she had gone to hear a concert and had struck up a friendship with a man with whom she had dinner and then went to the movies. Her friends, waiting with the cakes and packages, didn't know what to do. They stayed until 11:00 and then left. Joan never gave an explanation to them; her friends did not demand one. Anyway, it was all so clear that explanations would have been superfluous.

Some time afterwards, when I asked Joan how she could consider the adventure of an evening to be a "grand passion," she answered with a great deal of resentment that it was not her fault if it had lasted such a short time: the man she had met at the concert also had shown himself to be irresponsible, egocentric, and egotistical. When I asked her if she had ever thought that perhaps her ideal man didn't exist, she answered that I was a pessimist, and that, as a woman of old Europe, I was my husband's slave and could not understand her.

Joan did not convince me. That evening in the hospital, while I watched over the sleep of my sick husband, I concluded that certainly the most unhappy of all these casual friends were Joan and Susan because they were the most incapable of loving. I thought of the squandered beauty of Norma's face, of Ruth's melancholy, and of Alice's fear, and for a moment I hoped that they succeeded in finding serenity. For Joan and Susan, impatient girls, perhaps more egotistical than their rejected husbands, I felt only pain—a pain without hope.

Language

American English, I

G. A. BORGESE
Atlante americano, 1936, pp. 156-163

What have Americans done and what are they doing to their mother tongue which they carried with them, with few other possessions, on their humble ships as they crossed the sea?

The common saying in England is that they have massacred and barbarized it. But Americans like to say that they are shaping a new language, one that is very expressive and beautiful, to fit their own youthfulness. When you listen to them, you might get the impression that their linguistic work consists of demolishing their ancestors' home in order to build a new house with the same bricks. Once in a while, at more and more frequent intervals, they stick some new brick just out of their own furnace between the old bricks, right in full view, painted bright, even with brutal colors.

In addition to the two views, let a third one be allowed: Americans are not subverting the English language; on the contrary, they are leading it back, little by little, with more and more self-assured moves, toward its original radical spirit. To begin to grasp the truth hidden in this paradox, consider the example of slang which is the most obvious phenomenon of linguistic Americanism. What does the spirit of slang consist of, if not the invention and the adoption of words that are short, synthetic, and nervous, in keeping with the spirit that English has preserved in its treasury of national words, not flexuous and nobly draped like the words borrowed from France and the classical tradition?

The same remark should be made, or just about, for all the other phenomena of American English.

British English says *principal*, or *master*, which is the same as *maestro* or *magister*, or many other expressions, all (or almost all) of Latin origin. Once, on the spot now known as New York, lived Dutchmen in a little colonial harbor called New Amsterdam; for *owner* they said *baas*. The term pleased the Anglo-Saxons living there, and they took it with the city and all. Now Americans, when they want to refer to a clever man who is in charge, call him *boss*, and the very sound of it bears the imprint of strength.

Pepper is a universal word, with few exceptions. But why make it so long? Say *pep*, and that's all. In America a man of resources, a man with guts or pluck, or whatever the human or masculine expression may be which we Italians like in such cases, is "a man who has pep." This means that the Anglo or super-Anglo quality of these nervous words is not necessarily connected by genealogy to a pure Nordic root. *Fanatic* comes from Latin, but Americans, especially when they speak of people who are crazy about football, say *fan*. Advertisement comes from Latin also; but here this word-millipede usually ends up as *ad*. Americans are not concerned with purity but with intensity. And surely one of the most brilliant inventions of American speech and writing was the very Italian adjective *solo*, one of our words which has remained in the universal language of music. They attach it with no more ado to the word *flight*, so that they say *solo-flight*, as if it were a solo, a virtuosity similar to the one performed by a player or a singer, when they speak of the transatlantic flight of Lindbergh and his emulators. The term adds the charm of an art, a melodic whim, to the severe prestige of the mechanical and sportslike prowess.

Then, there are waif-words, words with no ancestry, neither Nordic nor Mediterranean, which exploded, spontaneous and barbaric, from the natural imitative expressivity of sounds. The most famous in the world is *bluff*. No matter what their origin, however, one characteristic unifies them all, and it is that sort of explosive charge which causes them to reach the desired meaning by the shortest trajectory. On the strength of this characteristic, American English is not a corrupted British English, but an English raised to the nth power.

The synthetic, and I would say pugnacious, nature of the vocabulary also appears in other aspects of the language, particularly in the syntax. British English has a different melody; or rather, it has a melody; American English does not. It does not like nuances, undulations, and half-terms; it is poor in chromatics and flats. Its objective is to say things with the greatest directness and the surest effects. The best results it can attain are of an epigraphic, lapidary sort. Sentences stand well on their feet, without swaying, joined to each other by precise connections. Adjectivation is functional, not voluptuous and decorative. The whole seems to stand vertically or to move like a marching column. The affirmative bent of American discourse was even parodied in the once-famous pop song, in which a Greek fruit peddler, accustomed to a much more lavish language, in order to adapt to the tastes of his transatlantic clientele, said: "Yes, we have no bananas." To think and write American means to think and write completely in prose—robust, pragmatic, fully committed to be translated without residue into conviction and action. Often, we taste an analogous flavor in ancient Latin. This does not mean that America has no poets, but their poets either are prosaic, realistic, and eloquent, or write a language that is terribly removed from usage, ethereal or dead, a soul alienated from the body of the nation. It's truly strange, but at no other time and in no other place after the end of classicism has such a clearcut distinction existed between genres as one can observe today in America. The novel is the novel, the drama is drama, lyric poetry is lyric poetry, prose is prose, and verse is verse. Hermaphroditic, ambiguous creations cannot breathe here. The so-called poetic prose cannot take root here. Thornton Wilder himself, whom we like so much, whom I admire so much, has not been able to gain full acceptance here exactly because they notice a redundance, a flaw, in his singing, soft prose. Free verse, too, in spite of Whitman, has withdrawn before the return of meter, well measured and locked in by rhyme, even more so than in countries with illustrious and scholastic traditions.

    One of the first impressions you receive as you disembark in New York is that of finding yourself before a country all inscribed and sculpted like an obelisk—so great is the importance of signs, ads, and road signs in the sky, on the walls, under one's feet. The intrusiveness of those writings, which spread and connect through the whole breadth of the country, has had and still has an incalculable impact on the evolution of the language. The motto, the slogan, the one-celled phrase which says all in one vibration, imbues the whole fabric of linguistic expression with its caustic quality. An additional impulse, tending to converge with the previous one, is evident in humor, such as in the brief dialogues made up of swift, biting repartees, and in the funny stories that make up such a large part of American conversation and that consist of a surprising twist of a moment of suspense at the end. A third line of influence is journalism, especially in headings, patterned on the elliptical telegraphic style. After articles, prepositions, and all other frills are cut out, what remains is only what is indispensable for meaning— bare, bony, cuneiform, stuck in the exactness of the newspaper column.

In order to understand what the press is and can be in America, go to one of New York's railway stations five minutes before a train is to depart. Look at that long line of crowded coaches, in which all the travelers hold symmetrically unfolded before their eyes the same multiple sheet, thirty or forty pages of printed paper. Coal, electricity, gasoline, and paper are the four highest consumption items in America. On the other hand, the incessant pulsating of the written or printed word (it is not without significance that America is the country of the typewriter, that piano without music) is only conceived of in terms of the spoken word. That is, Americans write just as they would speak in a living room or at a meeting. They are the most eloquent people in the world. Don't expect to encounter brothers of the taciturn, splenetic Englishman here. Even those who by nature would be inclined to be silent are forced by the uniform educational system to speak, and to speak well. Naturally, in this field also, standardization tends toward condensation and uniformity: everything must be said in the manner prescribed, and in no other. Some have claimed, with some exaggeration, that the average American lives on a vocabulary of 300 words. In any case, that doesn't deprive him of the mastery of his Webster Dictionary, which lists 408,000. He can go on explorations in there, whenever he needs to, taking off from the citadel of core words.

American pronunciation, unlike the British, tends to mark as much as possible the differences among vowels. Sounds are not entrusted exclusively to the lips and the esophagus, as happens in her-

metic Oxford, the capital of British elegance; chest sounds and perhaps nasal ones, too, increase range and intelligibility. This
language tends to become more and more communicative and
socially oriented, easier to adopt by the greatest number—good still
and always for theologians and poets, but useful also for Negroes
and children.

If one were to use a motto, in the American manner, one should
say that this language seeks to be a tool just for communication.
The English language expresses; the American language engraves.

American English, II

MARGHERITA SARFATTI
L'America, ricerca della felicità, 1937, pp. 130-131

The use of the word "to suppose" and of the expression "to be supposed to" is peculiar in all modes, persons, and tenses of American English. It is a code and a rule of behavior here.

The person who says "What am I supposed to do?" does not ask for opinions. He is giving himself up, hands tied, as a victim on the altar of a demanding god. The things one is supposed or not supposed to do in America are the elements of a detailed protocol. Perhaps this protocol is not longer nor more minutious than ours, if you think about it, but ours seems more flexible to us because of its long use. In America, it has the intransigence of a young divinity, the touchy ritual of any new cult. The stranger can rely on an abundance of smiling indulgence, and the one who sins against some article of the eternal "you are supposed to" is solicitously warned. An American, generously and kindly, does not even suppose that one might be doing it on purpose. But to persevere is diabolical; whoever does not amend is abandoned as a heinous offender. And why not? In Rome, do as the Romans do; in America, do as Americans are supposed to do.

Fantabulous

GIORGIO SOAVI
Fantabulous, 1963, p. 44

Glamorous, luxurious, attractive, unusual, positive, dramatic, gorgeous, NEW!, exciting, revolutionary, free, exclusive, infallible, enjoy, distinctive and pleasurable, gleaming, unquestionably, tremendous, surprising, de luxe, no extras, superb, definitely, thrilling, sensational, incredible, unimaginable, marvelous, unbelievable, extraordinary, colossal, gigantic, stupendous, supercolossal, supergigantic, superstupendous, absolutely positively, absotively posilutely supergigantic or stupendous or dramatic, it's too much, it's crazy, mad, professional. Professional is an adjective used for a shaving cream, a tape recorder, a camera. Incredibly (do you know why our Martini is so *incredibly* dry?), amateur, official, terrific. I went in to buy a nightgown for my wife. Undecided between a red and a grey, a smoky grey shading to white. The salesgirl helps me, holds the red gown up and shouts: "Sir, this one. Isn't it terrific?" Psychic, Sexciting, Appeteaser. Fantabulous. . . .

REFLECTIONS ON A
MYTHIC AMERICA

All the Italians who have written on America have made an attempt to go beyond superficial judgments and piecemeal observations. Whether they were actual or metaphoric travelers in the New World, their purpose was to discover and probe an unknown entity as thoughtfully and comprehensively as possible.

Curiously, several leitmotifs appear in each volume represented in this section. First, there is the "enigma" of America—an enigma that exists in the mind of the visitor for whom the American experience is something rare, for whom America cannot be a country with the customary dimensions, but one that has two different levels: the memories of a dream and the concrete presence of a repulsive-attractive United States. On the one hand, there are the expanses of virgin land, the gold rush, the pioneers, the ancient tribes, the fabulous rivers, the films, the black slaves, the promise of another chance on this earth, America as the private dream of the Westerner (so different from the images of other continents). On the other hand, there are the dehumanized cityscapes, the boring little lives of dutiful people, the desolate loneliness of the city street or restaurant, the violence, the racism, the "clean, sportive, chaste" youth—in Guido Piovene's words—the dull pursuit of an anesthetic existence. How can one possibly reconcile the two visions of America?

The other recurring theme is the preoccupation with European antecedents: how does America compare with what one already knows? European standards and categories cannot be imposed upon America, but what are the other standards to be used, in what category does America fit? To what extent is America a new and "primitive" country, to what extent a transplanted Europe? What does Europe see in its mirror beyond the oceans; has the promise been fulfilled or betrayed? What does the European traveler see of himself or herself upon approaching—burdened by the taboos and miseries of a repressive if glorious tradition—another way of life, a land most insist on viewing as "barbaric," "virgin," "fierce," and "untamed"? Again Piovene perceptively points to the need he feels to become estranged from his own roots. America offers the Italian writer a chance to breathe freely, to feel relieved of an overbearing atmosphere, cast off from a closed society, unburdened in a way that is vaguely threatening for some, exhilarating for others.

Finally, all these writers attempt to achieve an understanding of America as a totality. The contradictions they discover and the insights they gain become part of a new awareness of themselves and of their own background. This self-discovery, this paring down and reaffirming of the myth of America as the land of one's own soul, as the key to an understanding of the ideals, dreams, and terrible fallacies of the Western psyche, seems to be the central element in every text we have considered.

Which leads us to another observation: that, in spite of the efforts of writers present, past, and yet to come, there is no final statement possible on America, no text to reveal all that America has been and is for Italian observers. For any statement on this immense theme is bound to be personal, therefore partial, and ultimately inconclusive.

American Movies

MARIO SOLDATI
America primo amore, 1935, pp. 201-204

No more nor less than the serpentine seductions of Joan Craw-
ford would the formidable gun battles of Scarface, the famous
gangster film directed by Hawks and acted by Paul Muni, strike the
Italian public. But what American doesn't participate for real in
something similar at least once a year? One evening, in Cincinnati,
Ohio, I came out of a movie theatre. I had not been walking in the
street more than five minutes when, at a deserted intersection, the
alarm of a nearby bank suddenly rang. Three, four shadows sprung
from I don't know where and fled desperately. The same roar of
the police motorcycles followed without delay, the same piercing
explosions that a little earlier had been transmitted to me from the
innocuous sound track in the safety of the theatre.

In other words, in Europe our amusements are more modest but
more continuous. Our life is not so adventurous, but neither is it so
dreary. It is more stable, more civil, more human. We see our films
without expense and without tricks just by looking out from our
courtyard window.

America does not have courtyards. It is monotonous, dry, and
dark. Its long-standing puritanism has considered sins the things
that make life more pleasant. It has repressed and atrophied those
instincts which alone make life bearable: love, sociability, laziness,
gluttony. Meanwhile, the devil, chased from the body, has reenter-
ed by way of the spirit.

Once the puritan faith was dead, the spirit welcomed evil. The
formula of De Ritis—a puritan mind in a pagan body—is true only

if we reverse it: a pagan mind in a puritan body. The American body is as little pagan as you can imagine—clean, sporty, chaste. Cleanliness does not exalt the body. It isolates it from human contacts, intellectualizes it. Don't be too clean, Lawrence warned about Americans; it impoverishes the spirit. Sport, also. Above all, if practiced as it is in America: with discipline and regularity.

Finally, to feel the desire for making love, American students drink, overcoming in drunkenness the inhibitions of their nervous system—rediscovering in alcohol real life. Just the opposite of what happens among us.

So much for the body. The intelligence of Americans, so deprived of sensations; their life, so mechanical and regular; and their efficiency, so highly vaunted . . . have exactly the proud, diabolical, and sad characteristics of abstract knowledge. Americans make up for it with detective stories and movies: daydreamed sensations, vicarious adventures. The passions of America are reduced to a colossal masturbation.

Many will protest that the fantastic adventures, the desperate loves and the grandiose crimes, are signs of a powerful humanity and profound life. But the adventure undertaken mystically as an escape from yourself and from your country is the opposite of vitality. Love, when it is exaggerated, when it tends only to the perfect communion of souls, is sterile, malefic, destructive. And in regard to criminality, the madness of modern literary men has obscured its simple sense of death. We hear Shakespeare, Act I of *Macbeth*:

Present fears
Are less than horrible imaginings.
My thought, *whose murder yet is but fantastical*,
Shakes so my *single* state of man that *function*
Is smothered in surmise; and nothing is
But what is not.

Prodigious lines! They point to the intellectual origin of crime more clearly than all of Dostoevsky.

Detective stories and movies are not the effect but the cause of American crime. It doesn't matter that crime has chronologically preceded it. Contemplation, the solitary meditation on evil, if not transmuted into artistic forms, always causes that mental derangement, that gradual madness, that is the only true cause of a criminal act.

Arid America, therefore, boring America. But at intervals, owing to this very tiresomeness and aridity, directly out of the depths of great darkness, a livid and unnatural light illuminates the scene. The bomb explodes. And you are no longer living in thought but in the unreal reality of sin. You love, you kill, you earn a million no longer in the tranquil silver light of the screen, but in full relief, in full color, and yet with the anguish and exaggerated lucidity of a nightmare. Men and women whom absolute desire deifies, marvelously bloody cadavers, millions of dollars of dazzling greenbacks. In the long torpid tedium that precedes this sudden madness, the art of the cinema fascinates, excites, prepares for madness. And sometimes, conversely, who knows that it may not be sufficient to resolve it, to placate it. Think of the Elizabethan theatre. Such activity, sometimes sick and sometimes healthy, is perhaps the secret of the American movie industry.

American Literature: Its Origins and Present State

ELIO VITTORINI

Diario in pubblico, 1957, pp. 233-234

Elio Vittorini (1908-1966): A major Italian novelist, Vittorini was an enthusiastic Americanist during the 1930's. In addition to translating numerous works of American literature (Poe, Steinbeck, and Faulkner, among others), he attempted to publish an anthology entitled *Americana*. He succeeded in 1942, but only after the Fascist censors had eliminated Vittorini's commentaries on the selections he had included in his volume. *Americana* appeared in the originally planned form after the war. Vittorini's *Open Journal* (*Diario in pubblico,* 1929-1956) also contains numerous entries on American literature, including the material which the authorities had censored.

Vittorini was the founder and director of the literary journal *Il Politecnico* in the late 1940's, and later he codirected with Italo Calvino another seminal journal, *Il Menabo.* From a preoccupation with myth in literature, Vittorini moved on to a questioning of the validity of a literature which remained anchored in the world of nature. He then explored the relationship between literature and human "knowing" within the reality of a postindustrial society.

Several of Vittorini's works are available to the American reader: *Conversation in Sicily* first appeared in English in 1961; *The Red Carnation*, Vittorini's first novel, was published here in 1972; and *Women of Messina* and a *Vittorini Omnibus* appeared in 1973.

In 1945, in some of his journal notes, Cesare Pavese said about himself and Vittorini that they had been "saved" from the preciosity of an overripe literature by their journey to America, by their discovery of "barbarism." In the texts that follow, we hear Vittorini's voice define what that journey was, and who those Americans were that the Italian writers yearning for spontaneity and freedom found on the other shore.

(January 1941)

Even in a history of American literature, the first word that comes to mind and remains before us and gives us pause is that same word—land. Just as if it were a question of political history. And more, perhaps. For while political history does not usually include literary history, literary history always contains political history. It includes any and all histories at the same time; it is, in short, the history of man par excellence, within whatever framework of space and time we choose. We say "America," then. We say it, and we think of the atlas with the immense spread of the crowded colors, plains, mountains, snows high on the mountains, the icebergs up north, and the miles of shoreline facing the two oceans with those two great names—Atlantic and Pacific—and within that the ancient god, the desert, and the waterways, the railways, the highways, and houses, houses, houses.

The word "land" is very important to us today, in speech and in deed. But in the beginning there was simply the land; man discovered only more space. Just as the Spaniards and their descendants in the South up to this date, the French and English (and also the Dutch and Germans with them) added little or nothing new to the human consciousness after living for two centuries in the North. They cut down trees, built wooden stockades, cultivated the earth, savored again the lost flavor of the big hunt, increased and multiplied. It seems that the Pilgrim Fathers came from Europe full of disillusionment and weariness: they came to end, not to begin. Disappointed by the world, they no longer wanted the world. Only abstract furies agitated them—the idea of grace, the idea of sin, the ferocious prejudices of Calvinistic dualism. And they no longer had the energy to assert them in the old cities where the religious wars were fought. They fled as if they did not believe, as if they renounced the struggle. But there, on those coasts covered with hardwood trees, was the world again. They saw it and were again in the world, accepting, then also giving thanks, and from fatigue they changed to boldness, to faith.

In America, they found the necessary ferocity to practice those ferocious prejudices, to be in some way alive. They said nothing new; they added nothing to human consciousness; they discovered nothing for the human spirit. The colonizers lived only for those prejudices. And yet, writing to defend them or combat them, they already had a new voice. If we read Cotton Mather, the public accuser of "witches" and "heretics," or *The Bloudy Tenet of Persecution* of the enlightened Roger Williams, who struggled with so much fanaticism against their fanaticism, or the savage sermon "Sinners in the Hands of an Angry God" of the famous preacher Jonathan Edwards, we sense how different that voice is from the burgher's voice which had expressed or was still expressing the same ideas in Europe. Here there is the steady roar of hyperbole. This voice roars. And it will always be like this, a roaring voice, that will indicate the interior evolution of man in America.

* * *

(May 1946)

We find that there is no American author whose culture has not already gone beyond Shakespeare and Bacon. However rough in expression he may be, however breathless he may appear to us, however each of the words he pronounces may smell of the labor of a man who is newly returned to the woods, he has never once had a primitive stammer on his lips. Even reduced to rags, in his writing he will always wear something of the European past which is his past. He will have inside him a memory he cannot erase of all that man has learned. And however we may find that he has preserved it (as vision or music or technique), we find that his is a taste still flavored by a proximity to the courts, the universities, the churches of a class much older than his: an Elizabethan taste.

But in him, the common man who writes immersed in necessity, that style is no longer a luxury. The bold image is not bold in him.

Metaphor is not metaphor; hyperbole is not hyperbole. I mean to say that they are no longer gold and gems; they are not even emphatic. They are the same forms that exist in every English writer of the seventeenth century, and yet they are no longer the same. They are used differently. Exactly the way the letters of the alphabet are used. Just as the oldest peoples could use their so complicated arabesques to say sheep or moon. Or as one would use the carved wood of a galley to transport objects of common use—beds for sleeping, tables for eating, chairs for sitting.

For a long time—for two and a half centuries, almost three—we have seen American culture making objects of common use with the storied wood of the ships on which it came from Europe. We see it, in the beginning, artlessly rustic and humble. Then we see it impetuous, we see it wild, we see it become more and more original. And we will always see that it wields the treasures of European culture, at first in order to satisfy its rustic needs only, then also because of a more and more pressing need to affirm itself and refashion those treasures in its own way, to transform them, to replace them.

We see it wild and new, even naive at a certain stage, but not unfamiliar. This culture is the child of parents only one of whom is unknown. The other is famous, a gentleman, and has left his mark upon it. The technical knowledge of the time in which it was born is present in its blood; then it develops at the same rate as its impetuosity develops; it will continue to develop along with its originality and will become itself an original creation. That is, American culture will always have within it the awareness of European culture. It has all the years of human experience within its youth. And because it has all the history of mankind within, it is not a culture limited to America.

It marks a new point, but it recapitulates the culture of the entire world at the same moment it marks a new point. There is not a single moment of its development in which it does not recapitulate, at the same time marking a new point, the culture of the entire world. Even its originality is thus valid for the entire world.

The Struggle Against Idols

GIAIME PINTOR
Il sangue d'Europa, 1950, pp. 148-159

Giaime Pintor (1919-1943): A budding Americanist,
Pintor belonged to the youthful circle that clustered
in Turin around well-known and respected anti-
Fascist scholars and intellectuals. In the late 1930's,
after it had been thinned out by Fascist perse-
cutions, it included Natalia and Leone Ginzburg,
Carlo Muscetta, Carlo Levi, Giulio Einaudi (a
member of the publishing family), Massimo Mila,
and, marginally, Cesare Pavese. Pintor fought and
died as a partisan in World War II, leaving behind a
moving intellectual testament published posthu-
mously as *The Blood of Europe*.

A book always counts for what it doesn't set out to do, for that
margin of the unforeseen that it contains like a reserve of energy
and vigor. Such is Vittorini's anthology, *Americana*, published in a
collection of works of a character that is popular and easy to con-
fuse in a common critical approach. When one speaks of German
narrative or religious theatre, one alludes to a scholastic unity, to
cultural roots. But the book we wish to speak of counts for a
different reason: it is valuable as the straightforward message of a
people to the ones who have not touched their shores, and the
proud response of America to the problems of the world of the
future. At least this has been the success of Vittorini, and on this
polemical success can begin a more lively discourse than what one

would expect for a mere anthology. *Americana*—the brevity of the name suggests the richness of its intentions, evokes the visions of travelers rather than the study of philologists.

America has always been the object of a blanket evaluation for us. Perhaps its geographic compactness and the distance of the ocean have contributed to create this myth of a country that grows like a single body and takes form and assumes a shape according to its own habits. Immigrants came from all the countries of Europe, but the great voice of America immediately covered the din of different languages and merged the disparate peoples into a single race. Buildings, different from those in our cities, surged up along the two oceans. When this rush of life went beyond its initial phase, and left the prairie and the mines in order to become industry and power, a polemical tone took the place of the indulgent curiosity of the Europeans, until someone had the impression that a real conflict had erupted between the two civilizations, similar to the violent and inevitable clash of two successive ages.

This combination of diffidence and curiosity found its natural expression elsewhere in a rich sociology, above all, after the war (World War I), when America came into close contact with European life and imposed its own tastes and tendencies on it. Then this abstraction could be studied in its most obvious manifestations: total democracy and movies, Negro music and big business. Other phenomena remained indistinct in the shadows, too embryonic or too far away to strike eyes not accustomed to them. Among us in Italy sociology doesn't flourish, and the relations between the two peoples remained at the crude level of relations of the masses— influenced by the poverty of the immigrants and the noisiest aspects of advertising. And yet, the shape of America was too clear on the horizon by now not to excite the interest of intellectuals. Next to lyric books like that of Soldati and the flavorless documents of political journalism, some years ago appeared *America amara*, the first important study of the reactions of our intelligentsia to the now-mature aspects of American culture.

America amara is an exemplary book. Linguistically pure as few European writers are, and sensitive to the value of the word through a scrupulous literary education, Cecchi carries with him the limitations of the "region": he reacts to space as if it were an insuperable obstacle. Tuscany, that overcivilized region, is present in his every judgment, and the long-familiar profile of the Tuscan countryside is the standard for every other land. An indefatigable traveler, he is one of the most incapable of men in adapting himself to the surprises of the trip, one of the most obstinately enclosed in the prejudices of a single country.

Next to this geographic inferiority, Cecchi's political judgment is held back by another check, the characteristic inability of his generation to understand all those values that escape aesthetic appreciation, the tendency to convert facts of mores into pure curiosity and social situations into impulses of fantasy. This propensity in a writer can be a reason for superiority, and it has in fact liberated the literature of our century from tiresome ideological complexes and has given new life to it. At the same time, it is the first symptom of obscure dangers. Among us it has coincided, after the closing of a few more courageous experiences *(La Voce*, Gobetti)* with the affirmation of a school whose patrimony is quickly used up and whose major historic wrong will be to have lived in peaceful coexistence with Fascism.

In France, the mother country of all the modern literary colonies, the same phenomenon has been more conspicuous and convincing. One thinks of the absolute lack of foundation of the political pretensions of Gide, of the weakness of Valéry when he ventures to discuss temporal things, of the lovely and fruitless arabesque traced by Giraudoux in *Pleins pouvoirs*. The criticism of Cecchi, like that of all these others, rigorous and at times perfect on the horizontal plane of the page, has no validity whatever when it tries to develop in other dimensions, when it abandons the familiar terrain of prose poems in order to enter the more demanding domain of judgment. One witnesses then the vain spectacle of a scenographer who wants to make his sets habitable, or of a mathematician persuaded to carry his formulas onto the shifting sands of political economy.

Only reasons so strong, and another that we cannot argue about,

---

La Voce was an influential political and cultural journal (1908-1916). Piero Gobetti (1901-1926), a Piedmontese intellectual, was one of the first leaders of anti-Fascism in Turin.

but which decides every controversy definitively—the years which separate us—can explain the conflict in our understanding of the name America. Because where Cecchi has scrupulously collected a museum of horrors, where he has isolated sickness and decadence and described a world which it is impossible to believe in, we have heard a voice, deep and very close, the voice of our true friends and first contemporaries.

The presence of this America has filled up the emptiness and shadowy places of our souls. The myths of childhood, used up in a faded, good-natured dialect tradition, spring up again, brighter and fresher, on the highways of America. The youth of Saroyan, an Armenian-American, is ours, with the same discoveries and the same desires, a childhood where bicycles and newspapers have the enchanting presence which is denied to the worn-out objects of fairy tales. And the new legend is born among pianos and songs in unsteady cinematic images.

The abstract women of times past, the first who appeared on the horizon of our adolescence, were protagonists of resolute adventures on a screen in the provinces, and the unpronounceable names of the American movie stars marked the glorious stages of a sentimental education. After the War of 1914 had confused our fantasy with an ambiguous legend, before another war could reveal the true meaning of that episode from which our maturity had to spring, Hemingway had written *A Farewell to Arms*, the first clear example of how a man alone can find liberation from a tradition no longer valid, to remove himself with his own energy from the ambushes set by history.

Cecchi is unable to realize the enormous importance of all this, of the value of the precious cargo of spices and gold which the new war vessels have brought back from America. In his criticism of American writers, he insists on questionable philological points to justify what is first of all an existential incompatibility: the incompatibility between someone who has grown up in an atmosphere influenced by the open American spaces and someone who has confessed too frankly his own respect for "policemen on horseback" to be able to understand the impulses and reactions of an unruly crowd.

His name returns now at the head of this anthology as the author of a preface which is truly bitter in its refusal to make any effort to understand his adversary. But immediately afterwards, the pages that Vittorini has dedicated to the various phases of American culture represent the sharpest antithesis to the formula of Cecchi, turning upside down both his ideological content and critical method.

Vittorini knows that a purely musical reading of the selections is no longer useful to us and that, after the most recent studies of European criticism, to insist on that approach would mean losing the genuine flavor of the written word in order to give oneself up to pure sensibility. (In France, where the same historical evolution has reached a more advanced stage, academic criticism has plunged into a vortex from which it is difficult to recover.) Vittorini accomplishes the reversal of values necessary to keep on its feet a literary history that may also continue to be a universal history. Without realizing it, he proposes a radical thesis, a way to salvation, through which it will be the object itself, the concrete origin of inspiration, which will determine a scale of values and direct the interest of the critic.

Such a formula might provoke the easiest condemnations and recall polemics presently buried, if it was really a formula, if it corresponded to a doctrine, to some kind of neorealistic aesthetic. But it is first of all an invention and an outlet, a turning to what grows around us with the disinterested inquisitiveness of the living being and with that pure curiosity which gives birth to every valid judgment. Because at bottom what is a poetic revelation, if not the discovery of a new country, a glance that is suddenly arrested by figures at first indistinct, the emergence from the darkness of unknown words? All true poets, the true masters of the past, remain in our memory as governors of a province, discoverers of treasures they have left us as an inheritance. Certain hours of the day belong to them, as landscapes which art has redeemed belong to painters: every book, every completed work, remains like a signpost of man planted in the midst of a jungle.

In this progressive work of conquest and civilization, in this expansion of man beyond the boundaries of his primitive experience, America is found now as the most fertile and generous land. A century and a half ago, Germany emerged definitively from cultural prehistory and showed an unmistakable profile in the geography of European peoples. Fifty years ago, a group of intellectuals and writers of genius brought to completion a tiring labor of historic rapprochement and made a gift to the Western world of Russia, its land and its religious experience, its collective enthusiasms and its ills. America has now reached that point of equilibrium in which literature ceases to be first-hand experience and is not yet academic tradition. The writers who live at this time have the right to call themselves classics because in them, for the first time, a view of America that has no need for references is articulated.

Hawthorne and Melville, the major names of the last century, had already gathered the material for an American history. They had spoken at times with a voice that it is not possible to mistake, but the residues of an older history were still present in them. They felt the chains of a religious tradition; they could perhaps intuit the reasons for a new law, but could not lay the foundations for a new tradition.

Only the present generation has used its means of expression, its films and books, as weapons for a total war; has accompanied with the trust of its own words the progress of a century which asked for the commitment of all its forces; has known how to celebrate the new works of man in the same moment in which they were completed. As in every true literary revolution, the names that count among the American writers of today—Hemingway, Faulkner, Saroyan—are above all the inventors of a style. But theirs is a style in which the earthy matter is still fresh. It owes its fullness to the presence of new objects: new machines and new houses, new relations among men.

To be aware of this absolute privilege is not to exhaust the task of the critic, but it is the first condition for not misunderstanding the efforts of a people and a generation to express themselves. This understanding is found in the notes which Vittorini has placed before each group of writers. Free from every pedantic influence and supported by a vigorous and secure imagination, they are one of the most noteworthy examples of literary history lived by a writer. Certainly they are closer to classic examples like Mme de Stael's *Germany* or Heine's *The Romantic School* than to the usual work of professional critics. The fact that Vittorini wrote these pages a few months after *Conversation in Sicily* demonstrates what a force he is for our culture, how his name has already exceeded the limits of a contemporary reputation and has inscribed itself in a more profound and enduring history. . . .

The stupidity of an expression weighs on American civilization: a materialistic civilization, a civilization of producers. This is the pride of a race which has not sacrificed its own forces to ideological aspirations and has not fallen into the easy pitfall of "spiritual values," but has made its own life out of technology, has felt new affections born from the daily routine of collective work and new legends issuing from conquered horizons. Whatever the romantic critics may think, an experience so profoundly revolutionary has not remained without words. While in postwar Europe the themes of a decadent culture were taken up again, or formulas were adopted, like that of surrealism, necessarily devoid of a future, America was expressing itself in new fiction and in a new language. It was inventing cinematography.

Many feel what the American cinema is, with that ambivalence of sympathy and disdain which has been described as one of our irreducible European complexes, but no one perhaps has brought it to light with the necessary vigor. Now that an obligatory abstinence has cured us of the excesses of publicity and of annoying habit, we can perhaps recapture the meaning of that educative episode and recognize in American movies the greatest message that our generation has received. Certainly the film industry was born in Europe and had its first trials here, but scarcely out of infancy it became the mediocre appendix of our literature. The misunderstanding of a rigid aesthetic based on debatable assumptions caused debates over the most fatuous problems for years: who is the author of a film; what relationship does an actor have to the director? Only in Russia did the cinema recognize its way and follow it with the spontaneity of someone who doesn't seek a pedigree but trusts the impulse of his own energy. And when, some years after, it was reborn in America with the same easy spontaneity but endowed with a much greater capacity of expansion, the custodians of uncorrupted literary taste began to cry about industrialization, the decadence of the silent film, and other disasters of experimentation.

Yet, here also American capitalism and Russian proletarianism met in their resolute will to experience a world not yet discovered, to use with trust and energy the new instruments of man. Born as an expensive industry, subjected to the harshest laws of capitalistic economy, the American cinema was to become immediately the nourishment of the anonymous masses, to express their needs and preferences, to inaugurate the first dialogue between the great masses of the world and a unitary culture.

Then the movies entered our lives like an irreplaceable presence. Growing up at the same time we did, it taught us to see and structure reality according to new standards of measurement. It modified history and geography in our heads. It was both school and polemic, entertainment and myth. In this effort of expansion its importance was above all social since, as a weapon serenely revolutionary, it was abolishing political frontiers and fostering the acquisition of an awareness most urgent for our time—that of the unity of the human race. But on the aesthetic plane it had no less importance, for without movies, our eyes would see the world in another light. Today it is certain that the anonymous authors of American movies were the first to respond to Baudelaire's call to modern artists, the first to show how we are young and beautiful with our polished shoes and our bourgeois neckties. . . .

The important thing is to travel, answers a pioneer people to the mystics of the domestic hearth; and the old idol of the fatherland is smashed, it becomes human memory again, the land in which one believes and which one thinks of but which can enslave us no more. With this idol perish other superstructures rooted in the depths of our habits, much cowardice and laziness masked by noble words. America does not have cemeteries to defend. In this struggle against idols, it can recognize its mission: to struggle against the nonbelievers who continually repeat their error and prefer to human beings an orthodoxy or a rite, a political machine or a doctrine.

Coming in contact with this generous mission, the utopia of the New World resumes courage. While it is still pure theoretical statement in Marxist ideology, it becomes concrete example wherever man does not give in to the obscure dangers of mysticism and nostalgia, does not take refuge in neutrality and indifference, but freely and with the proper means confronts the duties of a problematical existence. This can happen in America; it can happen in Russia. In our words dedicated to America, much may be naive and inexact, much may apply to ideas which perhaps are extraneous to the historical development of the United States and its present reality. But it doesn't matter very much because, even if the continent did not exist, our words would not lose their significance. This America does not need a Columbus; it is discovered within us. It is the land we are striving to reach with the same hope and trust of the first immigrants and of whoever decides to defend, at the price of pain and error, the dignity of the human condition.

Yesterday and Today

CESARE PAVESE
La letteratura americana e altri saggi,
1959, pp. 193-196

Cesare Pavese (1908-1950): Poet, novelist, critic, and translator, Pavese wrote his doctoral dissertation on Walt Whitman and later introduced a number of American writers in Italy, foremost among them Melville. In his native Turin, where Gramsci studied and Pietro Gobetti had started the movement of *Giustizia e libertà*, he associated with the intelligentsia in a period which was very lively, both culturally and politically. The Pintors, the Levis, and the Ginzburgs formed his circle of friends, and later, in the 1940's, within the sphere of influence of the Einaudi publishing house, the young Pivano and the young Calvino were his protégés.

Pavese's poetry has just been made available to the American reader under the title *Hard Labor* (1976). The novels he wrote found immediate success and elicited a quantity of critical appraisals and acclaim. Among his novels which have appeared in English are *The Moon and the Bonfires* (1953), *The Devil in the Hills* (1959), *The House on the Hill*, and *Among Women Only* (both in 1968). *The Burning Brand* (1961) is a translation of Pavese's journal.

For Pavese, America was an essential presence—the central preoccupation in his critical essays, a crucial theme in his fiction, and ultimately, although he never visited here, very much a part of his personal life. His readers must remember the American landscapes he drew in *The Moon and the Bonfires* and the last poems he dedicated to his American love, as well as his perceptive pages on Melville, Sinclair Lewis, Edgar Lee Masters, and Sherwood Anderson. Pavese's criticism of American literature has been published in this country as *American Literature: Essays and Opinions* (1970).

Around 1930, when Fascism was beginning to look like "the hope of the world," some young Italians happened to discover America in their books—a pensive and barbaric America, happy and quarrelsome, corrupt, bountiful, heavy with the past of the whole world, and at the same time young and innocent. During several years those young Italians read, translated, and wrote, savoring the joy of discovery and rebelliousness which made official culture indignant but insured their success to the point where the regime was forced to tolerate them if it wanted to save face. It was no joke. We were then the country where Romanism had been reborn, where even land surveyors learned Latin. We were the country of Saints and Heroes, the country of God-given Genius. How could those nobodies, those merchants from the colonies, those uncouth billionaires, even dare to teach us about taste by having themselves read, discussed, and admired? The regime tolerated us, gritting its teeth and keeping on the alert, ready to catch a faux pas, an offensive page, a crude word, in order to catch us in the act and clobber us. It hit us a few times, but inconclusively. The aura of scandal and fashionable heresy surrounding the new books and their topics, the rebellious fury and the frankness which even the least attentive readers could feel pulsating through those translations proved irresistible to a public that had not yet been totally dulled by conformism and conventions. We can say in all frankness that, at least as far as trends and taste went, the new obsession did a lot to help nurture and keep alive the political opposition—however generic and futile—of the Italian "reading" public. For many people, an encounter with Caldwell, Steinbeck, Saroyan, and even the older Lewis brought the first breath of freedom, the first suspicion that not everything in the world of culture began and ended with the *Fasci*.

Obviously, for those who were aware, the true lesson went deeper. Those who did not limit themselves to leafing through the dozen or so amazing books that came out of the other continent in those years, those who shook that tree to bring down hidden fruit and also probed around it to explore its roots, soon realized that the expressive richness of that people came not so much from the flashy exploration of scandalous and really facile social theses, but from a stern aspiration which was already one hundred years old, an aspiration to fit everyday life, without exclusions, into language. And that inspired their constant effort to attune language to the new reality, to create in essence a *new* language, concrete and symbolic, thoroughly dependent on itself for justification and not on some traditional manner. That style, often vulgarized but still unusually striking in the most recent books, could easily be traced back to the initiators and the pioneers of the mid-nineteenth century, the poet Walt Whitman and the narrator Mark Twain.

At that point, American culture became for us something very serious and precious. It became a sort of great laboratory where, with quite different freedom and means, the same goal was pursued that the best among us were pursuing with less spontaneity perhaps but with as stubborn a determination: the creation of a modern taste, a modern style, a modern world. That culture seemed to us, in short, the ideal place for work and experimentation, for painstaking and hard-fought experimentation. That culture was not just the Babel of publicized efficiency and harsh neon-lit optimism which deafened and blinded naive people and, seasoned with Roman hypocrisy, would not have displeased even our own provincial militia leaders. We realized, in those years of study, that America was not *another* country, a *new* beginning in history, but just an immense theatre where our common drama was played out with greater frankness than elsewhere. And if, for a moment, we believed that it would be worthwhile for us to reject our own selves and our past in order to give our body and soul to that free world, that happened because history had shut us up in the absurd and tragicomic situation of nonexistence as a culture.

American culture allowed us to witness our own drama in those years, as if it were projected on a giant screen. It showed us a fierce, conscious, unceasing struggle to give a sense, a name, and some order to the new realities and the new drives of our individual and group life, to reconcile the ancient feelings and the ancient words of men with a changed world. As is natural in times of political stagnation, we were then content to study the ways in which those intellectuals from across the ocean had *expressed* that drama, how they had succeeded in *speaking* that language, to tell stories, to *sing* that story. We could not participate openly in the drama, in the story, in the test, and so we studied American culture a bit as one studies the past centuries, Elizabethan drama, or the "sweet new style."

Now the times have changed. Everything can be said; more than that, it has all pretty much been said. What happens is that the years go by, and more books than ever come to us from America. But today we open and close them without any trepidation. Once, even a minor work coming from there, even a mediocre film, moved us and elicited lively debates, forced us to side with it. Is it that we are growing old, or has a brief taste of freedom been sufficient to make us feel detached? The expressive and narrative summits of the American twentieth century will endure—Lee Masters, Anderson, Hemingway, Faulkner already live in the realm of the classics. But for us, not even the isolation of the war years has been sufficient to make us truly love whatever new thing reaches us now from out there. It happens at times that we read a book that awakens our imagination and our conscience; then we look at the date, and it is a prewar book. To be honest, we have the impression that American culture has lost its excellence, that spontaneous and knowing fury which placed it in the avant-garde of our intellectual world. And we cannot ignore the fact that this is happening just as America's fight against Fascism comes to an end or is suspended.

As the more brutal restrictions fell, we understood that many countries in Europe and in the world are today the laboratory where forms and styles are created; there is nothing to prevent anyone who has the will to do so, were he to be living in an old convent, to say a new word. But without a Fascism to oppose, that is to say without a historically progressive thought to keep alive, no matter how many skyscrapers and cars and armies it may produce, America will not be at the avant-garde of any culture any more. Without progressive political thinking and a progressive struggle,

America will rather risk giving itself up to a form of Fascism, even if it will do so in the name of its more cherished traditions.

* * *

Gone are the times when we discovered America. Within a decade, from 1930 to 1940, not only the Italians became acquainted with at least a half dozen contemporary American writers whose names will endure, but they rediscovered some of the nineteenth-century classics of that literature and got a glimpse of the basic continuity that links all the past and present creations of that people. That was also the decade when music and film seemed to shake up our blasé European sensibility. In this process of discovery, we even experienced the thrill of liberation and outrageousness which is inseparable from any encounter with a new reality, and which the Italian and European political climate certainly succeeded in fostering.

But that is all gone now. America now, the great American culture, has been discovered and given recognition, and we can foresee that for a few decades nothing will come to us from that country which can come close to the names and revelations that filled our prewar adolescence with enthusiasm. The Americans know it too, even if they don't say it too loud; they are busy with the conscientious job of cataloguing and researching the twenty years between the two wars. The truly important books that come to us now from America are not fiction or poetry anymore, but history books—interpretive, reflective books. Besides, all the new writers have lost that miraculous immediacy of expression, that inborn sense of earth and concreteness, the harsh wisdom that made us love then a Lee Masters, a Hemingway, a Caldwell. The Americans are now laboring on simple-minded complications with which we are very familiar. They may even bring fruit at a later date, but for the time being they add nothing to the crafty sophistication of us Europeans. As for film and all the rest, we would do better not to say anything. In short, it seems to us that today, after the war and the occupation, after strolling and conversing at length with us, the young Americans have undergone a process of spiritual Europeanization; they have lost a large part of the exotic and tragic directness which was their essence. But then, it may be that this, too, in history's game, is part of their destiny.

America Loved and Hated

GIORGIO SOAVI

America tutta d'un fiato, 1959, pp. 9-10, 19-20
28-31, 35-37, 91-93, 170-172

* * *

I spent three months in America in 1954. From my return until now I did not forget the memory of the American I saw, which fascinated me—the myth of that country. What is America doing? And why do I recall it so often? "Would you like to live there?" friends ask me. We Italians are excitable and dramatic and, proba- bly—as things stand now—we are not made for America. But we love it. We have observed it a great deal and, if we don't like it en- tirely, we remember so many things about that country that some- times we are here and we feel as if we were there. Yes, because Ital- ians, young people, exhibitionists, often live in their imagination as Americans. I don't recall having seen this phenomenon of imitation of other peoples on the part of Italians. Of the French? Certainly not. And not the Russians, Japanese, or English either. The Ger- mans. . . . With Americans, yes. Toward them we nourish feelings of amazement and irony, and we would like to imitate them a little.

I did not know what to do when I returned, but I knew one thing: that I didn't want to write in a journalistic way about them. It's true that America changes with lightning-like speed, and competent journalists are needed to keep up with its daily revolutions. I have written poetry because poetry, even when it has a narrative form like mine, strikes precisely like lightning.

Of all the peoples in the world, Americans, more than any others, have not lost sight of that fantastic world, the future. Americans have begun the future very early and with all the means at their disposal: accompanying Lindbergh to the airport on that rainy morning, creating economic complexes like the Tennessee Valley Authority, capable of turning whole regions upside down, encumbering the sky with skyscrapers. Everything is known about America. Tragedies, brutality also; perhaps the worst underworld on the globe is there. Will it be better or worse than Siberia? They will both be dreadful. We are now in the middle. Nevertheless, America is generous; it gives more than other peoples. In the middle of this great confusion, everyone is eating, while America gives away or sells its all, showy like its neckties and tough like its Constitution.

I have loved and hated it like a person that I love, and with the book finished, I regret having written certain spiteful things, certain ruthless things. Ruthlessness is good for people who are healthy and in good faith. I have faith, and perhaps one day I will write with more joy about America.

* * * *

We had tea on the ground floor of the Seagram's Building, in a huge salon with panels of dark wood called "The Four Seasons." It is the most chic spot in the city, together with the Hemisphere Club, which is on top of the Time skyscraper. The Four Seasons is the place for celebrities, or whoever believes he is one. Beyond the enormous windows the outline of the skyscrapers is visible—that Grand Canyon invented by man. These tall windows are decorated with copper curtains made of thousands of fine wires that vibrate and sway in the slightest breath, reflecting all the colors of the rainbow. A singular decoration made of piano wires hangs from the ceiling. It might seem to be a lamp, but in reality it doesn't emit light; you think of stalactites or of a monstrous brass cage. Some people whisper: "What is it for?" Few could say. They save face by saying: "Anyway, it's very beautiful."

Waiters dark-haired like bullfighters, with a dancing step, serve tea and pastries on trays in the form of a disc. No one raises his voice, no one laughs loudly. You would think it was a church or a bank. Here, someone whispered in my ear, people plot the most interesting love affairs and business deals in the city. Anything goes. Both sexes participate.

Needless to say, the air is "conditioned." You breathe that smell of fresh leather, of wet sawdust, which is the smell of summer in New York. It isn't hot outside today, and the temperature is mild, as if we were—let's say—in Versilia in May. So then, you say, why waste money and energy on air conditioners? The answer they give you is always the same: habit, laziness. By now, this country has imposed on itself the double torture of the year 2000: too much refrigeration and too much ice in summer; too much heat in winter.

There are days when it's hot outside. But in restaurants and movies, offices and libraries, you meet ladies who shiver and sneeze. The most provident carry a light coat or sweater with them. Sinusitis, headache, and bronchitis are the ills of the season. It is very difficult, perhaps impossible, to avoid iced water, iced broth, iced tea. And when I say iced, I mean with pieces of ice that float in the liquid like icebergs.

A strange country, granted. Perhaps the strangest that has ever existed. But I would hesitate to use irony. I am afraid that this will soon be the fate of Milan and of half of Europe.

* * *

Whoever finds that his office has become smaller does not need to ask if his reputation is in a decline. Someone said to me: "Do you know what an employee does as soon as he gets to his office? He measures it. If the measurements are the same as the day before, then he smiles at life like a man in an ad."

The skyscraper in which I am working (for a short time) is fifty stories high. My office is only at the halfway mark. The outside walls are alternately striped with grey cement and glass. When it is clear, the glass is blue. From afar, with its grey and blue lines, the skyscraper looks like the pajama pants of King Kong.

To live in a skyscraper is an exhilarating experience. I say "to live" because you don't come here only to work; often you eat both lunch and dinner there. The restaurant on the top floor, managed by an Italian, is probably the most elegant and the most popular in the city. There are, in addition, painting exhibits, photography shows, lectures, and films. Every so often, even a dance takes place here, with streamers and cotillions. More than the central office of a large industry, the building in which I live makes me think of an ocean liner with the stern driven into the ground and the prow lost among lights and haze.

Like all self-respecting skyscrapers, ours, too, has a platoon of

elevators. They are subdivided into various blocs, each corre-
sponding to a slice of the skyscraper. The first bloc of eight elevators serves the first nine floors and keeps to a speed that we would
call human or European. But the elevators that go only, let us say,
to the thirtieth floor (from the thirtieth to the fortieth), those have
a velocity or ascending thrust that is completely incredible. In comparison, the rockets of Gagarin and Titov are as restful as Neapolitan carriages. Personally, every time I go up to the thirty-third
floor I feel the panic of someone who is going—unprepared—into
orbit. The blood drops to my legs and my head spins. I often need
to lean against the metallic walls while a speaker, hidden who
knows where, broadcasts some notes of music. The contraption
goes at such speed that there isn't time to determine whether the
music is jazz or a Beethoven sonata.

The other morning I came into the office almost staggering. I let
myself fall into a chair, waiting with closed eyes to come to myself.
Suddenly I heard the voice of a colleague who, alarmed at my pallor, asked me if I felt well. "Would you like a cup of coffee?" she
added.

In fact, at that moment the young man who serves pastries and
coffee in paper cups in the various offices was passing by. He is
preceded by the sound of a little bell, similar to the one that an-
nounces the first sitting in the dining car in European trains.
"Thanks," I said. "I would gladly have a cup of coffee." Then,
after I got myself together, I asked how long it took to get used to
the elevators. "Oh," my colleague said, kindly, "you're young. In
six months you won't feel anything."

Another serious matter is catching an elevator to go from one
floor to another. The door opens for a fraction of a second and
then closes again. Since there is not one but eight elevators on the
landing, you never know where to run to. It takes an uncommon
quickness of reflex and spring. The opinion is widespread that the
engineer who set the timing was either an ex-athlete with an exceptional sprint or a first-class sadist. I have seen middle-aged
executives, still strong but with reflexes a bit slow, lose one elevator
after another. They become livid with rage, and in their hearts already feel the loneliness of retirement. But in a society like this one,
there isn't a tenth of a second to lose. Everyone in his way sets a little record every day. Here I realized that one cannot be allowed the

luxury of a pot belly or heavy thighs. I realized why executives continue to play tennis at well over fifty, in spite of grey hair and the beginning of varicose veins. They can't lose their spring. In a word, they must jump like crickets into the first elevator as soon as the boss calls them for an urgent job.

* * *

The more one lives in America, the more one realizes that the Italian newspapermen who work in Italy deserve being nominated en masse for beatification. The reader in Naples, Salerno, Viareggio, or Rome is unaware of what an investigation into the consumption of matches or motorcycles costs a reporter on a daily newspaper. Rather than furnish some information or a simple figure, an Italian official prefers facing the guillotine. I remember once in Rome I asked how many male and female voters there were. The official looked at me as one looks at a criminal, someone who sincerely wishes to deliberately subvert the values of Fatherland and Family. He said to me: "Well, my dear friend, you expect too much!"

Another time I was in Brussels. It was August, and in the Ministry of Foreign Affairs the European Defense Community (CED) was dying, thanks to the difficulties raised by Mendès-France. European illusions were crumbling like sand castles; there was a sense of catastrophe everywhere. At 8:00 in the evening, the correspondents of the Italian newspapers assembled in the foyer of a hotel and waited for the usual spokesman to announce some news and commit some calculated indiscretion. The spokesman appeared with a dark face; he wore a double-breasted blue pinstripe suit. If I remember rightly, the journalists were Sandro Volta, Giorgio Sansa, Francesco Maratea, Dante Benedetti, G. V. Sanpieri, and Lorenzo Bocchi. "Well," said Volta, "what's new?" The spokesman coughed, and with an accent that he claimed came from the school of the Foreign Office said: "Boys, I'm not about to give you the routine news now. Instead, I'll try to go beyond the facts and to effect a synthesis. In short, I'll give you an editorial."

In Italy, then, when they are disposed to speak, officials give you an editorial and no information. There is a profound contempt for facts. For example, I briefly interviewed a minister who recently visited the United States. He had nothing exceptional or explosive to reveal. Yet, when I asked him for authorization to publish what he had said to me, he warned: "Please tread very carefully. Tell, but don't tell."

In the United States, journalism is in its element; it moves with confidence and without loss of time. It is impossible for news to remain "secret" for more than twenty-four hours. No office resists the need, let us say almost the duty, to spread it on stenciled circulars.

"It's a real miracle," a friend once said to me. "The most recent formulas on the hydrogen bomb have not been published." The American newspaperman doesn't find locked doors. Generals, financiers, actors receive him every hour of the day. Photographers have free access to hospitals and can easily take pictures in prisons. I have seen a *Life* photographer say to Marilyn Monroe: "Now close your left eye; no, a more intelligent expression on your face; and now roll on the ground." The beauty of it is that Marilyn Monroe obeyed without a complaint. She knew that if she didn't behave well, the *Life* photographer could publish pictures that would be embarrassing and harmful to her career. Articles in American newspapers and magazines are often full of surprising information because it is easily obtainable. Not only that, but if in the middle of his coverage the journalist has a doubt, he can telephone the official, the actor, or the financier.

Ah, the telephones of the United States! They are much more useful, important, and efficient than the Statue of Liberty. Do you want San Francisco, Miami, Los Angeles, Las Vegas? No sooner has the operator requested that you don't put down the receiver ("Hold the line") than the call is there at your fingertips, as swift as a bolt out of the blue. And don't become impatient if you don't have the telephone number of the person you're seeking: the operator herself will look for it in the directory. If perchance you are nervous some day and happen to say something undiplomatic, she will reply smoothly: "Thank you, sir."

* * *

I have always had an instinctive respect for plumbers, but I had never imagined that they were a privileged class. In New York they are a sort of closed caste, powerful and rich.

Last month one of those mishaps happened in my house which in Italy are laughable but in America are catastrophes: the pipe under the sink became stopped up. Frankly, who in Italy gets upset over such a thing? There is always someone who will help out—either a real and proper plumber, or a garage attendant, or the porter. But here in New York it's entirely different. You are alone. The porter has other things to do and looks at you with the severe eye of a general on the battlefield. In short, it was a Saturday afternoon. On Saturdays, as one must understand, America rests. Bank clerks rest, as do factory workers, errand boys, school teachers—and plumbers. Only three or four plumbers in all of New York are ready for emergency work. But what must be done to convince them to come? If it rains, they don't stir. If you live too far away, they have "other urgent work." They are rich. Who can make them put themselves out excessively?

The afternoon the sink pipe became stopped up I was genuinely alarmed. If I found no one, I would have to have a very uncomfortable Sunday, without the possibility of washing a glass or cooking two eggs. The kitchen had the depressing odor of greasy and stagnant water. I believe that my voice trembled when I begged the plumber to come. He answered: "O.K., but not before 8:00."

At 8:00, an elegant gentleman knocked on the door. He wore a blue overcoat, black shoes, and the homburg of a State Department official. Rather surprised, if not intimidated, I asked him what he wanted. He answered with a tinge of irony: "Are you the one who telephoned, or did I make a mistake?"

In his right hand, he had an extremely proper bag of dark leather. I have seen doctors with less elegant bags. He took off his overcoat, opened the bag, and drew out a couple of tools. With the hand of a master, he fixed my poor pipe. The water was sucked down with a hearty, almost gay noise. He washed his hands in the bath tub and put his tools back in the bag. He said to me: "Would you mind if I left this bag with you for twenty-four hours? I must go out to dinner. I'll come get it tomorrow." I asked him what I owed him. He answered gently: "Fifteen dollars."

I suppose he noticed my sudden pallor. I said, trying not to show what a blow it was: "Yours must be a satisfying kind of work. You save people from disagreeable situations, a little like doctors. Only doctors are a little less expensive."

"Ah, really?" he exclaimed with real surprise.

"Yes," I answered. "My doctor charges ten dollars a visit."

"Oh," he said, laughing. "I generally charge ten dollars, too. But this is extra work. It's Saturday, sir. And in order to come here, I'll be late for dinner."

* * *

Not even the more and more frequent trips, by plane or boat, help destroy commonplaces. At the end of a more or less rapid excursion, tourists will recount at home the exaggerations they read before leaving but with redoubled enthusiasm. The images of a nonexistent or distorted America are multiplying. Till the end of time we are destined to read that: (1) American women are beautiful, but without femininity; (2) California oranges are gigantic, but tasteless; (3) New Yorkers, in their eagerness to work too much, don't enjoy life; (4) the mountains of Vermont are evocative, but they can't be compared to the Trentino Alps.

We certainly don't have to take the part of American women: they are not little, and they can defend themselves. But how can one call them "dull"? I would say that they are not always very beautiful, but they are pretty, wholesome, and simple. They have a straightforward way of telling you that they feel like having a drink with you, or that you "look like a very amusing uncle of theirs." They are not coquettish in the French sense of the word; they do not enjoy cheating. They like baseball, romanticism, blasé poets and songs. They detest being economically "dependent" on a man. Their aspiration is to buy stockings, and perhaps a fur coat, with their own paycheck. With fantastic energy they manage to keep house, give birth to children, go to the office, and organize a party for Saturday evening. Naturally, they have a big defect: if they happen to fall in love with someone else, they tell their husbands and divorce them. That's their way of being "dull."

I will never be able to understand how the people of New York got themselves the reputation abroad of being relentless workers. It must be a mystery of organized advertising. Besides, all you have to do is take a pencil and add it up. They work thirty-five hours a week. At five on Friday afternoons they take off, leaving the office or the factory, and you don't see them again until 9:00 Monday morning. On Saturday and Sunday they rest, and to keep from being bored, they invent a hobby for themselves—a pretext for passing the time: they grow roses, paint, write comedies, perhaps some send anonymous letters (and thus, in my opinion, McCarthyism was born).

With all this, every time they meet an Italian, Americans half close their eyes and sigh: ah, lucky you, with that miraculous country, and the sun, the good wine, whole days free, without cares. Is that clear? We are still the country of *dolce far niente*. The sun, the good wine, Posillipo, and "Ohi, Maré." Americans, too, like us are slaves of ready-made expressions. No one disabuses them of the idea that "from the Alps to Mount Etna" we are only concerned with the tunes of ditties and songs. Who will convince the reader from Long Island or Detroit that a Neapolitan works (or seeks work) seven days out of seven? Who will explain to a clerk in Chicago or a coed in San Francisco that Italy is the country of moonlighting and that every Italian has (or at least knows how to do) three different jobs?

Sometimes I go around on foot in New York and make a note of the things I see and the people I meet: the children who play with a patched-up ball on 46th Street, the lovers who hold hands in front of St. Patrick's Cathedral, the old man who plays the accordion, the blind man with a parrot who sells chances on the wheels of fortune of Bari, Naples, and Rome. I like this humble, somewhat sad America—that is, an America outside of the propagandistic schemes, a bit in contrast to cinerama, prosperity, and modernity.

Every so often, however, I think of the remarks of that French writer from whom a Parisian weekly requested not real articles but pieces of picture postcards. And then I, too, wonder: is this the America that the reader wants?

There is still a certain secret America, bitter and unpleasant: in some provincial corners, or in some New York slums, I am sure that Charlie Chaplin's tramp exists. Unfortunately, Chaplin is no longer the fashion in these parts.

Mythic America

GIANFRANCO CORSINI
America allo specchio, 1960, pp. 9-13

Gianfranco Corsini (1921-): Corsini is a journalist with wide experience as a correspondent in England and the United States and as a writer for Italian and American magazines. During the late 1930's he belonged to the Resistance, and in 1943 he joined the Communist party. He is presently literary editor and specialist in American affairs for the Roman newspaper *Paese Sera*; in addition, he is affiliated with the University of Salerno as a professor of American literature. Corsini has visited the United States annually since 1958, the year on which his book *America in the Mirror* is based. He has written other books on the United States: *Dissenting America* (1966), *The Great American Crisis* (1974), *A History of the North American Indians* (1974), and *America Two Hundred Years Later* (1975).

I arrived in the United States at the end of 1958, when the streets and shops of New York were beginning to be illuminated with Christmas decorations. My first impressions of America were of the children who gaily chased each other around the ice rink of Rockefeller Center, in the shadow of a huge, multicolored fir tree. I set out from here again—after two long stays—at the beginning of 1960, carrying with me the picture of the same lights and of a holiday crowd joyfully preparing to celebrate, in peace and plenty, the end of a decade.

The mythic America of our childhood and adolescence seemingly paraded, as in a colossal cinemascope, before my eyes. But the experience of five months, the encounters with places and people on this immense continent, the things seen, read, or thought, conspired against the natural tendency to idyllic simplification.

When speaking about the United States for the first time, it is in fact difficult to separate oneself from the European tradition that wants a concise and immediate definition of the New World. Defining America in a word, categorizing and fixing it in authoritative terms, is part of the mythology of this last half century and is the fruit of a static vision of American reality as something antithetical (in a positive or negative sense, according to the point of view) to the culture of our Old Continent.

The interest of past travelers consisted above all in *verifying* current opinions on the culture of the United States and on the "American way of life" in the light of this traditional mythology. When they came to the United States, they usually approached it as a homogeneous and isolated entity whose social system served as the starting point for an ideological polemic to develop back home. Meanwhile, the United States' relations with the rest of the world represented only a marginal element of their inquiry.

America "sweet" or "bitter," accepted or rejected, are the two poles between which swings a whole literature bent on gathering certain superficial and spectacular elements of American life rather than on analyzing in depth fundamental components and surprising contradictions. Moreover, such an analysis appears to us today to be historically bound to a period in which the United States still appeared to be basically cut off from the rest of the world, in spite of its participation in World War I.

Since the last war—and above all since the formation of NATO—the attitude of European observers toward the United States has remained substantially the same. The *defense* or *condemnation* of the "system" in terms of the American government's foreign policy did not alter the assumption according to which the United States represented a reality in isolation, invulnerable from abroad and, in a certain sense, unchangeable. Behind the *dynamic* appearance that they wanted to attribute to the American way of life and political stance was hidden a vision of the United States which was still *static* and antihistorical, a vision fed by the artificial perpetuation of a myth that was increasingly more removed from reality.

Therefore, the first thing that strikes anyone who goes to the United States today with an objective and realistic attitude is the evident inadequacy of the preconceived method of investigation Europeans have used up to now. Not only does such a method have no foundation or justification, but also the international situation has changed in such a way as to provoke, even within the United States, the first symptoms of radical transformations. America it-self appears to be committed to reestablish the truth, intent on scrutinizing itself in the mirror, perplexed, attentive, conscious of its own restlessness and its own complexity.

For Europeans who, like this writer, have grown up in the shadow of the American myth, who have hidden a sheriff's badge under the bed or shouted "Americans go home" through the streets, who have read Hemingway together with Leopardi and have felt saved and menaced by America in the space of a genera-tion—for all of us it is difficult to suddenly liberate ourselves from the numerous preconceived ideas matured over a period of years. But in reappraising the phases of our enthusiasm and our delusions, in reliving our constant relation to the reality of Ameri-ca, we feel that little by little—even within ourselves—America has been transformed finally from myth into reality. While a genera-tion grew up, America also grew up with it, with leaps and contra-dictions. With all the complexes of the past overcome, we feel that today we Europeans and our American cousins are beginning to move on a terrain of equality.

Circumstances that in the past prevented us from overcoming so many reciprocal complexes (the intellectual superiority of Europe on one side, which was set against the pride of that country called upon to protect Western civilization with armed force) today create the possibility of a meeting between adults without preconceived ideas, wanting only to deal with reality. When a European "looks at America today," Mario Einaudi wrote recently, "what he sees he can like or dislike," but "what he cannot do is reject America without knowing . . . what it is." Neither can he accept it, it must be added, without seeing its contours clearly and without sounding its complexity in depth. "The incapacity to look at facts without preconceived ideas and without dogmatic attitudes," Einaudi continues, "has brought some of the most sagacious European political commentators to affirm that American society has less mobility today than it did in the nineteenth century."

If the Buffaloes Stampede

GIORGIO SPINI

America 1962, 1962, pp. 105-106

Giorgio Spini (1916-): Professor Spini teaches modern history at the University of Florence and is chairman of the Italian Committee to Coordinate Studies in American History. He is a militant member of the Socialist party and chairman of the Socialist Institute of Historical Studies. An antifascist, Spini served in World War II as a liaison officer between the Allies and the Italian Resistance. In addition to *America 1962,* he has written a number of other books, including *The Autobiography of Young America* (1968), and has edited a two-volume work, *Italy and America* (1976).

A people is never a "nation of sheep" as long as there are some who are not resigned to living like sheep. And the American people, essentially, are not a nation of sheep. If anything, they are a nation of buffaloes who tend to keep on ruminating peaceably in their pasture as long as it is possible; but once they are needled, they charge, holding their heads low, like an avalanche, and woe to whoever is in their path. They tried to live ruminating in peace during World War II, until Pearl Harbor started them and then they charged, massacring with their terrible horns Hitler, Mussolini, and Japan, with no pity or mercy. The late Joseph Stalin had the bad idea of poking at them again, precisely in one of their most sensitive spots, that is, by giving them the impression that they were be-

ing treated as stupid beasts, easy to trick. And they charged again—
butting, without paying attention to the fine points. We can thank
God if with the fury of their gut reaction they did not cause even
more disasters than came out of it. Now they are beginning to feel
unsure about the road to take. So there they stand pawing and
snorting, torn between a great desire to send everybody to the devil
and start chewing cud again on the prairie, and a great fear of what
might happen to them in the future. But if tomorrow, after much
snorting and shaking of their huge heads, the buffaloes make up
their minds to stampede again, Lord have mercy on the ones they
find in their path. They do not belong to the species of those slimy,
slippery, spineless animals we so often find under our feet. They
are big, heavy beasts, full of energy to burst, who do everything
they put their minds to very seriously. They are still capable of
rushing, perhaps at any moment, in new directions, with the same
violence with which storms or polar frosts rush in after killer heat
waves on their continent. They are perhaps of a race rather close to
those other big beasts roaming way over in the East on the Russian
plains. One thing is sure: under their leathery rough skin they have
ingenuity to burn, and at times they can show they are much shrew-
der animals than many believed them to be. All it takes is for them
to decide to get moving; then you will see things that will take your
breath away.

True, they have hard heads. A friend of mine who teaches phy-
sics in an American university was telling me that if ever they become convinced that they need to take that road, they are capable
of creating a society that is more collectivistic than a Soviet collective. All the while they will continue to swear fearlessly by "rug-
ged individualism" and to repeat that America is the country of
private enterprise. It's useless to hope that they will adjust to patterns that are not from back home. One of the reasons why the extreme Left, Socialist or Communist, has ended in disaster in the
United States is that it smelled too German or Russian, or perhaps
like a ghetto and too little like buffalo. But, on a moment's notice,
they are accustomed to sweeping away all that's old and to starting
everything again, without wasting much time in lamenting. The
potential New Left has the enormous advantage of being totally

and unequivocally of pure buffalo race. It's not for nothing that it also likes so much charging with heads butting, instead of debating ideologies. The New Left springs up from old indigenous spiritual roots. It often walks almost unconsciously in the footsteps of prairie prophets like William Jennings Bryan. It has the same sad, manly face of an Abraham Lincoln. We had better not expect it to speak the language of our Marxists. But, exactly because of this, we may hope that it will have something new to bring to history.

Crossing the Southwest

GUIDO PIOVENE
De America, 1954, pp. 339-344

I reached the Grand Canyon by crossing a Navajo reservation. While the Grand Canyon is one of the major tourist attractions (Baedeker gives it three stars), the reservation is a desolate prehistoric land, cut off from all main routes, visited only by federal agents, teachers, doctors, missionaries, and some curiosity-seekers like myself. It is one of the bleak and splendid domains the Indians have left in America. Calling the lands of the Indians "Red lands" —as it is done—is inadequate, in spite of the fact that red is their dominant color. This red goes through all tones and gradations, from vermilion to purple to orange; it pales down to a pinkish white and deepens into a purple violet verging on black. It can be extremely delicate as when, for example, wide expanses of sky appear within faraway circles of rocky ridges as softly hued as flowers. The colors of the evening sky are the same as those of the earth, with trails of a pale blue. Sulphur yellow, verdigris, and sea-green vein the red. As you drive, you begin to believe that your windshield is colored, and even your thoughts are stimulated by a mysterious exaltation, almost by a hidden violence.

These spaces look deserted, although 70,000 Indians live here scattered in their nomadic life. The pine woods, where the Indians gather turpentine, are deserted; deserted the arid plains, which look as if they were dyed; deserted the rocks, striped, cut razor-sharp, often in the shape of monsters, elephants, and turtles, with an incredibly detailed wealth of heads, combs, and legs. A lonely snow-capped mountain, formerly believed to be a deity, now rechristened

San Francisco, rises all to itself in the distance. The region I am traveling through now contains many petrified forests. The fallen tree trunks lying on the ground are from 150,000 to 250,000 years old, and their fibers have turned from wood into a metallic substance. When they are cut and polished, they look like semiprecious stones. At times, when the plain widens, giving a sea-like quality to the depths of blue air and a shimmering which seems to announce a mirage, one almost has the physical sensation of traveling toward the afterlife. The rare living creatures look like apparitions—such as the birds fluttering by in three hues of blue, turquoise, cornflower, and delft; or a flock tended by a very old lady; or a man on horseback; or a man standing atop a solitary rock looking down as if from a window. Outside of the forests, only the painted rocks throw shadows.

Clusters of houses surrounding a hospital, a school, a mission, or a service station are scattered along the road which crosses the reservation, but men are visible only in the larger villages, which here they call "cities." I had to stop in one of them, Tuba City, on the steps of a dry goods store. Ten or twelve Indians were seated by me; not one said a word, and they all looked straight ahead. They wore the absent expression of mathematicians or musicians. They are, in fact, gifted in music and abstract thought.

In the lonely regions that look deserted and are inaccessible to all but those who know the trails, the red canyons gape in the middle of the forest, similar to underground temples whose roofs have been lifted, with 1,000 meter deep gorges. These are the places of mysterious dread and of sinister fantasies. From the bottom of one of these canyons soars a needle of rock where legend says that a woman in the shape of a spider lives.

Speaking of other continents, such as Africa or Asia, it is customary to say that open spaces and mountain ranges suggest millenary wisdom. The American landscape never does so. It is sublime because it is inhuman. It is abstract, impervious to man. It is never wise but exalted and absorbed in itself. It is never ancient, not even with an antiquity of millennia. It is astral, geologic, anterior to life. It has no age, like monsters. Nature is admirable in other places because of its affinity with man; here, because of its aloofness. A civilization that was born yesterday lives next to it, not connected to it, but seemingly immersed in a different dimension of time and space, a civilization devoted to a different brand of comfort and asceticism, fighting an ascetic battle for an anesthetic comfort. When speaking of America, one must remember that the most modern nation in the world includes spaces such as these, deserts that remain barren or are colonized by necessity. America includes the cruelty of an essentially lonely nature where no one dreams of resting in the open air, a nature dominated by a mythology devoid of characters, of true personifications and even of divinities, ruled over by Powers and Forces. It would not be credible if Americans were not carrying it inside them, if their character were not in part shaped by it, either through resemblance or contrast. Man can sometimes be understood through the landscape. Nature in America has three chords: the exalted sublime; the chimeric, the dream of an Earthly Paradise; and the pleasant fakery, like a cold smile, of the artificially contrived resort areas.

The profoundest joy that nature can offer in America is the feeling of greatness, not because one feels embraced by the divine, but because one feels alienated from oneself, never here, but always "somewhere else," hurled away into a random point of the cosmos . . . .

Canyons are viewed from above, since they are created by erosion, and one climbs downward toward the depths, instead of climbing upwards, either on foot or on muleback. The excursion is made difficult by the horrible dryness of this desert of stones, closed among vertiginous walls, till the river bed is reached. For us who remain at the top, the Grand Canyon gapes like an underwater vision, as if the ocean had dried up and we were contemplating its bottom. It is a labyrinth of grotto-like valleys with its blocks of stone squared off temple-like, submerged 1,400 meters below us— red, orange, purple—according to the time, like darkening embers right after sunset, bluish and cold later. The Grand Canyon is the closest embodiment of our childhood fantasy of the inaccessible mountain realm, inhabited only by evil forces. Our Alps, at their fiercest, look hospitable when compared with this necropolis, immense and naked in its cruel colors. The Colorado River runs hidden except at certain points where one can see it shine briefly. On a moonless night, as the abyss had disappeared in darkness, I saw shooting stars crossing over it and seemingly plunging in it. Jupiter, moon-like, brightened with its light an entire zone of the sky. But away from it the sky was crowded with more stars than I have ever seen in other parts of the world, so much so that the stars were like a veil, as if everything had become a Milky Way. It would have been impossible to humanize this sky, to pick out constellations, to find in the signs of a mythology other than the measureless mythology of astral forces. The sky, too, was sublime because it was removed from men, absolute and uncharted. It led me back to the thoughts I have already expressed, on the quality of the Nature to be found at the heart of this civilization.

An American Church

GUIDO PIOVENE

De America, 1954, pp. 437-441

If you want to understand a people, you must study the major expressions of its religious life. Without them, nothing can be explained, not even facts that appear to be remote from it and those that belong to practical life. If I have described in detail the Mormon Church and its capital, it's not so much as a homage to the Church of the Latter Day Saints, in spite of its one million members, its notable holdings, and its wealthy temples in Salt Lake City as well as in Manti, Saint George, and Logan in Utah, Mesa in Arizona, Idaho Falls in Idaho, Cardston in Canada, and Laie in Hawaii. The Mormons are only the one hundred fiftieth part of the American population. Their church is important mainly for another reason: it is the only church born in America and developed in America, nourished by indigenous religiosity. Some of its characteristics can therefore be found in all the other organized churches as they have developed on this continent. Hence, the Mormon Church is worthy of attention, not for its own sake but as a key to understanding some trends in all the other churches.

Convinced that they are the only ones who, through the revelation received by Joseph Smith, have restored the genuine teachings of Christ and the structure Christ imposed on the church, the Mormons are neither Catholic nor Protestant. Both groups, the Catholic and the Protestant, seem to them to have deviated from the divine teachings. The same thing, as a matter of fact, is believed by another church we observed, the Christian Scientist; in religious as well as in economic and social matters, Americans constantly look for the "third way." On the other hand, it is obvious that the Mormon Church brings together elements of discordant religions. It is connected with Islam because of polygamy (even if today this practice is deferred until heavenly life) and because of its corporeal and materialistic conception of the afterlife, in which even family relationships and carnal relations are perpetuated. It is puritanical-Calvinistic in attributing religious value to success in business, the divine reward for the one who obeys the Laws. The Mormon Church is antipoverty; its virtuous man is most often well-to-do. This gives it the appearance of a business; its Vatican is made up of hotels, stores, rental property, and insurance companies. A bit of Catholicism can be detected in its authoritarian, strictly hierarchical organization. One notices in it, therefore, the American tendency to arrive at a sort of super-religion, which goes beyond all others and is a synthesis of them. This is an important trend, even if the results are often clumsy.

Another characteristic aspect is that the afterlife is not static but "progressive" and demographic. Even when in God's presence, man will continue to be active forever, to progress, to perfect himself and to fecundate, thereby enriching the celestial grounds with new bodies and new souls. Happiness must be attained on this earth (health, prosperity, and fecundity) and must be increased in a paradise not dissimilar from this earth. There is no conflict between this world and the other, no denial of worldliness. It's an optimistic religion, with no cult of pain. There is no hell, and at the end of time God will redeem everyone, placing each at different levels according to merit. There will be a certain number of people who will live (the word "live" means literally to dwell) right next to the Father, just as on this earth only some of the Mormons are admitted to the Temple. Also, this church has the cult of health. The health of the body is a religious duty. The instruction and training of intellectual and artistic abilities is also a religious duty; ignorance is sin. The church supports theatre, music, architecture, and even dance. In the great circular tabernacle, open to all and rising next to the Temple (8,000 people can be seated in it), one of the largest and best of all existing organs, with 11,000 pipes, plays Bach and Beethoven daily for Mormons and "Gentiles." It was built when the Mormons were fighting for their survival. The atmosphere in this city, as we were saying, is one of refinement and culture, even though the culture is conformist and paternalistic.

The democratic spirit and the "visionary" temperament of the American soul are visible in other aspects of this faith. In the bosom of the church, prophets, ministers, teachers and evangelists must continue to live, and they are common people with common jobs. The whole truth has not been revealed yet; revelation, then, is also progressive, going on and on. It is, therefore, an article of faith to believe in the apparitions of angels, in prophecies, visions, revelations, and miracles, in the gifts of healing and of speaking unknown tongues. God appears and speaks continuously, in person, to the men who implore a revelation. The true church makes its truth manifest because it proceeds almost enveloped in the physical presence of God and in a sort of continuous revelation. Whoever knows American history, even in a cursory way, knows that beliefs such as these grow spontaneously in the souls of the crowd here and take different forms.

But there are other points of even greater significance. Among the revelations contained in the holy book, the *Book of Mormon*, there is one—as we saw—that says the descendants of the Hebrew family that fled Jerusalem six centuries before Christ endowed America with a splendid civilization. After his resurrection and his ascension to heaven, Christ came to America, repeated his revelation and fulfilled for that people a true and real ministerial function similar to the one the Pope has among us. This belief expresses well a constant inclination of American religiosity, which nourishes the lay culture also: the inclination to take one's departure not from the suffering Christ but from the triumphant Christ. The crucifixion is overshadowed and only one moment is highlighted—the redemption, the victory over sorrow and death. The American Mormons did not see Christ's tears, only his triumph when death was overcome and done away with.

The Mormons' central belief, however, is the one contained in the tenth article of their faith, which says textually: "We believed in the literal gathering of Israel and in the restoration of the Ten Tribes; that Zion will be built upon this [the American] continent; that Christ will reign personally upon the earth; and that the earth will be renewed and receive its paradisiacal glory." The reader should not be misled. The Mormons believe they are the core of the "true" Israel; they are, therefore, basically anti-Semitic. The full Gospel, integrated by Christ's second predication and the *Book of Mormon*, was given to America only, and it must spread from here. The study of the Bible and its correct interpretation show that America, and not Palestine, had been chosen by God and His prophets as the Holy Land, the Promised Land. The Hebrew family that left Jerusalem to cross the ocean was, then, the only one to understand properly the words of the prophets. In order to fulfill God's commandment completely, allowing the true believers to accomplish their mission, America remains in effect—even among the misbelievers—the land of law and liberty. The fabled primitive American people of the Mormon mythology were the most Christian of peoples, the people God Himself ruled after dying elsewhere. America, all of America, North and South, will be the Zion foreseen by the prophecies. Here Christ will come in His final return to earth to transform it into paradise, from here He will rule over the peoples. His coming will be preceded by four signs: an angel with the gospel, a celestial messenger, the descent of Elijah, and the reunion of the Saints—the Mormons—who because of that are called the "Latter Day Saints."

Synthesis of religions, religious duty to attain redemption through the overcoming of economic and physical want, war on sickness, cult of health and success, instruction, assimilation of heaven and earth, sense of mission, waiting for an earthly Paradise, a new Pentecost, a second Coming: Aren't these the inclinations or beliefs we found in all the churches and sects rooted in America? We found them in varying combinations, now here, now there, in sophisticated or naive forms, in popular movements that last as long as the exaltation of a religious revival as well as in the permanent churches, including those which have, in other lands, a different appearance and different substances. Those beliefs impregnate American civilization, even in its practical manifestations, even among the sixty million people who are called atheistic because they do not belong to a specific church. And American civilization finds in them its own mythology.

LITERATURE

IV

Before the 1920's, Italian interest in American literature was sporadic and limited. Whitman and Poe were known, and Cooper's romances were popular, but deep or sustained enthusiasm was rare. In this early period, the dominant Italian critic of American literature was Enrico Nencioni. Between 1867 and 1896, he published studies in the periodical *Nuova Antologia* which later appeared in his book, *Saggi critici di letteratura inglese* (1897). The title, *Critical Studies of English Literature*, is revealing: only three out of forty-nine essays are devoted to American writers; the remainder are English. Even well into this century, Italians regarded American literature as a mere appendage of British literature, lesser in both quality and quantity. Nevertheless, Nencioni, for one, did grasp the potentiality of American literature to create a distinctive New World identity. In a passage of rather Chateaubriandesque inspiration, he wrote: "Poetry truly American, the true echoes of Mississippi and Missouri, Virginia and Maryland, has a rude, primitive quality, a music natural and magnetic like that of vast lakes and wind among lianas, or impetuous and violent like that of great deafening cataracts."

Given the cultural elitism of Italian intellectuals in the 1920's, it is not surprising that the view of American literature as poor relation to a long and admirable English literary tradition should persist. The elder generation of Italian critics who discovered American literature in the 1920's—Emilio Cecchi, Carlo Linati, and Mario Praz—all held this opinion. Like Nencioni, they were all more prolific critics of English than American literature. By this time, the distinctive identity of American literature had become encapsulated in the term *barbarismo*. (Our word "barbarism" would fail to render the complexity of associations which *barbarismo* sums up; "primitivism" comes closer.) *Barbarismo* is the literary expression of the idea of the "New World"—America as a young country, close to nature, less civilized and therefore more primitive than the Old World. For the academic-based and conservative critics of this first generation, *barbarismo* carried pejorative connotations; they found the lack of tradition to be a serious and even insurmountable barrier to the creation of significant literature. In spite of this negative outlook, however, Praz, Cecchi, and Linati did furnish the impetus for further study and introduced a number of important American writers to the Italian public. Why did they bother with a literature they disapproved of? As Praz wrote apropos of Hemingway: "To a literature overripe with culture, as ours was in the Twenties . . . I offered as a curative the example of an art which seemed to spring from virgin soil."*

The key word here is "curative" for, as was mentioned before, at every level everything American appeared to Italians as having almost miraculous healing powers, as fulfilling a function of renewal for a tired, overrefined, perhaps corrupt civilization—even if some Italians, like Praz himself, opted for the values of the "old" and felt deeply uneasy when faced with the "new."

In the 1930's, several factors led to a new wave of discovery of American literature. The Fascist cultural milieu, which strongly discouraged any interest in things foreign, was reflected in the weary and uncreative Italian literature characterized by Praz as "overripe with culture." Rebelling against restrictions that stifled their own creativity, young writers followed where the first generation had led but arrived at different conclusions. They, too, accepted the concept of *barbarismo*, but they did not define it as a manifestation of infantile crudeness. For Elio Vittorini and Cesare Pavese—the leading *americanisti*, as they came to be known—*barbarismo* was positive and vital, a renewal of literature in nature, uninhibited by a lifeless tradition. Translating and writing about

*"Hemingway in Italy," *Partisan Review*, 15 (1948), p. 1089.

American literature enthusiastically, Pavese and Vittorini saw it under many guises: as the avant-garde of world literature, as a truly democratic and hence unique literary achievement, as inspiration and model for their own poetry and fiction. Entirely different in critical method and temperament, both were insightful and original critics. Inevitably, after the war their interest in American literature waned: the period of discovery was over, the Italian political and cultural climate had altered radically, and not less significantly, perhaps, the *americanisti* themselves had changed. Now grown older and mature as writers, they were making their own literature.

As the generation of Pavese and Vittorini fell silent in the post-war period, a new group of writers concerned with American literature emerged: the scholars. From the time of the American occupation on, American literature has become widely disseminated in Italy and is studied in Italian universities. As Agostino Lombardo tells us in his essay, "American Literature in Italy Today," it is now seen both more fully and more objectively than in the past.

Babbitt

ANTONIO GRAMSCI
Note sul Machiavelli, sulla politica e sullo
stato moderno, 1955, pp. 352-354

It would be interesting to analyze the reasons for the great success *Babbitt* has had in Europe. It's not a great book; it is constructed schematically, and even the mechanics of it are too obvious. It has more cultural than artistic importance; the critique of mores prevails over art. It is a very important cultural fact that in America there would be a realistic literary current which begins by being a critique of mores. That means that self-criticism is expanding, in other words that a new American civilization is being born aware of its strengths and its weaknesses. The intellectuals are moving away from the dominant class in order to become an integral part of that civilization and a true superstructure, not just an inessential, indistinct element of the corporate structure.

European intellectuals have already lost this function, at least in part. No longer do they represent cultural self-awareness or the self-critical conscience of the dominant class. They have again become the direct agents of the dominant class, or they have estranged themselves completely from it, becoming a separate caste with no roots in national popular life. They laugh at Babbitt: they are amused by his mediocrity, his naive stupidity, his conformist way of thinking, his standardized mentality. They don't even pose the question "Are there Babbitts in Europe?" The problem is that the standardized petty bourgeois does exist in Europe but his standardization, instead of being national (and in a big nation like the United States), is regional and local. The European Babbitts are of a historic brand inferior to the American Babbitt. They are a national weakness, whereas the American is a national strength. They are more picturesque but also more stupid and more ridiculous. Their conformity centers around a rotting and debilitating superstition, while Babbitt's conformity is naive and spontaneous, and centers around an energetic and progressive superstition.

According to Linati, Babbitt is "the prototype of today's American industrialist"; instead Babbitt is from the middle middle class and his most characteristic mania is to rub elbows with "modern industrialists," to be like them, to be able to exhibit their moral and social "superiority." The ideal to attain and the social model is the modern industrialist, while for the European Babbitt the ideal and the model are provided by the bishop's assistant, the petty nobility of the provinces, the division head in the Ministry. This lack of critical spirit among European intellectuals must be noted. In the preface of his book on the United States, André Siegfried contrasts the American taylorized worker to the artisan in a Parisian luxury trade, as if the latter were the prevalent type of worker in Europe. European intellectuals generally think that Babbitt is an exclusively American type, and they congratulate their old Europe on it. Anti-Americanism is comical even more than stupid.

The petty bourgeois in Europe laughs at Babbitt and therefore at America, which is supposedly populated by 120 million Babbitts. The petty bourgeois cannot look at himself objectively and cannot understand himself, just as the imbecile cannot understand he is an imbecile (without which he would demonstrate he is an intelligent man). And so imbeciles are the ones who do not know they are, and petty bourgeois are those philistines who do not know they are philistines. The European petty bourgeois laughs at the peculiar American philistinism but does not notice his own. He does not know he is the European Babbitt, inferior to the Babbitt in Lewis's novel inasmuch as the latter tries to escape, to stop being Babbitt. The European Babbitt does not fight against his philistinism; he wallows in it and thinks that his voice and his quack-quack of a frog stuck in the mud is a nightingale's song. In spite of everything, Babbitt is the philistine of a country on the move; the European petty bourgeois is the philistine of conservative countries rotting in the stagnating marsh of commonplaces about great traditions and great culture. The European philistine thinks he discovered America with Christopher Columbus and that Babbitt is a puppet born to amuse him, the man burdened by centuries of history. Meanwhile, no European writer has been able to give us a portrait of the European Babbitt, that is, to show an ability for self-criticism. Only the one who does not realize his stupidity is truly stupid and obtuse.

Notes on American Writers

ELIO VITTORINI

Diario in Pubblico, 1957, pp. 271, 122-123, 137-138, 162, 97

(November 1946)

American literature is the only one to coincide, right from its birth, with the modern age, the only one that can be called entirely modern. All other literatures have preserved Renaissance and medieval characteristics, even in their contemporary manifestations. To write about them . . . is also to write about humanism and the Middle Ages. When one writes about American literature, however, one is writing only about the modern age, and modernity can be singled out, understood for itself, studied as such.

(January 1941)

With Emerson and Thoreau, the great contradiction which was inside America began to reveal itself. Culture was robust and deep in them as in the most cultured whole men of Europe, Carlyle or Goethe. Ralph Waldo Emerson was not content with absorbing Plato, Plotinus, Montaigne, and whatever there is that is still contemporary in every classic. In the same way, Henry Thoreau meditated over Greek texts, mulling over them by himself in the journal which was both his life and his work. He continuously effected a revision of values, selecting from among the many juices which form the lymph of human consciousness. Ultimately, the assimilation had a truly expressive function in them; it had finally become, as it had meant to be for so long, expression. Full-fledged at last, complete; expression through assimilation. With some essays and some poems by the one ("Hamatreya," "Days," "The Problem") and with *Walden* and a small part in the *Journals* by the other, it was in America that the human spirit was taking a step forward.

Emerson and Thoreau were saying something more than what Europeans had said up to that time. More than Goethe on the individual, on human individuality, on ethics and God. More than Carlyle on history. Emerson's theories on art as a manifestation of experience and as the higher discovery of truth are still fundamentally valid today. His other theory on self-reliance, a manifesto of nonconformity, and Thoreau's theory of civil disobedience have found a worthy follow-up only dozens of years later. Yet, they spoke coldly, with ice on their lips. The powerful new voice rose with them in metaphysical roars, without revealing the wild beast. And they enriched the human spirit only intellectually, not in its flesh and blood; they enriched it with abstract furies.

A further step was needed: it was necessary to get to Poe, Hawthorne, and Melville to find really concrete words. They really dealt with the flesh; they worked with blood and unchained the new force entire. They did not have the reserved restraint their predecessors, Emerson and Thoreau included, had had. What was inside man? Was there corruption, sickness, damnation? *"L'Amérique est pourrie,"* Cooper's Frenchman had said, *"avant d'être mûre."* It was *pourrie* because it lived on prejudices, conventions, and inhibitions. But inside it had an unripe voice, savage, not civilized, not *mûre* at all, the voice of youthful ferocity. That's where the great contradiction lay, and Thoreau and Emerson, as we have said, had started drawing it out of the dark recesses that gave it birth.

Since, however, Emerson and Thoreau also were enslaved by prejudices, conventions, and inhibitions while they proclaimed the need to free man, they only knew how to teach passive defense, separation, abstraction, and individual solitude. The teachings were once again for a "purity" which was a limitation of life, like that of the puritans. The contradiction, if it was revealed, was not explained or properly recognized. It was not openly dealt with. They understood, for example, that America, as a new world, in order to be a new world—and a new beginning of man in the world —had to recapitulate "everything" of the old. They recognized that fact, and yet they excluded suffering, "evil," from this totality. But Poe, Hawthorne, and Melville accepted suffering and evil first of all. As masters of physical reality, they accepted, first of all, the shedding of blood. They said that since there is also corruption in man, long live corruption and damnation. This is the way to free man from his own decadence. *"Viva la muerte!"* And they explained the contradiction. They showed that it was life; it was a great contradiction!

(January 1941)

Much more than Howells, and more also than James, a woman, Emily Dickinson, gave the most that the human spirit can give when it is in subjection—whether consciously or unconsciously—to ways of life prescribed by traditional values. We are placing her here with Howells and James because she was close to them in cultural development, and because her life, as portrayed in her poems, gives her the air of a Jamesian character who might have acquired her fierce melancholy without going through a process of mystification. But Emerson, whose spiritual isolation she understood with perfect clarity, was her point of departure. A house, a garden, and the everyday eternity of her solitude gave her the voice which spoke with the energy of the greatest poets. There was no protest in her, no legend, no vital historical significance. But there was, condensed in the pure diamond of her poetry, the special fulfillment human beings find in realizing—and it is no game—that they are unfulfilled. And this may be an elementary thing, now that Dickinson has expressed it. This may be just as elementary a thing as the simplest achievements of literature from the time of the Greek poets on.

(March 1941)

Hemingway is perfectly cruel with subtlety. He also makes mistakes at times in the same sense that Faulkner makes mistakes. For example, in *The Sun Also Rises*, he gives naturalistic interpretations of certain behavior and does not attain the symbolic level. But that is a defect in calculation, an error in perspective, on his part and never a qualitative mistake. His sense of the qualitative is always present in the structuring of his prose; it is efficacious, and that has to do, I believe, with the manner in which his art is twofold. While Faulkner's art is two-dimensional, from the most capillary images of his prose to the most explicit gestures of his characters, Hemingway's art has a "linear" duplicity. Symbols are born in Hemingway without gestation; rather they come forth by elision, suggestion, and repetition of images, as Minerva out of Jupiter's head. In Hemingway's every page we find accepted as an ancient fact of humanity that the ways of purity are akin to the ways of corruption; and that purity is ferocious, and that every vague aspiration to cruelty is an aspiration to purity; then, we find a stoic ideal implicit.

Hemingway's symbols come from stoicism. That is why they seem to lack a motive or to be impressionistic, particularly when he describes and speaks of Spain and Africa. He tells a story without motivation. He does not say anything that describes or explains, and yet he succeeds in convincing us that life is youth, only youth, a fearless riot, and that only in youth is there purity. It does not matter if man is consumed or destroyed; he will still be a man in his stoicism, knowing how to drink hemlock. According to Hemingway, then, the last gesture of Socrates is the essential gesture of man; it is not a gesture of self-destruction, but of fulfillment, a last thanks to life given in bitterness and boredom.

(December 1937)

In this sort of universal literature written in one language which is today's American literature, the most American ends up by being precisely the one who does not carry the American card and America's particular past within him, the one who is freest of local historical precedents and who is, in short, open to the common culture of humanity. Perhaps he is even someone who has just arrived from the Old World and who carries the weight of the Old World on his back, but carries it as if it were a cargo of spices and aromatic essences, not of ferocious prejudices. America for him will be a stage of human civilization. He will accept it as such, and he will be American in that sense—pure, new, and without anything of America that is already dead and smells. He will be American 100 percent. With his cargo from the Old World, which is just a cargo of aromatic essences, he will only render special, concrete, definitive his own being American. He will make America richer, and he will cause the Old World to be left even further behind. . . .

Hemingway and Us

ITALO CALVINO

Il contemporaneo, November 13, 1954, p. 3

Italo Calvino (1923-): Today, Calvino is one of the best-known Italian novelists and probably the most imaginative mind to come out of the post-World War II generation. He was a member of the Resistance and also part of the group that clustered around the Einaudi publishing house in Turin, a group which included Cesare Pavese. Most of his works have been translated into English: *The Baron in the Trees* (1959), *The Non-existent Knight* and *The Cloven Viscount* (1962), *Cosmicomics* (1968), *t-zero* (1969), and *Invisible Cities* (1974). Unlike Pavese, Vittorini, and Pintor—who never came to the United States— Calvino has been a frequent visitor and has made the American cityscape an element of his fictional world.

The article included in this volume was written by the younger Calvino. It reflects his early preoccupations, and documents the reevaluation process taking place in the Italian literary world in the early 1950's.

There was a time when for me and for many others, my contemporaries or thereabout, Hemingway was a god. And those were great times, which I remember with satisfaction, without even a hint of the ironical indulgence one may feel in considering youthful fads and enthusiasms. Those were serious times, and we lived them seriously and at the same time with bravado and pure hearts. In Hemingway we could have also found a lesson in pessimism, of individualistic detachment and superficial involvement in the crudest experiences. That was also in Hemingway, but either we were not good readers or we had other things on our minds. In any case, what we learned from him was an open and generous attitude of pragmatic involvement—which was technical and moral at the same time—in the things that had to be done. We learned to look at the world with clear eyes, to refuse self-contemplation and self-pity, to grasp swiftly what life experience could teach and the worth of a person through a quick exchange of words or a gesture. But very soon we started to become aware of Hemingway's limitations and defects. His political universe and his style, to which I was heavily indebted in my first literary efforts, appeared narrow and easily transformed into mannerism. That life of his, with its philosophy of sanguinary tourism, began to inspire diffidence in me, and even dislike and repulsion. But today, after about ten years, as I draw up the accounts of my apprenticeship with Hemingway, I can close the books in the black. "You didn't do it, old man," I can tell him, indulging in his style for the last time. "You didn't succeed in becoming a *mauvais maître*." Since today Hemingway is a Nobel Prize winner (a fact which means absolutely nothing) the occasion is as good as any other to put on paper ideas I have long carried inside me. These notes on Hemingway precisely aim at defining both what Hemingway was for us and what he is now, what estranged us from him and what we still find in his pages and in no others.

In those times, what pushed us toward Hemingway undoubtedly was a suggestion poetic and political at the same time, a hazy enthusiasm for active anti-Fascism as opposed to a purely intellectual opposition to Fascism. As a matter of fact, to be frank, there was a point when it was the Hemingway-Malraux constellation that attracted us, symbolizing international anti-Fascism and the Spanish war front. Fortunately, we Italians had had D'Annunzio, who had vaccinated us against "heroic" inclinations, and the aestheticizing tendencies of Malraux soon became apparent to us. For some in France—for Roger Vailland, for example (who is a nice guy, anyway, a little superficial but authentic)—the Hemingway-Malraux duo was a fundamental influence. The definition of *dannunziano* was also used for Hemingway, at times not inappropriately. But Hemingway uses a dry point; he almost never dribbles. He is never overblown; he keeps his feet on the ground. (Almost always; for example, I can't stand Hemingway's "lyricism." "The Snows of Kilimanjaro" is, in my view, his worst work). He usually stays close to the concrete. All of these characteristics are in violent contrast to the *dannunziano* style. And then, in any case, let's be cautious about giving definitions: if one can be called *dannunziano* just because he likes an active life and beautiful women, then long live the *dannunziani*! The problem is not one of terms, however. Hemingway's myth of activism belongs to another trend of contemporary history, much more recent and still problematical.

The Hemingway hero wants to identify with the actions he performs; he wants to be the sum of his acts. His identity is to be found in his adherence to a manual or somehow practical technique. He tries to have no preoccupation or commitment other than to know how to do one thing well: fishing skillfully, hunting, blowing up a bridge, watching a *corrida* as it should be watched, even making love well. But around him, there is always something he wants to escape from, a sense of the vanity of everything, a sense of despair, defeat, and death. Whether he is fighting a shark or defending a position against the *falangistas*, the Hemingway hero concentrates on exact obedience to his code, those rules of competition which he feels he must impose on himself with the seriousness of moral dictates. He hangs onto that because outside of that there is emptiness and death. Hemingway does not even mention this fact, for his first rule is understatement. One of the most beautiful and personal of his short stories, "Big Two-Hearted River," is simply an account of the things a man does when he goes fishing alone, goes up a river, finds a good spot to raise his tent, cooks, wades into the river, puts the bait on the hook, catches small trout, throws them back into the water, catches a bigger one, and so on and so forth. The story is nothing more than a bare list of gestures, brief and clear transitional images, and a few generical and half-hearted notations on emotions, such as "he was really happy." It is a very sad story, permeated by oppressiveness and an undefinable anguish which hems it in on every side, the more so as nature appears serene, and the man's attention is concentrated on his fishing operations. . . .

Hemingway, as is well known, does not bother with philosophy. But his poetics have much more than a casual connection with an American philosophy tied directly to a "structure" and to a milieu concerned with practical activities and concepts. A neopositivism proposing a closed system of rules of thought—a system whose validity is nowhere else than in itself—corresponds to the allegiance which the Hemingway hero gives to his ethical-sports code—sole certainty in an unknowable universe. Hemingway's style, which exhausts the unattainable reality of feelings and thoughts by making lists of gestures and repartees in sketchy conversations, corresponds to behaviorism, which equates human reality with paradigms of behavior. . . .

All around is the horror of the vacuum of existential nothingness. *Nada y pués nada y nada y pués nada*, thinks the waiter in "A Clean, Well-Lighted Place." "The Gambler, the Nun, and the Radio" closes with the idea that everything is opium for the people, that is, an illusory protection against a universal sickness. We can see in these two short stories, both written in 1933, the expression of an approximative Hemingway existentialism. But we must not believe just these more explicitly "philosophical" statements; rather we must believe his general manner of portraying what is negative, senseless, and desperate in contemporary life, beginning way back with *Fiestà* (1926) with its eternal tourists, erotomaniac and hard-drinking. The emptiness of the dialogue, with its pauses and divagations—whose most obvious antecedent must be found in the "evasive" dialogue skirting the abyss of despair among Chekhov's characters—is in tune with the whole spectrum of dilemmas of twentieth-century irrationalism. The middle bourgeoisie in Chekhov, defeated from all points of view but not having lost their awareness of human dignity, dig in their heels under the first blows of the hurricane and maintain their hope in a better world. Hemingway's expatriates are plunged into the hurricane body and soul. The only resistance they can offer is to ski well, shoot lions well, establish rapports between man and woman and between man and man; techniques and qualities that certainly will still have a value in that better world of the future, which, however, they do not believe in. There was World War I between Chekhov and Hemingway; and reality took on the guise of a great massacre. Hemingway refuses to be on the side of the massacre; his anti-Fascism is one of the certain, clear-cut "rules of the game" upon which his life-view is based. Yet he accepts the massacre as the natural milieu of contemporary man. The novitiate of Nick Adáms—the autobiographical character of his first and most poetic short stories— is a training in withstanding the world's brutality. It begins in "Indian Camp," where his physician father operates on a pregnant Indian woman with his fishing knife while her husband, unable to withstand the sight of her suffering, silently cuts his own throat. When the Hemingway hero searches for a symbolic ritual to represent this conception of the world, he will not find anything better than the *corrida*, thus letting in suggestions of primitivism and barbarism, following D. H. Lawrence and a certain kind of ethnology.

It is in such a tormented cultural landscape that Hemingway must be placed. And at this point we can look back to Stendhal for comparison, an author who has often been mentioned in connection with him. Not an arbitrary name, this one, but rather suggested by Hemingway's declared predilection, and justifiable on the basis of a certain analogy in the programmatic sobriety of their styles—much more skillful and Flaubertian in the modern author— and of a certain parallelism in biographical elements and at times in localities (a "Milanese" Italy). Stendhal's hero is midway between the rationalist lucidity of the seventeenth century and the Romantic *Sturm und Drang*, between the Enlightenment's pedagogy of the heart and the Romantic exaltation of amoral individualism. The Hemingway hero finds himself at the same crossroads one hundred years later, when bourgeois thought has become impoverished. Its best inheritance has gone to a new class, and yet it still goes on developing, along dead-end paths, partial and contradictory solutions. From the old trunk of the Enlightenment branch out the American pragmatic philosophies; and the Romantic tree bears its last fruit in existentialist nihilism. Stendhal's hero, while a son of the French Revolution, still accepted the world of the Holy Alliance and submitted to the rules of the game dictated by its hypocrisy in order to fight his individual battle. Hemingway's hero, while he has seen the great alternative of the October Revolution open up, accepts the world of imperialism and moves amid its massacres, also fighting, with lucidity and detachment, a battle he knows in advance is lost.

Hemingway's fundamental intuition is that war is the most truthful image, the "normal" reality of the *bourgeois* world in the imperialist era. When he was barely eighteen, even before the American intervention, he managed to reach the Italian front, just to see what war was like, first as an ambulance driver and then as the manager of a mess hall, going back and forth among the Piave trenches on a bicycle. . . . What he understood about Italy, and how he could already see in the Italy of 1917 the Fascist face and the proletarian face in opposition to each other, were told in 1929 in the best of his novels, *A Farewell to Arms*. How he understood the Italy of 1949 was told in his novel *Across the River and into the Trees*, less well conceived than *A Farewell to Arms* but interesting in many respects. Nevertheless, all that he never understood, since he was unable to get outside his tourist self, could be the subject of a long essay.

Hemingway's first book (1924; published with additions in 1925), whose tone was set by his World War I memories and by those of the massacres in Greece, where he was a journalist, was entitled *In Our Time*. The title in itself doesn't say much, but is charged with a cruel irony if it is true that Hemingway was quoting from a verse in the *Book of Common Prayer*: "Give peace in our time, O Lord." The flavor of war as recorded in the brief chapters of *In Our Time* was decisive for Hemingway, just as the impressions described in *Tales from Sebastopol* were for Tolstoi. I don't know whether it was Hemingway's admiration for Tolstoi that caused him to seek a war experience, or whether the war was the origin of his admiration for Tolstoi. For surely the participation in war described by Hemingway is not the one Tolstoi described, nor is it the one described by another author Hemingway loved, the minor American classic, Stephen Crane. Hemingway's is the war fought in foreign countries, seen with the detachment of the outsider; we find prefigured here what was going to be the attitude of the G.I. in Europe.

But what interests us most in Hemingway is not his witnessing the reality of war, nor his denunciation of massacres. Just as no poet is completely identified with the ideas he embodies, Hemingway cannot be totally identified with the crisis of the culture that is his background. In spite of the limitations of behaviorism, to define man by his actions—by his being or not being up to the tasks that face him—is certainly a good and right way to interpret human existence. And this very definition of man is best exemplified by characters who are more concrete than the Hemingway hero, whose actions are almost never "work"—except when it is an unusual kind of work, like hunting sharks—or a specific fighting duty. His bullfights, for all their technical brilliance, leave us cold; but the clear and serious precision with which his characters know how to light a camp fire, throw a line, or position a machine gun, that interests us and is of use to us. We would give up all of the showiest, most celebrated Hemingway for one of those moments when he speaks of man's perfect integration with the world and with the things he does, for those moments when man is at peace with nature even while struggling with it, and is in harmony with humankind even in the heat of battle. If one day someone succeeds in writing, as a poet, about workers and their machines, about the precise operations of their jobs, he will have to go back to those moments in Hemingway, extracting them from the framework of futility, brutality, and boredom, and replacing them in the organic context of the modern world of productive work from which Hemingway picked them and isolated them. Hemingway understood something about how one lives in this world with open eyes and without tears, without illusions and mysticism, how one lives alone without anguish, and how one is happier with companionship than alone; above all, he elaborated a style that fully and exactly expresses his conception of life and that, if it at times reveals its limitations and faults, in its best moments, as in the Nick Adams short stories, can be considered the most sober and immediate language of modern prose, the most devoid of dribble and pomposity, the most limpidly realistic. . . .

Spoon River

FERNANDA PIVANO
America rossa e nera, 1964, pp. 64-66

I was a young girl when I saw the *Spoon River Anthology* for the first time. Pavese had brought it to me one morning after I had asked him to explain the difference between American and English literature. He had been so amused by my question; he had moved his pipe from one side of his mouth to the other to conceal a smile, and he had not answered me. Naturally, I was put off by it, and when he gave me the first "American" books I looked at them with great suspicion.

I opened the *Spoon River Anthology* halfway through and found a poem that ended this way: "Kissing her with my soul upon my lips, it suddenly took flight." Who knows why these lines took away my breath; it is so difficult to explain the reactions of adolescents. Perhaps they reminded me of an epigram of Plato that I had found in the *Palatine Anthology* (in those days I read ancient Greek easily and I continuously leafed through everything I found in the library). Or perhaps it pleased me that a poet was concerned again with what happens when a man kisses a girl. Who knows? What I do know is that only much later did my interest fix on other reasons which at first I perceived confusedly and then, partly because of Pavese's words and partly because of my increasingly perceptive reactions, I explained to myself with some clarity.

There is no doubt that for an adolescence like mine, weary of the stuff—epic at all costs—in vogue in our prewar period, the lean simplicity of the poems of Masters and their humble subject matter, revolving around little ordinary facts lacking in heroism and mixed mostly with tragedy, were a great experience. With time the experience deepened, as I detected in the themes of that subject the world that inspired it: the revolt against conformity, the brutal frankness, the desperation, the denunciation of a false morality, the antimilitaristic, anticapitalistic, antiprejudiced irony—the necessity and impossibility of communication. In these characters who had not succeeded in making themselves understood, and who had not themselves understood, in their drama of poor human beings swept away by an incontrollable destiny, I found a more and more subtle fascination as I learned to recognize them. In order to recognize them better, I undertook to translate them, almost for the purpose of imprinting them on my mind.

Naturally I did not say this to Pavese. I feared that he wouldn't take me seriously. But one day, after several years spent refashioning these portraits in Italian—always the same but always a little different—he found my manuscript in a drawer. I was ashamed like a thief while he slowly leafed through it, turning up the corners of the pages with long nervous fingers. I waited with a pounding heart for him to say something to me. But he only said: "Then you have understood that there is a difference between American and English literature." He smiled and took the manuscript away with him.

He convinced Einaudi to publish it. Those were happy days, although they were already beset by the beginning of the war. To obtain the authorization of the censor, the permit to publish was requested for an *Anthology of S. River*, and the permit was granted to the anthology of this new saint. (Or at least so Pavese told me; who could say if he was serious or not?) The book appeared in the middle of the war, a little before the publishing company was confiscated. Pavese brought me the first copy in a café in Turin in front of the railroad station. I came from one village, and he from another. He was already wanted by the authorities and had wrapped a large, comical scarf around himself, concealing half his face. He told me that the scarf was enough to disguise him completely. Both of us had eyes that glistened a bit while we stood there looking at that thin little book, that was only a selection from the real anthology, with its white cover bordered with green and its paper a little rough to the touch of hands numb with cold. A waiter brought us two cups of something colored (they called it coffee or chocolate in those days), and he was very offended when he realized that we hadn't even tasted it. Then Pavese left for his village, and I for mine with the little book under my coat, not knowing that a few days later the authorities would confiscate it.

Pavese told me the story of the confiscation while we were eating a cutlet of breaded rabbit, which was presented with the name "chicken alla Milanese." Einaudi had been very clever and had exploited his permit to publish to the limit. The authorities decided that confiscation was necessary because of the immorality of the cover. A cover was substituted with unusual submissiveness. Thus, the book began to circulate with the speed of a best seller, and many young people like me were able to make the acquaintance of these poems. I remember one day that I went to see an exhibition of a painter now famous. With great emotion, I recognized written on a white wall, with a large brush (there were not yet flu masters and felt tips), a verse from the anthology with the title underneath: *Spoon River*. It was an abbreviated title, as we had immediately gotten used to saying it, as if with a wink. Because for those of us who were young then, *Spoon River* meant many things: purity, faith in the truth, a horror of superstructures. Perhaps it meant love of poetry; certainly it meant love of *that* poetry.

This love was inspired by reasons that were political, moral, and aesthetic—certainly motives that were very different from those that had inspired it in America twenty years before.

The Influence of American Literature in Italy FERNANDA PIVANO

America rossa e nera, 1964, pp. 215-219

A conference was recently organized in Rome to discuss Italy's position in regard to American culture in general and, naturally, to American literature in particular. Many university professors of English literature, as well as some doctoral students in American literature, were present. One of the participants read an account of what has happened in Italy in the field of American literature since the end of the war; another read a paper on the part Cesare Pavese had in difffusing this literature among us. Many students, attending with scholarships from every city, listened attentively. The walls were covered with books, periodicals, and newspapers—in short, with everything indispensable to the pursuit of university or "scientific" studies, as professors like to call work of a philological nature.

Of the old guard, those who popularized American literature in Italy without being university professors, there was no one. Cecchi made a brief pro forma appearance; Vittorini remained in Milan. As for me, I had too small a role in this matter to consider myself a party to the issue, but a residue of youthful fanaticism had induced me to accept the invitation of the young professors, some of whom were my friends. There, in the middle of so many bibliographies and so many catalogues, I felt a little like a shipwrecked sailor, and I asked myself if what I was feeling was a wee bit of envy or really only nostalgia.

It is clear that these university lecturers study American literature as they might study Greek history or archaeology. They speak of the various American currents of literary criticism as their colleagues in other branches speak of Croce and De Sanctis or Montaigne and Sainte-Beuve. They succeed in separating the writers from their lives and analyzing their pages like microbes under a microscope. To do this, they combine the results of hundreds of volumes written on the same subject, and they are very fine, as only specialists know how to be. They publish their studies in technical reviews and read them among themselves, exchanging congratulations and enlarging the catalogues and bibliographies—just as scholars of Latin literature or paleography do. The only difference is that these studies are almost always in a negative key. I mean a professor of Latin literature or paleography chooses these subjects because he loves them, and he analyzes them because he believes he can help others in new analyses. In contrast, these students of American literature seem to aim above all to show the weaknesses and drawbacks of a field of study which they themselves have freely chosen.

In one burst of openness and enthusiasm, the young scholars even put Pavese's critical studies under the microscope. Naturally, an imaginary Pavese came out of this, for the position of Pavese, his criterion of judgment, was so different from theirs. And I then understood that we oldsters could not feel any envy over the availabiltiy of so much material for study, but only a great nostalgia. When I was working on my thesis on Melville, between 1939 and 1940, I did not find a single book on the subject in the library (notwithstanding the fact that it was a classic and not a "modern" that could excite the suspicions of the authorities of that time); but precisely because of this technical difficulty, an enthusiasm was born in me, an interest, a strange sensation of doing something useful, even in the practical sense, in that practically very useless area which is the study of literature.

Today, the young professors speak about this kind of enthusiasm with courteous self-importance, with philological exactness they condemn all the errors committed in the field of criticism in those years. The not-so-young professors make use of these errors to resume their old refrain that an autonomous American literature, cut off from English literature, does not exist, and that up to this time people have concerned themselves with American literature only as a fad. One might answer that it was a very uncomfortable fad which sent Pavese to prison and which resulted in the arrest of even an insignificant person like myself. But today, as was the case twenty years ago, it is useless to try to dislodge convictions so deeply rooted. More than by them, we are amazed by the very young, the "scientists" who under their magnifying glass, illuminated by the reflectors of entire specialized libraries, have discovered that Pavese made errors.

The most serious mistake, which truly scandalizes them, is the one regarding Edgar Lee Masters and the *Spoon River Anthology*. Pavese liked this book very much—perhaps not as much as it might seem from the publisher's blurbs he wrote in his own hand for one of the innumerable Italian editions of the book, but he did like it a lot. Evidently he wasn't the only one, judging from the number of copies in circulation. It is understood, of course, that this is not a standard of judgment, because the novels of Liala also sold many copies; but in those years there was no intellectual—let us speak plainly—who did not read those pages without a shiver. It was not a fashionable work, but books of poetry never are. It was not written by a famous poet; no one knew this poor, unsuccessful lawyer, almost dead of starvation and the author of rivers of illegible verses. Nor did the work awaken political interest, either because of its philo-Fascism like certain of Ezra Pound's speeches or for its anti-Fascism like certain of Hemingway's articles.

Yet, reading this book, our generation of intellectuals dreamed of sincerity. In those years, the fanfare of Fascist rhetoric had reached its zenith. It spoke in terms of *bourgeois* and anti*bourgeois* with a terminology stolen from nineteenth-century French artists and perverted in its meaning. A *bourgeois* was no longer the crass and insensitive philistine, egotistical and reactionary about art, but whoever revealed that kind of obtuseness about politics. On the other hand, whoever believed in heroics, in the so-called uncomfortable life, in wars of expansion and conquest, in the renunciation of his own personality and private life, was un*bourgeois*. Only the most prosaic, most vulgarized echo rebounded from D'Annunzio's aesthetics; when he was in public, the un*bourgeois* forced himself to hold in his stomach and thrust out his chest. The family existed for the greater development of the State; houses had to be monumental to give a sense of the power of the State; the headlines on the front pages of daily newspapers had to be huge to demonstrate how important was the State for the people.

Everyone in our generation knew these things, but that time has passed and has canceled or smoothed over everything. These things no longer matter to young people, even if they know them. To intellectuals, then, it was tiresome, for example, that in a novel approved by the Fascist censor you could not speak of corrupt politicians or of suicides, of poverty or of brothels, etc.—not because writers loved these things, but because these things were part of real life. In fact, it was easier to find a corrupt politician than the conquerors of nations so loved by the propaganda of that time. What is more, he was rather more charming, in spite of everything.

When those innocent American books appeared in people's hands—mediocre books if you wish, books in which men acted like human beings, full of weaknesses and defects, wanted humble ordinary things, and expressed themselves in a sincere and subdued language—I believe that many of us felt like adolescents in front of certain films forbidden to minors. Pavese's famous statement, that the American literary world appeared in those times to be "something more than a culture," but rather a promise of life, a call of destiny, did not provoke smiles among our generation because it exactly reflected our state of mind during those years. That is why the first Americans we fell in love with, under the impetus of Pavese and Vittorini, were not always the classics, neither old nor modern, but at times second-rate authors.

Of the modern classics, we first fell in love with Sherwood Anderson and Masters, because for us they were the champions of that sincerity of expression that in those years seemed the most unattainable dream. It was not only their subject matter that fascinated us. Certainly it was a very exciting subject matter, very interesting, almost like a film of Tom Mix or Charlie Chaplin, or like the words of certain popular songs that come from America. But a simple ethnic document cannot engross an entire generation for years at a time.

No one thought much about it when as adolescents we read the translations of Pavese and Vittorini and were moved by their enthusiasm to discover with them an unsuspected world and an authentic language, full of reality. And it was Pavese who reviewed the history of this experience at the end of the war . . . .

American Literature in
Italy Today

AGOSTINO
LOMBARDO
The Sewanee Review 68 [1960]: pp. 368-374*

Agostino Lombardo (1927-): Professor of English at
the University of Rome and editor of the first Italian
scholarly journal devoted to American literature,
Studi Americani, Lombardo is the author of many
scholarly works and is a well-known Americanist. He
is a frequent visitor to American universities and has
been active in bringing about the systematic study
of American literature on the university level in Italy.
His latest book is *The Devil in the Manuscript* (1974).

If American literature played an active part in Italian culture before and during World War II, in the years immediately following
the war it became a flood. While many authors had been translated, translations now followed so fast on each other's heels as to
be overpowering. There was a moment in which only American
books, films, and records seemed to exist in Italy. Everything was
translated, without the slightest discrimination. What had been an
interest determined by serious cultural or political reasons became a
fashion. The influence of twentieth-century American literature on
Italian writing, especially Italian fiction, reached its height: unfortunately, however (except in the case of a few writers, such as
Calvino), it did not reach Italian authors in the direct way which
had been so valuable to Pavese or Vittorini, but at second or third

*This essay is an excerpt from Professor Lombardo's introduction
to a special issue of *The Sewanee Review* devoted to American literature in Italy. It was written in English.

hand. Italian prose became, very often, the translation of a translation, and the so-called Italian neorealism became to a large extent
nothing but ersatz American fiction—and that not of the best.

But this was an explosion, a boom. Gradually, the situation
changed: and America in the first place lost its mythological quality. The changed political situation played an important part in this.
Once liberty was regained, America as a symbol, America as a
common denominator, had no more reason to exist—and for many
it assumed rather the form of a political adversary. . . . But if this
refusal of contemporary American literature implies a political
stand, there is also an awareness of the earlier misunderstanding, of
the false perspective in which American literature had been placed.
Pavese himself clarifies the situation excellently in an essay of 1946:

We are accustomed to considering the United States as a country which
entered world culture with a warm, persuasive and unmistakable voice only
in the ten years which followed the great war, and the names of Dewey and
Mencken, Lee Masters and Sandburg, Anderson, O'Neill, Van Wyck
Brooks, Waldo Frank, Gertrude Stein, Dreiser, Carlos Williams, Hemingway and Faulkner seemed to us the sudden explosion, inexplicable and unexpected, of a social or academic crust which, in spite of occasional protests or cracks—something was known of Poe and of Whitman—had remained intact from the beginnings of the colony. . . . We shared the sensation of those "young Americans" of being new Adams, alone and
resolute, who had come out not from Eden but from a jungle, freed of all
burdens of the past, fresh and ready to walk on the free earth. . . . But
now it turns out that those young Americans were wrong. Their explosion
was not the first nor, above all, the greatest in American history. . . . In
reality it was not American culture which was renewed from the bottom in
those years; it was we who seriously came into contact with it for the first
time. Now not a day passes without voices from across the Atlantic reaching whoever cares to listen, voices which recall, evoke and explain a whole
rich tradition in which at least one great revolution, one great "renaissance," had already taken place.

After the "boom," then, and after the "myth," Italian culture
went in search of the more authentic values in the American tradition. It is true that indiscriminate translation continued and that
the invasion of amateurs and propagandists continued and even in-

creased in periodicals and newspapers, but meanwhile the classics were being translated: from Melville to Hawthorne, Whitman to Mark Twain, and James to Poe. Likewise the damage done by improvised critics was offset by the work done by authentic critics in the more serious periodicals and journals. . . . The regular flow of American writers, artists, and scholars into Italy—and likewise the frequent visits of Italian intellectuals to America—have insured that a less arbitrary or conventional picture prevails (and this more authentic America is faithfully reflected in Guido Piovene's *De America*). The political struggle, whether on one side or the other, tends, it is true, to deform it once more; but at the same time direct knowledge prevents propaganda having, at least among intellectuals, its full effect. American books now arrive regularly, specialized libraries are set up, the tools are available for the scholars. The prestige of American literature is growing in Italian universities; American authors are introduced in the syllabuses of English studies; the first regular specialized courses are beginning.

The situation is too fluid and active for a precise balance to be drawn up. Some tendencies, nevertheless, are already observable, and some conclusions can be reached. The first of these conclusions is that the period which can be considered as the third phase of the Italian experience with American literature shows a great decrease of interest, if not by the public certainly by the critics and by the cultural circles in general, in many of the twentieth-century writers who attracted almost the whole of the attention before and during World War II. Saroyan and Cain, Caldwell and Steinbeck among fiction writers, Masters, Lindsay, and Sandburg among poets, hold less and less place in critical discussions. In this sense the times when Italy was "discovering America" are indeed over. The interest instead—and this is the second conclusion—is turning more and more to the American "classics" of the nineteenth century and to the truly great writers of the twentieth: Faulkner, Hemingway, Wolfe, Fitzgerald, and then Eliot and Pound.

The third conclusion is that in the period after World War II Italian culture has taken an ever-growing interest in American poetry, not only that of Whitman, Poe, Sandburg, and Masters, but also of Melville and Emily Dickinson, and—much more—of Eliot, Pound, Stevens, and William Carlos Williams. . . . Certainly it is possible to make a number of reservations as to the way in which American poetry has been and often is examined, above all in connection with the indiscriminate way in which certain poets (Ezra Pound is a case in point) have been exalted, the more especially because such lavish praise can cause harm not only to Italian studies but also to Italian poetry. At times, too, the interest rises from snobbery rather than from any real intellectual need. But there is no doubt that, on the whole, it is a proof of maturity and a clear symptom of the new attitude towards American literature.

This is also demonstrated by the fourth conclusion: in Italy, side by side with the interest in the poetry, a remarkable interest has grown up in American criticism, and not only in that of Matthiessen, but also of the "new critics." Various studies and translations have appeared, but what is most significant, American critical methods are often, for better or worse, adopted by Italian critics—especially by such, as is only natural, as are concerned with American literature (Cambon is an example of the best). This presents certain dangers, but in the last analysis it can only lead to an enriching of Italian criticism—which needs this opening, tied as it has been for many years to the single, though valuable and necessary, teachings of Croce. In this way the living relation between the philosophies of the two countries has been very useful (from which springs also the interest in American criticism)—a relation no longer concentrated only on the thought of Dewey (whose "presence" in Italy, thanks also to Croce, has been extremely active, and has had obvious repercussions also in the field of pedagogics), but which is supported by the whole problematics of contemporary thought.

While much work remains to be done, while many authors (Cooper, Irving, and Howells, for example) must still be revalued and studied on a new basis, and while many extraliterary prejudices and obstacles must still be removed, there seems to be no doubt, judging from what has been set out above, that Italian studies in American literature are proceeding along the right lines. This is not the moment of discoveries, nor that of enthusiasm, and certainly Italian-American studies lack now that literary and human, political and moral warmth which characterized them, but also distorted and adulterated them, in earlier years. This is the moment of study, of research—and it is no coincidence that the first serious histories of American literature, by Salvatore Rosati and Carlo Izzo, have been published in the last few years, and that the first European periodical devoted to American studies (*Studi Americani*) has appeared in Italy. The results of this study, nevertheless, may lead in a much more lasting manner, even if less ostentatiously, both to a true understanding of American literature and to that enrichment of human consciousness which springs from a search into and acquisition of any part of truth.

SUMMING UP

V

Reflections on America

GUIDO PIOVENE
De America, 1954, xvii-xxii

Besides making a summary diagnosis of America at an important turning point of its history, I have proposed to write a tentative interpretation of American civilization, as we can foresee it and project it in the future, in these the middle years of the century. Here to some extent a certain degree of poetic imagination is bound to be mixed in with factual observation. A civilization is in fact the translucent transposition a people makes of itself and which it shows others, almost its own projection into infinity. It is like the cone of shadow which the earth unknowingly projects into space. It is formed by unconscious forces and the visions which are born from them. Everything that finds a place in between, what we call everyday life, is a sequence of episodes that often contradict it. A simple observer, even the most attentive and subtle, always lets the sense of a civilization escape him.

America to a large extent is a country still unaware of itself, and this I have repeated many times. I would like to add that the remainder of the world is not in a different situation vis-à-vis America. The world contains America but knows it little and badly. For the European, America is mostly a sum of bookish notions, in addition to a certain number of conventional opinions and in some cases a purely immediate experience. It is seldom an experience lived culturally and intellectually. It looks as if this enormous physical being belonged only to a very small extent to the world of intellect, for itself and for others.

European intellectualism and European conceit find an easy solution. To the extent that they understand America, it is a pure and simple derivation of Europe, almost an immense buildup of exotic vitality upon the old European enlightenment. What they do not understand is attributed to the infantilism and the quasi-barbarity of a primitive people. But there is an error in these current opinions which prevents comprehension and even genuine interest. America is not at all an appendage of Europe; it is not a Europe transported to the other side of the ocean. It is different, and its being different may make it an enigma for the average man. One must make an effort in order to interpret it.

Like those faces by Leonardo da Vinci which emerge, smiling and abstruse, from a background of abstract spaces, America is a civilization of crowds and factories emerging from a prehistoric backdrop of forests and canyons. Different does not mean incompatible, but rather endowed with elements that demand an effort of focusing and of acclimation to be understood and assimilated. Precisely because of this, for the European America can be the complementary civilization, that Other, that extraneous term which is needed to create a new civilization. Knowing America, as fate has decreed we should do, marks the end of the fierce European narcissism which has not been toned down even by the communist influence. Intellectual Western Europe, as a matter of fact, will never bring itself to view communism as it is, but insists only on the prospects of its own assimilation of it. This method does not even yield fictitious results when one is dealing with America. Here Europe is called upon to face something different from itself.

My vision of America is mostly a vision of space—space with the counterpoint of the rhythms of a great indigenous civilization in the process of developing. We face here a natural vastness which becomes a spiritual dimension and a dimension of the modern mind. This is what I mean when I say, time and again, that intelligence today cannot be conceived as detached from spatial vastness. Visually, American civilization is a mixture of a decrepit prehistoric nature and modern technology.

A writer who affords us the physical sensation of America (immense, oblivious spaces in which extraordinary adventures take place obscurely; as a critic wrote, caves, ruins, islands, open fires, hidden treasures, floods, rivers, drunks, and corpses; but all immersed in nature yet, with little history and little awareness), Mark Twain in *Tom Sawyer* writes an instructive passage about the cave where the body of the unfortunate Injun Joe is found. Hungry, thirsty, trapped underground, the fleeing assassin has broken off a stalagmite in order to gather the drop of water which falls every twenty minutes: "That drop was falling when the Pyramids were new; when Troy fell; when the foundations of Rome were laid; when Christ was crucified; when the Conqueror created the British Empire; when Columbus sailed; when the massacre at Lexington was 'news.' It is falling now, it will still be falling when all these things shall have sunk down the afternoon of history and the twilight of tradition and been swallowed up in the thick night of oblivion." It is a rhetorical commonplace and exactly because of that, the truth, the appropriateness, and the prominence of that stalagmite in Twain's landscape are striking, placed as it is in the middle of children's adventures and beside the body of a murderer. In Mark Twain the relationship that emerges spontaneously is not between the modern and the ancient or between contemporary life and past civilizations, but that between a summary of human history and the world outside history, an astral world in which man has not yet appeared or has been forgotten.

In America two sets of terms are in contact, the cosmic and the immediate, the astral and the human. A technological civilization adorns landscapes of a decrepit nature, immensely older than the European. I don't know if in America what counts most is the youthfulness of the operating civilization or the age of the environment. This detachment between the human and the sublime, indifferent background tears man away from himself, empties him of history, and transforms him into an abstraction. America's space is mythological, but the mythological beings that oversee it do not have the appearances of ours. They are neither Jupiter nor Venus nor the Christian saints. They are abstract ethereal Forces. They are also intellect, pure mathematics, and technology which attempt to capture those Forces and become identified with them. This civilization exalts, more than the values of the human and Christian person, the supreme value of detachment, the value of pure investigative intelligence, and almost a different measure of man. There is always something abstract in it. It seems to me worthy of note that abstract and related forms of art invented in Europe—this art of Forms and Forces, not human, or human in a different manner—have found their dwelling in America and have become the norm of a culture. Here a cosmic civilization replaces an historical one. Here humanity forgets in part its history or stores it in libraries and in archives, like operations in the memory of its computers. Here man becomes detached from his own face. It is not surprising that Europeans would find it a little difficult to become accustomed to America. They can sense this, even if everyday life and the habitual human relations seem easy and innocent.

One inevitable question is whether or not America is moving toward a civilization which will be Christian. I am convinced that in our post-Christian phase of the world other forms of religious life are being elaborated under the yet-obligatory Christian label. A different religious life, I said, because of the positive values it contains, not only different by defect or hypocrisy. The religious panorama in America shows two apparently contradictory aspects: disputes and intransigence on the part of churches and sects, which are prompted by practical causes and the struggle to survive; and a tendency to believe that all cults are interchangeable, to transform all religions into a single motivation adorned by different mythologies. This is the tendency a French writer has labeled theism. What is most specific in Christianity is dissolving unnoticed. In my book, in any case, I have attempted to indicate that the American Christ is a Christ without the cross, who is born, one would say, from his triumph over suffering and death, a Christ whose passion is left in the shadows and whose resurrection only is brought into full light, a Christ who is all healer and all savior. In Christianity transplanted beyond the ocean, in this religion that's antisuffering and antideath, the redemption plays an almost exclusive role.

Such a religion leaves its imprint on the nonreligious aspects of life also. The obligation to enjoy comfort, the refusal to be content with the status one has achieved, the almost ascetic imperative to make money, to spend, to buy new products so as to become the new tool for collective deliverance are not related to the joy of living. Their origin is rather to be found in a religious command, which says that one must fulfill the redemption in oneself and in others. It looks as if right from the beginning something in American civilization had reacted against the idea of original sin and this concept could not be intimately accepted any more. I do not believe that experience could modify it, make it more suffering-oriented, more tragic in a European sense. It already has its bias. The Redemption looms on the horizon; this civilization can fail, but it cannot become other. It's not a civilization of work, either. It is dominated, rather, by an Edenic ideal, the ideal of a natural life made painless by technological comfort. If work is the everyday norm of the American man, his ideal is vacation. Even their major vices, like alcohol and gambling, must be viewed as part of an Edenic ideal. American detachment, which I have mentioned so often, is not Christian and stoic. It is attained by satisfying needs, thereby silencing individual egotisms.

If I should now define in a few words, necessarily inexact, what seems to me to be the dream of American civilization, I would define it thus: a flight of each individual into his own personal sphere and into his own eccentricities. Thanks to this, a general satisfaction arises in which each person ceases to attract intellectual energies, and there emerge an impersonal quality of inquisitive mind, a new nature, a sort of pool of intellects, techniques, and religions.

I have already said that the sense of a civilization and its nature have nothing to do with, or rather contradict at times, its everyday appearance. The sense of a civilization is poetic-religious; it is not used in immediate experience and it is not fragmented into *tranches de vie*. Casually observed, American civilization is the glorification of the common man. But its fundamental religious idea, the Redemption, combined with the doctrine of evolution that prevails in this culture, orients it toward a "surpassing" of man. A hint of "superman" mythology can be seen, if one look through and through in the texture of this culture which prizes victory, intelligence, and humanistic pride.

I was walking one day in New York in the neighborhood of the George Washington Bridge. On the façade of a church, whose denomination I do not know, I read an inscription which I did not pay attention to at the moment but which later, as I thought about it, became for me the motto of the still potential civilization of the United States: "Intelligence is the glory of God." Let us think of the characteristics, which for me are the fundamental ones, of American civilization: syncretism, inclining toward individualism only in order to satisfy man, but then by that path inclining toward a depersonalized universal human intelligence; a civilization of abstraction and detachment, more mathematical than historical, with Pythagorean aspects, favorable also to vast bureaucracies tending toward universalism; a civilization in which the liking for man and the will to cooperate with man, even with the one met by chance never to be seen again, is immensely stronger than the so-called bond. A civilization that brings together in the same endeavor such disparate races, in which blood separates but mind unites, carries within it the experimental notion of unity based on the objective data of research and on the truths all human intellects have in common. Public taste is drawn to psychoanalysis, surrealism, and whatever aims at transforming the obscure into the rational and the unhappy into the happy.

I see here the outlines of a civilization founded on the lucid values of the mind—syncretistic, intellectualistic—which today is still in its childhood stage. The task of this overseas country, laden with irrationality, is probably to elaborate the rationalistic civilization of our post-Christian world. It may be that the task will not be brought to term, since nature fulfills only a minimal portion of its own hypotheses. Perhaps I am in error. We have posited a *tabula rasa*. Therefore, the chances of error as we pronounce a judgment are maximal.

Bibliography

Although several books about the American impact on Italian literature were written after World War II, there has been no study of the wider range of contacts between Italian writers who informed and influenced Italian opinion and the American reality. Therefore the following list of works consists almost entirely of primary sources, both those from which the present anthology has been compiled and other similar works which for various reasons (such as repetition of material, lack of topicality, or inability to obtain permission to reprint) are not represented in this collection.

For the opinions of Italian travelers to the United States in the nineteenth century, the reader is advised to consult Andrew J. Torrielli, *Italian Opinion of America as Revealed by Italian Travelers 1850-1900* (Cambridge, Mass.: Harvard University Press, 1941; rpt. New York: Kraus Co., 1969).

d'Agostino, Nemi. "Mondo vecchio e mondo nuovo." *La Fiera Letteraria* 8 (1953): 5.

_____. "Pavese e l'America." *Studi Americani* 4 (1958): 399-413.

Amoruso, Vito. "Cecchi, Vittorini, Pavese e la letteratura americana." *Studi Americani* 6 (1960): 9-71.

Antonioni, Michelangelo. "Che mi dice l'America." *L'Espresso* (April 6, 1970): 5-11.

_____. "Frigida America." *La Fiera Letteraria* 2 (1947): 12.

Bacino, Ezio. *America bifronte.* Florence: Vallecchi, 1957.

Barzini, Luigi, Jr. *Gli Americani sono soli al mondo.* Milan: Mondadori, 1952.

_____. *Nuova York.* Milan: Giacomo Agnelli, 1931.

Berti, Luigi. *Boccaporto.* Florence: Parenti, 1940.

Borgese, G. A. *Atlante americano.* Modena: Guanda, 1936.

Calvino, Italo. "Hemingway e noi." *Il contemporaneo* 1 (November 13, 1954): 3.

Cecchi, Emilio. *America amara.* Florence: Sansoni, 1940.

_____. *Scrittori inglesi e americani.* Milan: Mondadori, 1946.

Corsini, Gianfranco. *America allo specchio.* Bari: Laterza, 1960.

Dolci, Danilo. "Alcuni appunti su esperienze educative sperimentali in USA." Unpublished notes, 1973.

Fernandez, Dominique. *Il mito dell'America negli intellettuali italiani dal 1930 al 1950.* Trans. A. Zaccaria. Rome: Sciascia, 1969.

Golino, C. L. "On the Italian Myth of America." *The Italian Quarterly* 3 (1959): 19-33.

Gramsci, Antonio. *Note sul Machiavelli, sulla politica e sullo stato moderno.* Turin: Einaudi, 1955.

Heiney, Donald. *America in Modern Italian Literature.* New Brunswick, N.J.: Rutgers University Press, 1964.

Ianni, Constantino. *Il sangue degli emigranti.* Milan: Edizioni di Comunità, 1965.

"Un' inchiesta fra i narratori." *Galleria* (1954): 314-326.

Linati, Carlo. *Scrittori anglo-americani d'oggi.* Milan: Corticelli, 1932.

Lombardo, Agostino. "L'America di Vittorini." *Criterio* 5-6 (1958): 354-368.

_____. "La critica italiana sulla letteratura americana." *Studi Americani* 5 (1959): 9-49.

_____. "Introduction to Italian Criticism of American Literature." *The Sewanee Review* 68 (1960): 353-374.

_____. "Tradizione americana." *Studi Americani* 2 (1956): 285-301.

Lucentini, Mauro. *America che cambia.* Milan: Rizzoli, 1967.

Pavese, Cesare. *La letteratura americana e altri saggi.* 3rd ed. Turin: Einaudi, 1959.

Piazzesi, Gianfranco. *La svolta dell'America.* Milan: Rizzoli, 1972.

Pintor, Giaime. *Il sangue d'Europa.* Turin: Einaudi, 1950.

Piovene, Guido. *De America.* Milan: Garzanti, 1954.

Pivano, Fernanda. *America rossa e nera.* Florence: Vallecchi, 1964.

_____. *La balena bianca e altri miti.* Milan: Mondadori, 1961.

Praz, Mario. *Cronache letterarie anglo-sassoni.* Rome: Edizioni Storia e Letteratura, 1950-1966.

_____. "Hemingway in Italy." *Partisan Review* 15 (October, 1948): 1086-1100.

_____. *Viaggi in occidente.* Florence: Sansoni, 1955.

Prezzolini, Giuseppe. *Tutta l'America.* Florence: Vallecchi, 1958.

Ronchey, Alberto. *L'ultima America.* Milan: Garzanti, 1967.

Ruggiero, Amerigo. *America albino.* Turin: Einaudi, 1934.

Sarfatti, Margherita G. *L'America, ricerca della felicità.* Milan: Mondadori, 1937.

Soavi, Giorgio. *America tutta d'un fiato.* Milan: Mondadori, 1959.

_____. *Fantabulous.* Milan: Mondadori, 1963.

Soldati, Mario. *America primo amore.* Florence: Bemporad, 1935. (rpt. Milan: Mondadori, 1959).

Sorelli, Antonio. *Questa è l'America.* Milan: Edizioni L'Alpe, 1945.

Spini, Giorgio. *America 1962.* Florence: La Nuova Italia, 1962.

Tomasi, Silvano M., and Engel, Madeline H., eds. *The Italian Experience in the United States.* Staten Island, N.Y.: Center for Migration Studies, Inc., 1970.

U.S.A. Al di là di un mito. Turin: Einaudi, 1968.

Vittorini, Elio. *Diario in pubblico.* 2nd ed. Milan: Mondadori, 1957.

Index

ABOUT THE EDITORS

Angela M. Jeannet, associate professor of Italian and French, Franklin and Marshall College, Lancaster, Pennsylvania, specializes in twentieth-century Italian and French literature. She has written articles for *Italica, Symposium,* the *Italian Quarterly,* and other journals. She is presently researching material for a study on Italo Calvino.

Louise K. Barnett, assistant professor of English, Douglass College, Rutgers University, New Brunswick, specializes in American studies. She has written articles for *Forum Italicum, Studi Americani, Italian Quarterly,* and other journals. Her previous books include *The Ignoble Savage* (Greenwood Press, 1975).